TORONTO GUIDEBOOK 2019

SHOPS, RESTAURANTS, ATTRACTIONS & NIGHTLIFE

The Most Positively Reviewed and Recommended by Locals and Travelers

EGP Editorial

TORONTO
GUIDEBOOK
2019

SHOPS, RESTAURANTS, ATTRACTIONS & NIGHTLIFE

TORONTO GUIDEBOOK 2019
Shops, Restaurants, Arts, Entertainment & Nightlife

ISBN-13: 978-1722118037
ISBN-10: 1722118032

INDEX

TORONTO GUIDEBOOK 2019

Shops, Restaurants, Arts, Entertainment & Nightlife

This directory is dedicated to Toronto Business Owners and Managers who provide the experience that the locals and tourists enjoy. Thanks you very much for all that you do and thank for being the "People Choice".

Thanks to everyone that posts their reviews online and the amazing reviews sites that make our life easier.

The places listed in this book are the most positively reviewed and recommended by locals and travelers from around the world.

Thank you for your time and enjoy the directory that is designed with locals and tourist in mind!

TOP 500 SHOPS

The Most Recommended by Locals & Trevelers

(From #1 to #500)

#1
Kensington Market
Category: Farmers Market, Used, Vintage, Consignment, Local Flavor
Average price: Modest
Area: Kensington Market
Address: 34 St Andrew St
Toronto, ON M5T 1K6
Phone: (416) 593-0616

#2
Cabaret Vintage
Category: Thrift Store, Used, Vintage, Consignment, Women's Clothing
Average price: Expensive
Area: Niagara, West Queen West
Address: 672 Queen St W
Toronto, ON M6J 1E5
Phone: (416) 504-7126

#3
Blue Banana Market
Category: Home Decor, Jewelry, Cards & Stationery
Average price: Modest
Area: Kensington Market
Address: 250 Augusta Ave
Toronto, ON M5T 2L7
Phone: (416) 594-6600

#4
Just You Sarah & Tom
Category: Toy Store, Flowers & Gifts
Average price: Modest
Area: Koreatown, Palmerston
Address: 624 Bloor Street W
Toronto, ON M6G 1K7
Phone: (416) 535-4619

#5
Courage My Love
Category: Used, Vintage, Consignment, Jewelry
Average price: Modest
Area: Kensington Market
Address: 14 Kensington Avenue
Toronto, ON M5T 2J7
Phone: (416) 979-1992

#6
Mountain Equipment Co-Op
Category: Sports Wear, Outdoor Gear
Average price: Modest
Area: Entertainment District
Address: 400 King St W
Toronto, ON M5V 1K2
Phone: (416) 340-2667

#7
Lavish & Squalor
Category: Women's Clothing, Men's Clothing
Average price: Expensive
Area: Entertainment District, Queen Street West, Downtown Core
Address: 253 Queen St W
Toronto, ON M5V 1Z4
Phone: (416) 599-4779

#8
Toronto Eaton Centre
Category: Shopping Center
Average price: Modest
Area: Downtown Core
Address: 220 Yonge Street
Toronto, ON M5B 2H1
Phone: (416) 598-8700

#9
Haute Classics
Category: Women's Clothing, Used, Vintage, Consignment
Average price: Modest
Area: Yonge and St. Clair, Deer Park
Address: 1454 Yonge Street
Toronto, ON M4T 1Y5
Phone: (416) 922-7900

#10
Tap Phong Trading Company
Category: Home Decor, Kitchen & Bath, Hardware Store
Average price: Inexpensive
Area: Chinatown, Kensington Market, Downtown Core
Address: 360 Spadina Avenue
Toronto, ON M5T 2G4
Phone: (416) 977-6364

#11
Rolo
Category: Gift Shop
Average price: Modest
Area: Yorkville
Address: 24 Bellair Street
Toronto, ON M5R 2C7
Phone: (416) 920-0100

#12
Come As You Are
Category: Adult
Average price: Modest
Area: Alexandra Park
Address: 493 Queen St W
Toronto, ON M5V 2B4
Phone: (416) 504-7934

#13
Fashion Crimes
Category: Accessories, Women's Clothing
Average price: Expensive
Area: Entertainment District, Queen Street West, Downtown Core
Address: 322 Queen St W
Toronto, ON M5V 2A2
Phone: (416) 592-9001

#14
Balisi
Category: Shoe Store, Accessories, Women's Clothing
Average price: Expensive
Area: Niagara, West Queen West, Trinity Bellwoods
Address: 711 Queen Street W
Toronto, ON M6J 1E6
Phone: (416) 203-2388

#15
Good Egg
Category: Bookstore, Kitchen & Bath
Average price: Modest
Area: Kensington Market
Address: 267 Augusta Ave
Toronto, ON M5T 2M2
Phone: (416) 593-4663

#16
White Toronto
Category: Bridal
Average price: Exclusive
Area: Yorkville
Address: 19 Hazelton Avenue
Toronto, ON M5R 2E1
Phone: (416) 849-9196

#17
The Beguiling
Category: Bookstore, Comic Books
Average price: Modest
Area: Palmerston
Address: 601 Markham Street
Toronto, ON M6G 2L7
Phone: (416) 533-9168

#18
Seduction Love Boutique
Category: Lingerie, Adult
Average price: Modest
Area: Church-Wellesley Village, Downtown Core
Address: 577 Yonge St
Toronto, ON M4Y 1Z2
Phone: (416) 966-6969

#19
Anthropologie
Category: Women's Clothing
Average price: Expensive
Area: Yorkville
Address: 80 Yorkville Avenue
Toronto, ON M5R 2C2
Phone: (416) 964-9700

#20
Secrets From Your Sister
Category: Lingerie
Average price: Expensive
Area: Palmerston, Seaton Village
Address: 560 Bloor Street W
Toronto, ON M6G 1K1
Phone: (416) 538-1234

#21
Linda Penwarden Jewellery
Category: Jewelry
Average price: Expensive
Area: Mount Pleasant and Davisville
Address: 631 Mount Pleasant Road
Toronto, ON M4S 2M9
Phone: (416) 484-1843

#22
Uncle Otis Clothing
Category: Men's Clothing
Average price: Expensive
Area: Yorkville
Address: 26 Bellair St
Toronto, ON M5R 2C7
Phone: (416) 920-2281

#23
Chapters
Category: Bookstore
Average price: Modest
Area: Entertainment District, Downtown Core
Address: 142 John St
Toronto, ON M5V 2E3
Phone: (416) 595-7349

#24
Sonic Boom
Category: Music & DVDs
Average price: Modest
Area: The Annex
Address: 782 Bathurst Street
Toronto, ON M5R 3G3
Phone: (416) 532-0334

#25
Change of Scandinavia
Category: Lingerie
Average price: Modest
Area: Entertainment District, Queen Street West, Downtown Core
Address: 315 Queen St W
Toronto, ON M5V 2A4
Phone: (416) 977-7667

#26
The Optic Zone
Category: Eyewear & Opticians
Average price: Modest
Area: Corktown, St. Lawrence, Downtown Core
Address: 33 Jarvis Street
Toronto, ON M5E 1N3
Phone: (416) 362-3937

#27
Brown's A Short Man's World
Category: Men's Clothing
Average price: Expensive
Area: Alexandra Park
Address: 545 Queen Street W
Toronto, ON M5V 2B6
Phone: (416) 504-5937

#28
Lululemon Athletica
Category: Sports Wear, Women's Clothing, Yoga
Average price: Expensive
Area: Queen Street West
Address: 342 Queen St W
Toronto, ON M5V 2A2
Phone: (416) 703-1399

#29
So Hip It Hurts
Category: Sports Wear, Watches
Average price: Expensive
Area: Entertainment District, Queen Street West, Downtown Core
Address: 323 Queen Street W
Toronto, ON M5V 2A4
Phone: (416) 971-6901

#30
Game Centre
Category: Music & DVDs
Average price: Modest
Area: Downtown Core
Address: 730 Yonge Street
Toronto, ON M4Y 2B7
Phone: (416) 925-4951

#31
Outer Layer
Category: Cards & Stationery, Gift Shop
Average price: Modest
Area: Queen Street West
Address: 577 Queen Street W
Toronto, ON M5V 2B6
Phone: (416) 869-9889

#33
Black Market Vintage Clothing
Category: Used, Vintage, Consignment
Average price: Inexpensive
Area: Entertainment District, Queen Street West, Downtown Core
Address: 256 Queen St W
Toronto, ON M5V 1Z8
Phone: (416) 599-5858

#32
Scout
Category: Jewelry, Cards & Stationery
Average price: Modest
Area: High Park, Roncesvalles
Address: 405 Roncesvalles Avenue
Toronto, ON M6R 2N1
Phone: (416) 546-6922

#34
Shanti Baba
Category: Jewelry, Hobby Shop, Tobacco Shop
Average price: Modest
Area: Alexandra Park
Address: 546 Queen St W
Toronto, ON M5V 2B5
Phone: (416) 504-5034

#35
Show Room
Category: Men's Clothing, Women's Clothing
Average price: Expensive
Area: Entertainment District, Queen Street West, Downtown Core
Address: 278 Queen Street W
Toronto, ON M5V 2A1
Phone: (416) 977-3888

#36
Condom Shack
Category: Adult
Average price: Modest
Area: Entertainment District, Queen Street West, Downtown Core
Address: 231 Queen St W
Toronto, ON M5V 1Z4
Phone: (416) 596-7515

#37
Getoutside
Category: Shoe Store
Average price: Modest
Area: Entertainment District, Queen Street West, Downtown Core
Address: 437 Queen Street W
Toronto, ON M5V 2A5
Phone: (416) 593-5598

#38
The Hudson Bay Company
Category: Department Store
Average price: Expensive
Area: Downtown Core
Address: 176 Yonge Street
Toronto, ON M5C 2L7
Phone: (416) 861-9111

#39
MAC Cosmetics
Category: Cosmetics & Beauty Supply
Average price: Expensive
Area: Entertainment District, Queen Street West, Downtown Core
Address: 363 Queen St. West
Toronto, ON M5V 2A4
Phone: (416) 979-2171

#40
Labour of Love
Category: Jewelry, Gift Shop
Average price: Modest
Area: Cabbagetown
Address: 242 Carlton Street
Toronto, ON M5A 2L2
Phone: (416) 923-8988

#41
Social Butterfly
Category: Women's Clothing, Lingerie, Accessories
Average price: Expensive
Area: Riverdale
Address: 315 Danforth Ave
Toronto, ON M4K 1N7
Phone: (416) 466-5872

#42
Hanji
Category: Cards & Stationery
Average price: Modest
Area: Koreatown, Palmerston
Address: 619 Bloor Street W
Toronto, ON M6G 1K8
Phone: (647) 349-2095

#43
North Standard Trading Post
Category: Fashion
Average price: Expensive
Area: Parkdale, Roncesvalles
Address: 1662 Queen Street W
Toronto, ON M6R 1B2
Phone: (647) 348-7060

#44
Solutions
Category: Home Decor
Average price: Modest
Area: Mount Pleasant and Davisville, Yonge and Eglinton
Address: 2329 Yonge Street
Toronto, ON M4P 2C8
Phone: (647) 430-8750

#45
The Paper Place
Category: Cards & Stationery
Average price: Modest
Area: Niagara, West Queen West
Address: 887 Queen St W
Toronto, ON M6J 1G5
Phone: (416) 703-0089

#46
One Million Comix & Next Move Games
Category: Bookstore, Hobby Shop
Average price: Modest
Area: Church-Wellesley Village, Downtown Core
Address: 531 Yonge Street
Toronto, ON M4Y 1Y5
Phone: (416) 934-1615

#47
Holt Renfrew
Category: Department Store
Average price: Exclusive
Area: Yorkville, Downtown Core
Address: 50 Bloor Street W
Toronto, ON M4W 3L8
Phone: (416) 922-2333

#48
Eliot's Bookshop
Category: Bookstore
Average price: Inexpensive
Area: Downtown Core
Address: 584 Yonge St
Toronto, ON M4Y 1Z3
Phone: (416) 925-0268

#49
69 Vintage Store
Category: Used, Vintage, Consignment
Average price: Modest
Area: West Queen West, Beaconsfield Village
Address: 1100 Queen St W
Toronto, ON M6J 1H9
Phone: (416) 516-0669

#50
Bergo Designs
Category: Furniture Store
Average price: Expensive
Area: Distillery District
Address: 55 Mill Street
Toronto, ON M5A 3C4
Phone: (416) 861-1821

#51
Smash
Category: Furniture Store, Antiques
Average price: Expensive
Area: The Junction
Address: 2880 Dundas St W
Toronto, ON M6P 1Y8
Phone: (416) 762-3113

#52
Pandemonium
Category: Bookstore, Music & DVDs, Vinyl Records
Average price: Modest
Area: The Junction
Address: 2920 Dundas Street W
Toronto, ON M6P 1Y8
Phone: (416) 769-5257

#53
Coal Miner's Daughter
Category: Women's Clothing, Jewelry, Accessories
Average price: Modest
Area: Koreatown, Palmerston
Address: 587 Markham Street
Toronto, ON M6G 2L7
Phone: (647) 381-1439

#54
Model Citizen
Category: Accessories, Women's Clothing, Men's Clothing
Average price: Modest
Area: Kensington Market
Address: 279 Augusta Ave
Toronto, ON M5T 2M1
Phone: (416) 703-7625

#55
Maison De La Presse
Category: Books, Mags, Music & Video
Average price: Modest
Area: Yorkville
Address: 99 Yorkville Ave
Toronto, ON M4W 1A7
Phone: (416) 928-2328

#56
John Fluevog
Category: Shoe Store
Average price: Exclusive
Area: Entertainment District, Queen Street West, Downtown Core
Address: 242 Queen Street West
Toronto, ON M5V 1Z7
Phone: (416) 581-1420

#57
Made You Look Jewellery
Category: Jewelry
Average price: Expensive
Area: Parkdale
Address: 1338 Queen St W
Toronto, ON M6K 1L4
Phone: (416) 463-2136

#58
Nick's Shoe Repair Shop
Category: Shoe Repair, Shoe Store
Average price: Modest
Area: The Annex
Address: 169 Dupont Street
Toronto, ON M5R 1V5
Phone: (416) 924-5930

#59
Body Blue
Category: Shopping
Average price: Modest
Area: Riverdale
Address: 199 Danforth Ave
Toronto, ON M4K 1N2
Phone: (416) 778-7601

#60
Active Surplus
Category: Electronics
Average price: Inexpensive
Area: Entertainment District, Queen Street West, Downtown Core
Address: 347 Queen Street W
Toronto, ON M5V 2A4
Phone: (416) 593-0909

#61
Trove
Category: Accessories, Shoe Store, Women's Clothing
Average price: Modest
Area: Palmerston
Address: 791 Bathurst Street
Toronto, ON M5S 1Z5
Phone: (416) 516-1258

#62
Urban Barn
Category: Furniture Store, Home Decor
Average price: Modest
Area: Niagara, West Queen West, Trinity Bellwoods
Address: 610 Queen Street W
Toronto, ON M6J 1E3
Phone: (416) 364-6664

#63
Peach Berserk
Category: Women's Clothing
Average price: Expensive
Area: Niagara, West Queen West
Address: 81 Shaw Street
Toronto, ON M5V
Phone: (416) 829-8676

#64
GUFF
Category: Thrift Store, Antiques, Furniture Store
Average price: Modest
Area: Leslieville
Address: 1142 Queen Street East
Toronto, ON M4M 1L2
Phone: (416) 913-8025

#65
Dufferin Mall
Category: Shopping Center
Average price: Inexpensive
Area: Brockton Village
Address: 900 Dufferin Street
Toronto, ON M6H 4A9
Phone: (416) 532-1152

#66
Citizenry
Category: Shopping, Cafe
Average price: Inexpensive
Area: West Queen West, Trinity Bellwoods
Address: 982 Queen Street W
Toronto, ON M6J 1H1
Phone: (647) 458-6672

#67
B & J Trading Company
Category: Home Decor, Kitchen & Bath
Average price: Inexpensive
Area: Chinatown, Kensington Market, Downtown Core
Address: 378 Spadina Avenue
Toronto, ON M5T 2G5
Phone: (416) 586-9655

#68
New Balance Toronto
Category: Shoe Store, Sports Wear
Average price: Modest
Area: Yonge and St. Clair, Deer Park
Address: 1510 Yonge Street
Toronto, ON M4T 1Z6
Phone: (416) 962-8662

#69
The Purple Purl
Category: Arts & Crafts
Average price: Modest
Area: Leslieville
Address: 1162 Queen St E
Toronto, ON M4M 1L4
Phone: (416) 463-1162

#70
Fraiche
Category: Accessories, Arts & Crafts, Women's Clothing
Average price: Modest
Area: Queen Street West, Downtown Core
Address: 348 Queen Street W
Toronto, ON M5V 2A2
Phone: (416) 341-8606

#71
Doll Factory By Damzels
Category: Women's Clothing
Average price: Modest
Area: Leslieville
Address: 1122 Queen Street E
Toronto, ON M4M 1K8
Phone: (416) 598-0509

#72
Ladybug Florist In the Village
Category: Florist
Average price: Modest
Area: Church-Wellesley Village, Downtown Core
Address: 513 Church Street
Toronto, ON M4Y 2C9
Phone: (416) 922-9971

#73
West Elm
Category: Furniture Store
Average price: Modest
Area: Liberty Village
Address: 109 Alantic Ave
Toronto, ON M6K 1E2
Phone: (416) 537-0110

#74
Bootmaster
Category: Men's Clothing, Shoe Store
Average price: Expensive
Area: Downtown Core
Address: 609 Yonge Street
Toronto, ON M4Y 1Z5
Phone: (416) 927-1054

#75
Bicyclette
Category: Women's Clothing
Average price: Modest
Area: Niagara, West Queen West, Trinity Bellwoods
Address: 880 Queen St W
Toronto, ON M6J 1G9
Phone: (416) 532-8048

#76
Girl Friday
Category: Accessories, Women's Clothing
Average price: Modest
Area: Niagara, West Queen West, Trinity Bellwoods
Address: 740 Queen Street W
Toronto, ON M6J 1E9
Phone: (416) 364-2511

#77
M0851
Category: Accessories, Women's Clothing, Men's Clothing
Average price: Expensive
Area: The Annex
Address: 38 Avenue Road
Toronto, ON M5R 2G2
Phone: (416) 920-4001

#78
Reflections Vintage & Antiques
Category: Used, Thrift Store, Vintage, Consignment, Accessories
Average price: Modest
Area: Downtown Core
Address: 676 Yonge Street
Toronto, ON M4Y 2A6
Phone: (416) 944-0333

#79
Betsey Johnson
Category: Accessories, Women's Clothing
Average price: Expensive
Area: Yorkville
Address: 102 Yorkville Avenue
Toronto, ON M5R 1B9
Phone: (416) 922-8164

#80
Chosen Vintage
Category: Used, Vintage, Consignment
Average price: Modest
Area: West Queen West, Trinity Bellwoods
Address: 960 Queen Street W
Toronto, ON M6J 1H1
Phone: (647) 346-1993

#81
Shopgirls Gallery Boutique
Category: Women's Clothing
Average price: Expensive
Area: Parkdale
Address: 1342 Queen Street W
Toronto, ON M6K
Phone: (416) 534-7467

#82
Winners
Category: Shoe Store, Men's Clothing, Women's Clothing
Average price: Modest
Area: Downtown Core
Address: 444 Yonge St
Toronto, ON M5B 2H4
Phone: (416) 598-8800

#83
Heel Boy
Category: Shoe Store
Average price: Modest
Area: Niagara, West Queen West, Trinity Bellwoods
Address: 773 Queen Street W
Toronto, ON M6J 1G1
Phone: (416) 362-4335

#84
Lush
Category: Cosmetics & Beauty Supply
Average price: Expensive
Area: Ryerson, Downtown Core
Address: D202 - 1 Dundas St W
Toronto, ON M5B 2H1
Phone: (416) 646-5874

#85
The Outer Layer
Category: Cards & Stationery, Gift Shop
Average price: Expensive
Area: The Annex
Address: 430 Bloor Street W
Toronto, ON M5S 1X5
Phone: (416) 324-8333

#86
The Monkey's Paw
Category: Bookstore
Average price: Modest
Area: Little Portugal
Address: 1229 Dundas Street W
Toronto, ON M6J 1X6
Phone: (416) 531-2123

#87
Harry Rosen
Category: Men's Clothing
Average price: Exclusive
Area: Ryerson, Downtown Core
Address: 218 Yonge St
Toronto, ON M5B 2H6
Phone: (416) 598-8885

#88
Pandora
Category: Jewelry
Average price: Expensive
Area: Financial District, Downtown Core
Address: 200 Bay Street
Toronto, ON M5J 2J3
Phone: (416) 360-1467

#89
Spoof
Category: Women's Clothing
Average price: Inexpensive
Area: Entertainment District, Queen Street West, Downtown Core
Address: 350 Queen Street W
Toronto, ON M5V 2A2
Phone: (416) 456-9228

#90
Grassroots Environmental
Category: Kitchen & Bath, Skin Care, Department Store
Average price: Modest
Area: The Annex
Address: 408 Bloor Street W
Toronto, ON M5S 1X5
Phone: (416) 944-1993

#91
iQliving
Category: Home Decor, Kitchen & Bath
Average price: Expensive
Area: Greektown, Riverdale
Address: 542 Danforth Avenue
Toronto, ON M4K 1P8
Phone: (416) 466-2727

#92
Ferré Sposa
Category: Bridal
Average price: Modest
Area: Dovercourt
Address: 934 Bloor St W
Toronto, ON M6H 1L4
Phone: (416) 535-8999

#93
Vintage Depot
Category: Used, Vintage, Consignment
Average price: Inexpensive
Area: Kensington Market
Address: 70 Kensington Ave
Toronto, ON M5T 2K1
Phone: (416) 596-6513

#94
Frock
Category: Accessories, Women's Clothing
Average price: Expensive
Area: Roncesvalles
Address: 97 Roncesvalles Ave
Toronto, ON M6R 2K9
Phone: (416) 516-1333

#95
Midtown Digital
Category: IT Service& Computer Repair, Electronics, Computers
Average price: Modest
Area: Yonge and St. Clair, Deer Park
Address: 1391 Yonge Street
Toronto, ON M4T 1Y4
Phone: (416) 533-2001

#96
ZANE
Category: Accessories, Leather Goods
Average price: Expensive
Area: Niagara, West Queen West, Trinity Bellwoods
Address: 753 Queen Street W
Toronto, ON M6J 1E5
Phone: (647) 352-9263

#97
Homesense
Category: Home Decor
Average price: Modest
Area: Downtown Core
Address: 195 Yonge St
Toronto, ON M5B 1M4
Phone: (416) 941-9185

#98
BMV Books
Category: Bookstore, Music & DVDs
Average price: Inexpensive
Area: The Annex
Address: 471 Bloor Street W
Toronto, ON M5S 1X9
Phone: (416) 967-5757

#99
House Of Energy
Category: Cafe, Jewelry
Average price: Inexpensive
Area: Kensington Market
Address: 145 Augusta Avenue
Toronto, ON M5L 2L4
Phone: (647) 557-7168

#100
The Papery
Category: Cards & Stationery
Average price: Modest
Area: Yorkville
Address: 124 Cumberland Street
Toronto, ON M5R 1A6
Phone: (416) 962-3916

#101
BYOB Cocktail Emporium
Category: Home Decor
Average price: Modest
Area: West Queen West, Trinity Bellwoods
Address: 972 Queen St W
Toronto, ON M6J 1H1
Phone: (416) 858-2932

#102
Friendly Stranger
Category: Personal Shopping
Average price: Modest
Area: Entertainment District, Queen Street West, Downtown Core
Address: 241 Queen Street W
Toronto, ON M5V 1Z4
Phone: (416) 591-1570

#103
Harvest Wagon
Category: Florist, Fruits & Veggies
Average price: Modest
Area: Rosedale, Summer Hill
Address: 1103 Yonge St
Toronto, ON M4W 2L7
Phone: (416) 923-7542

#104
Honest Ed's
Category: Department Store, Outlet Store
Average price: Inexpensive
Area: Palmerston
Address: 581 Bloor Street W
Toronto, ON M6G 1K3
Phone: (416) 537-1574

#105
Vocado
Category: Women's Clothing
Average price: Modest
Area: Liberty Village
Address: 171 E Liberty Street
Toronto, ON M6K 3P6
Phone: (647) 347-7153

#106
Silly Goose Kids
Category: Toy Store
Average price: Modest
Area: The Danforth
Address: 2054 Danforth Ave
Toronto, ON M4C 1J6
Phone: (647) 341-4400

#107
Dollarama
Category: Discount Store
Average price: Inexpensive
Area: Downtown Core
Address: 730 Yonge Street
Toronto, ON M4Y 2B7
Phone: (416) 924-1064

#108
Seekers Books
Category: Bookstore
Average price: Inexpensive
Area: The Annex
Address: 509 Bloor Street W
Toronto, ON M5S 1Y2
Phone: (416) 925-1982

#109
A & C Video Games
Category: Videos, Video Game Rental
Average price: Inexpensive
Area: University of Toronto, Downtown Core
Address: 706 Spadina Avenue
Toronto, ON M5S 2J2
Phone: (416) 923-3066

#110
Gifts from the Earth
Category: Hobby Shop
Average price: Modest
Area: The Danforth
Address: 320 Avenue Danforth
Toronto, ON M4K 1N8
Phone: (416) 465-4579

#111
Groovy
Category: Shoe Store
Average price: Modest
Area: Entertainment District, Queen Street West, Downtown Core
Address: 323 Queen Street W
Toronto, ON M5V 2A4
Phone: (416) 595-1059

#112
Artscape Wychwood Barns
Category: Art Gallery
Average price: Expensive
Area: Wychwood
Address: 601 Christie Street
Toronto, ON M6G 4C7
Phone: (416) 653-3520

#113
Value Village
Category: Thrift Store
Average price: Inexpensive
Area: Downsview
Address: 1030 Wilson Avenue
Toronto, ON M3K 1G6
Phone: (416) 633-2623

#114
Metro Cigar
Category: Tobacco Shop
Average price: Modest
Area: Downtown Core
Address: 712 Yonge Street
Toronto, ON M4Y 2B3
Phone: (416) 923-8047

#115
Cyclemania
Category: Bikes
Average price: Modest
Area: Riverdale
Address: 281 Danforth Ave
Toronto, ON M4K 1N2
Phone: (416) 466-0330

#116
Ecotique
Category: Shopping Center
Average price: Expensive
Area: High Park, Roncesvalles
Address: 191 Roncesvalles Avenue
Toronto, ON M6R 2L3
Phone: (416) 516-2234

#117
Bizzy B's Stamp and Scrap
Category: Specialty School, Art Supplies, Office Equipment
Average price: Modest
Area: Bloor-West Village, Swansea
Address: 2100 Bloor Street W
Toronto, ON M6S 1M7
Phone: (416) 203-0433

#118
Tiffany & Company
Category: Watches, Jewelry
Average price: Expensive
Area: Discovery District, Yorkville, Downtown Core
Address: 85 Bloor Street W
Toronto, ON M5S 1M1
Phone: (416) 921-3900

#119
Club Monaco
Category: Men's Clothing, Women's Clothing
Average price: Expensive
Area: Discovery District, Yorkville, Downtown Core
Address: 157 Bloor St W
Toronto, ON M5S 1P7
Phone: (416) 585-4101

#120
Manulife Centre
Category: Shopping Center
Average price: Modest
Area: Yorkville, Downtown Core
Address: 55 Bloor Street W
Toronto, ON M4W 1A5
Phone: (416) 961-2311

#121
Lululemon Athletica
Category: Sports Wear
Average price: Expensive
Area: Yorkville
Address: 153 Cumberland Street
Toronto, ON M5R 1A2
Phone: (416) 964-9544

#122
Chinatown Centre
Category: Shopping Center
Average price: Inexpensive
Area: Alexandra Park, Chinatown, Downtown Core
Address: 222 Spadina Ave
Toronto, ON M5T 2C2
Phone: (416) 599-8877

#123
Exposures Photography
Category: Photographers, Photography Store
Average price: Modest
Area: Downtown Core
Address: 4 Wellesley Street West
Toronto, ON M4Y 1E7
Phone: (416) 929-0566

#124
Labl Studio
Category: Sewing & Alterations, Bridal
Average price: Modest
Area: Parkdale
Address: 52 Seaforth Avenue
Toronto, ON M6K 1N6
Phone: (416) 504-1504

#125
Urban Outfitters
Category: Women's Clothing, Men's Clothing, Home Decor
Average price: Expensive
Area: Downtown Core
Address: 235 Yonge St
Toronto, ON M5B 1N8
Phone: (416) 214-1466

#126
The Devil's Workshop
Category: Jewelry
Average price: Modest
Area: Niagara, West Queen West, Trinity Bellwoods
Address: 890 Queen Street W
Toronto, ON M6J 1G3
Phone: (416) 855-4321

#127
Eye Spy
Category: Furniture Store, Antiques, Home Decor
Average price: Modest
Area: Leslieville
Address: 388 Carlaw Ave
Toronto, ON M4M 2T4
Phone: (416) 461-4061

#128
Sophia's Lingerie
Category: Lingerie, Women's Clothing
Average price: Expensive
Area: Greektown, Riverdale
Address: 527 Av Danforth
Toronto, ON M4K 1P7
Phone: (416) 461-6113

#129
Type Books
Category: Bookstore
Average price: Modest
Area: Niagara, West Queen West, Trinity Bellwoods
Address: 883 Queen St W
Toronto, ON M6J 1G5
Phone: (416) 366-8973

#130
Longboard Living
Category: Sporting Goods
Average price: Modest
Area: Kensington Market
Address: 202 Augusta Avenue
Toronto, ON M5T 2L8
Phone: (416) 901-7787

#131
She Said Boom!
Category: Bookstore, Music & DVDs
Average price: Inexpensive
Area: High Park, Roncesvalles
Address: 393 Roncesvalles Ave
Toronto, ON M6R 2N1
Phone: (416) 531-6843

#132
The Clay Room
Category: Arts & Crafts
Average price: Modest
Area: Riverdale
Address: 279 Danforth Ave
Toronto, ON M4K 1N2
Phone: (416) 466-8474

#133
Regal Hardware
Category: Hardware Store
Average price: Modest
Area: Riverdale
Address: 800 Queen Street E
Toronto, ON M4M 1H7
Phone: (416) 466-8577

#134
Drake General Store
Category: Bookstore, Hobby Shop
Average price: Expensive
Area: West Queen West, Beaconsfield Village
Address: 1144 Queen St W
Toronto, ON M6J 1J3
Phone: (416) 531-5042

#135
Public Butter
Category: Used, Vintage, Consignment
Average price: Modest
Area: Parkdale
Address: 1290 Queen St W
Toronto, ON M6K
Phone: (416) 535-4343

#136
GelaSkins
Category: Accessories
Average price: Modest
Area: The Junction
Address: 2738 Dundas Street W
Toronto, ON M6P 1Y3
Phone: (416) 519-1360

#137
Malabar
Category: Costumes
Average price: Expensive
Area: Downtown Core
Address: 14 McCaul St
Toronto, ON M5T 1V6
Phone: (416) 598-2581

#138
Suspect Video and Culture
Category: Videos, Video Game Rental, Bookstore, Music & DVDs
Average price: Inexpensive
Area: Koreatown, Palmerston, Seaton Village
Address: 605 Markham Street
Toronto, ON M6G 2L7
Phone: (416) 588-6674

#139
The Workroom
Category: Fabric Store
Average price: Modest
Area: Parkdale
Address: 1340 Queen Street W
Toronto, ON M6K
Phone: (416) 534-5305

#140
Energia Athletics
Category: Sports Wear, Yoga
Average price: Modest
Area: The Danforth, Riverdale
Address: 164 Danforth Avenue
Toronto, ON M4K 1N1
Phone: (416) 406-6664

#141
Scooter Girl
Category: Toy Store
Average price: Modest
Area: High Park, Roncesvalles
Address: 187 Roncesvalles Avenue
Toronto, ON M6R 2L5
Phone: (416) 534-2211

#142
Knife
Category: Kitchen & Bath
Average price: Exclusive
Area: Little Italy
Address: 249 Crawford Street
Toronto, ON M6J 2V7
Phone: (647) 996-8609

#143
Macklem's Baby Carriage & Toys
Category: Children's Clothing, Baby Gear & Furniture
Average price: Expensive
Area: High Park, Roncesvalles
Address: 2223 Dundas Street W
Toronto, ON M6R 1X6
Phone: (416) 531-7188

#144
MeepleMart
Category: Toy Store, Hobby Shop
Average price: Modest
Area: Chinatown, Downtown Core
Address: 247 Spadina Ave
Toronto, ON M5T 3A8
Phone: (416) 835-6910

#145
Iceman Video Games
Category: Videos, Video Game Rental
Average price: Exclusive
Area: Kensington Market
Address: 206 Augusta Avenue
Toronto, ON M5T 2L6
Phone: (647) 748-7022

#146
Balisi
Category: Shoe Store
Average price: Expensive
Area: Greektown, Riverdale
Address: 439 Danforth Ave
Toronto, ON M4K 1P4
Phone: (416) 463-4848

#147
MarsHall
Category: Department Store
Average price: Modest
Area: Ryerson, Downtown Core
Address: 382 Yonge Street
Toronto, ON M5B 1S8
Phone: (416) 979-0378

#148
Kitchen Stuff Plus
Category: Kitchen & Bath
Average price: Modest
Area: Church-Wellesley Village, Downtown Core
Address: 703 Yonge Street
Toronto, ON M4Y 2B2
Phone: (416) 944-2718

#149
Bling Bling On Queen
Category: Art Supplies
Average price: Inexpensive
Area: Alexandra Park, Queen Street West
Address: 448 Queen Street W
Toronto, ON M5V 2A8
Phone: (416) 365-0880

#150
Te Koop
Category: Accessories, Luggage
Average price: Modest
Area: Entertainment District, Queen Street West, Downtown Core
Address: 421 Queen Street West
Toronto, ON M5V 2A5
Phone: (416) 348-9485

#151
Mjolk
Category: Furniture Store
Average price: Exclusive
Area: The Junction
Address: 2959 Dundas St W
Toronto, ON M6P 1Z2
Phone: (416) 551-9853

#152
Spectacle
Category: Eyewear & Opticians
Average price: Expensive
Area: West Queen West, Trinity Bellwoods
Address: 752 Queen Street W
Toronto, ON M6J 1E9
Phone: (416) 603-0123

#153
Studio1098
Category: Jewelry, Bridal
Average price: Expensive
Area: Summer Hill
Address: 1098 Yonge Street
Toronto, ON M4W 2L6
Phone: (416) 944-1098

#154
Cole Haan
Category: Shoe Store
Average price: Expensive
Area: Discovery District, Yorkville, Downtown Core
Address: 101 Bloor Street W
Toronto, ON M5S 2Z7
Phone: (416) 926-7575

#155
Above All Electronic Surplus
Category: Computers, Electronics
Average price: Modest
Area: Koreatown, Palmerston, Seaton Village
Address: 635A Bloor Street W
Toronto, ON M6G 1K8
Phone: (416) 588-8119

#156
General Tao
Category: Cards & Stationery, Toy Store
Average price: Modest
Area: Bickford Park
Address: 853a Bloor Street W
Toronto, ON M6G 1M3
Phone: (416) 516-4404

#157
Wonder Pens
Category: Office Equipment
Average price: Modest
Area: Little Italy, Trinity Bellwoods
Address: 906 Dundas Street W
Toronto, ON M6J 1W1
Phone: (647) 461-2426

#158
Grreat Stuff
Category: Men's Clothing
Average price: Modest
Area: Niagara, West Queen West, Trinity Bellwoods
Address: 870 Queen Street W
Toronto, ON M6J 1G3
Phone: (416) 533-7680

#159
Dudley Hardware
Category: Hardware Store
Average price: Modest
Area: Church-Wellesley Village, Downtown Core
Address: 511 Church Street
Toronto, ON M4Y 2C9
Phone: (416) 923-5751

#160
Fresh Collective
Category: Accessories, Women's Clothing
Average price: Modest
Area: Niagara, West Queen West, Trinity Bellwoods
Address: 692 Queen Street W
Toronto, ON M6J 1E7
Phone: (416) 594-1313

#161
Value Village
Category: Thrift Store
Average price: Inexpensive
Area: Brockton Village
Address: 1319 Bloor St W
Toronto, ON M6H 1P3
Phone: (416) 539-0585

#162
Due West
Category: Women's Clothing, Men's Clothing
Average price: Expensive
Area: Entertainment District
Address: 431 Queen Street West
Toronto, ON M5V 2A5
Phone: (416) 593-6267

#163
Northbound Leather
Category: Lingerie, Leather Goods
Average price: Expensive
Area: Downtown Core
Address: 586 Yonge Street
Toronto, ON M4Y 1Z3
Phone: (416) 972-1037

#164
Your Feel Good Soap Company
Category: Cosmetics & Beauty Supply
Average price: Modest
Area: Niagara, West Queen West, Trinity Bellwoods
Address: 616 Queen Street W
Toronto, ON M6J 1E4
Phone: (647) 834-9347

#165
Lavishy Boutique
Category: Jewelry, Accessories, Gift Shop
Average price: Modest
Area: The Junction
Address: 3095 Dundas Street W
Toronto, ON M6P 1Z9
Phone: (416) 767-6240

#166
EQ3
Category: Furniture Store, Home Decor
Average price: Expensive
Area: Liberty Village
Address: 3-51 Hanna Avenue
Toronto, ON M6K 3S3
Phone: (416) 533-9090

#167
TOWN
Category: Cards & Stationery
Average price: Modest
Area: Brockton Village, Bloordale Village, Wallace Emerson
Address: 1187 Bloor Street W
Toronto, ON M6H 1N3
Phone: (647) 748-8696

#168
Aritzia
Category: Accessories, Women's Clothing
Average price: Expensive
Area: Entertainment District, Queen Street West, Downtown Core
Address: 280 Queen St W
Toronto, ON M5V 2A1
Phone: (416) 977-9919

#169
Meg
Category: Accessories, Women's Clothing
Average price: Modest
Area: Niagara, West Queen West, Trinity Bellwoods
Address: 849 Queen Street W
Toronto, ON M6J 1G4
Phone: (416) 364-3983

#170
Curry's Art Store
Category: Home Decor, Art Supplies
Average price: Modest
Area: Downtown Core
Address: 490 Yonge Street
Toronto, ON M4Y 1X5
Phone: (416) 967-6666

#171
Boutique Cherie
Category: Women's Clothing, Accessories, Jewelry
Average price: Modest
Area: Koreatown, Palmerston, Seaton Village
Address: 609 Bloor St W
Toronto, ON M6G 1K5
Phone: (416) 532-1222

#172
La Di Da Boutique
Category: Jewelry, Accessories
Average price: Modest
Area: The Danforth
Address: 128 Danforth Ave
Toronto, ON M4K 1N1
Phone: (416) 849-5388

#173
Indigo Books Music & More
Category: Bookstore
Average price: Modest
Area: Yorkville, Downtown Core
Address: 55 Bloor St W
Toronto, ON M4W 1A5
Phone: (416) 925-3536

#174
Gadabout
Category: Antiques, Used, Vintage, Consignment
Average price: Modest
Area: Leslieville
Address: 1300 Queen St E
Toronto, ON M4L 1C4
Phone: (416) 463-1254

#175
Little Island Comics
Category: Comic Books
Average price: Modest
Area: Palmerston
Address: 742 Bathurst Street
Toronto, ON M5S 2R6
Phone: (416) 901-7589

#176
Cat's Cradle Clothing Boutique
Category: Accessories, Women's Clothing
Average price: Modest
Area: Downtown Core
Address: 596 Yonge Street
Toronto, ON M4Y 1Z3
Phone: (416) 920-8216

#177
Durumi Apparel
Category: Women's Clothing
Average price: Modest
Area: Alexandra Park, Queen Street West
Address: 416 Queen Street W
Toronto, ON M5S 2R2
Phone: (647) 727-2591

#178
Placewares
Category: Shopping
Average price: Inexpensive
Area: St. Lawrence, Downtown Core
Address: 92 Front Street E
Toronto, ON M5E 1C4
Phone: (416) 603-1649

#179
Designer Fabrics
Category: Fabric Store
Average price: Inexpensive
Area: Parkdale
Address: 1360 Queen Street W
Toronto, ON M6K 1L7
Phone: (416) 531-2810

#180
RW & Company
Category: Men's Clothing, Women's Clothing
Average price: Modest
Area: Downtown Core
Address: 260 Yonge St
Toronto, ON M5B 2L9
Phone: (416) 591-7247

#181
2 For 1 Movies
Category: Videos, Video Game Rental, Music & DVDs
Average price: Inexpensive
Area: Swansea
Address: 2444 Bloor St W
Toronto, ON M6S 1R2
Phone: (416) 767-0110

#182
Red Pegasus
Category: Toy Store, Jewelry, Cards & Stationery
Average price: Modest
Area: Little Italy, Bickford Park
Address: 628 College St
Toronto, ON M6G 1B4
Phone: (416) 536-3872

#183
Matter of Time
Category: Antiques, Vinyl Records
Average price: Modest
Area: Leslieville
Address: 229 Jones Avenue
Toronto, ON M4M 3A5
Phone: (647) 678-5437

#184
Joe Fresh
Category: Men's Clothing, Women's Clothing, Children's Clothing
Average price: Inexpensive
Area: Casa Loma
Address: 396 St Clair Ave W
Toronto, ON M4P 3N3
Phone: (416) 410-3736

#185
Exile Vintage
Category: Thrift Store
Average price: Expensive
Area: Kensington Market
Address: 62 Kensington Avenue
Toronto, ON M5T
Phone: (416) 596-0827

#186
Mabel's Fables
Category: Bookstore, Toy Store
Average price: Modest
Area: Mount Pleasant and Davisville
Address: 662 Mount Pleasant Rd
Toronto, ON M4S 2M9
Phone: (416) 322-0438

#187
Freedom Clothing Collective
Category: Women's Clothing, Jewelry
Average price: Modest
Area: Dovercourt, Dufferin Grove
Address: 939 Bloor Street W
Toronto, ON M6H 1L5
Phone: (416) 530-9946

#188
Stella Luna
Category: Thrift Store
Average price: Modest
Area: Parkdale, Roncesvalles
Address: 1627 Queen Street W
Toronto, ON M6R 1A9
Phone: (416) 536-7300

#189
Adornments on Queen
Category: Home & Garden
Average price: Modest
Area: Corktown
Address: 338 Queen Street E
Toronto, ON M5A 1S8
Phone: (416) 955-4791

#190
Noah's Natural Foods
Category: Health Market, Grocery
Average price: Expensive
Area: The Annex, Downtown Core
Address: 322 Bloor St W
Toronto, ON M5S 1W5
Phone: (416) 968-7930

#191
Urban Outfitters
Category: Women's Clothing, Men's Clothing
Average price: Expensive
Area: Alexandra Park, Queen Street West
Address: 481 Queen St W
Toronto, ON M5V 2A9
Phone: (416) 203-8633

#192
VC Ultimate
Category: Sports Wear
Average price: Modest
Area: Dufferin Grove
Address: 962 College St
Toronto, ON M6H 1A5
Phone: (416) 531-1339

#193
Klaxon Howl
Category: Shopping
Average price: Expensive
Area: Niagara, West Queen West
Address: 877 Queen Street W
Toronto, ON M6J 1G5
Phone: (647) 436-6628

#194
Ask Computers
Category: Computers, IT Service, Computer Repair
Average price: Modest
Area: Corktown, St. Lawrence
Address: 111 Front Street E
Toronto, ON M5A 4S5
Phone: (416) 862-9595

#195
RedLetter
Category: Shopping
Average price: Modest
Area: Yorkville
Address: 128 Cumberland St
Toronto, ON M5R 1A6
Phone: (647) 340-7294

#196
Risque Clothing
Category: Women's Clothing
Average price: Modest
Area: The Annex
Address: 404 Bloor Street W
Toronto, ON M5S 1X5
Phone: (416) 960-3325

#197
Valhalla Cards & Gifts
Category: Cards & Stationery, Gift Shop
Average price: Modest
Area: Niagara, West Queen West, Trinity Bellwoods
Address: 791 Queen Street W
Toronto, ON M6J 1G1
Phone: (416) 203-6328

#198
Toronto Barber & Beauty Supply
Category: Cosmetics & Beauty Supply
Average price: Modest
Area: Discovery District, Downtown Core
Address: 100 Dundas St W
Toronto, ON M5G 1C3
Phone: (416) 977-2020

#199
Andalous Imports
Category: Arts & Crafts
Average price: Modest
Area: Downtown Core
Address: 425 Yonge Street
Toronto, ON M5B 1T1
Phone: (416) 593-5689

#200
Village Shoe Boutique
Category: Shoe Store
Average price: Modest
Area: Dovercourt
Address: 898 Bloor St W
Toronto, ON M6H 1L1
Phone: (416) 533-8889

#201
BMV Books
Category: Bookstore, Music & DVDs
Average price: Inexpensive
Area: Mount Pleasant and Davisville, Yonge and Eglinton
Address: 2289 Yonge St
Toronto, ON M4P 2C6
Phone: (416) 482-6002

#202
Zara
Category: Men's Clothing, Women's Clothing
Average price: Modest
Area: Entertainment District, Queen Street West, Downtown Core
Address: 341 Queen Street W
Toronto, ON M5V 2A4
Phone: (647) 288-0545

#203
Out On the Street
Category: Men's Clothing
Average price: Modest
Area: Church-Wellesley Village, Downtown Core
Address: 551 Church Street
Toronto, ON M4Y 2E2
Phone: (416) 967-2759

#204
Vintage Mix 1
Category: Used, Vintage, Consignment
Average price: Inexpensive
Area: Little Portugal, Ossington Strip, Beaconsfield Village
Address: 186 Ossington Ave
Toronto, ON M6J
Phone: (416) 534-7767

#205
Knitomatic
Category: Knitting Supplies
Average price: Modest
Area: Casa Loma, Wychwood
Address: 1378 Bathurst St
Toronto, ON M5R 3J1
Phone: (416) 653-7849

#206
Studio Brillantine
Category: Home Decor
Average price: Expensive
Area: Parkdale
Address: 1518 Queen Street West
Toronto, ON M6R 1A4
Phone: (416) 536-6521

#207
Black Daffodil
Category: Women's Clothing
Average price: Modest
Area: The Junction
Address: 3097 Dundas St W
Toronto, ON M6P 1Z8
Phone: (647) 726-9400

#208
Winners
Category: Department Store, Men's Clothing, Women's Clothing
Average price: Modest
Area: Yorkville
Address: 110 Bloor Street W
Toronto, ON M5S 2W7
Phone: (416) 920-0193

#209
Winners
Category: Men's Clothing, Women's Clothing
Average price: Modest
Area: St. Lawrence, Downtown Core
Address: 35 Front St E
Toronto, ON M5E 1B3
Phone: (416) 362-0213

#210
Joe Fresh
Category: Department Store
Average price: Modest
Area: Church-Wellesley Village, Downtown Core
Address: 60 Carlton Street
Toronto, ON M5B 1J2
Phone: (416) 596-7209

#211
Penny Arcade Vintage
Category: Used, Vintage
Average price: Modest
Area: Little Portugal, Beaconsfield Village
Address: 1177 Dundas Street W
Toronto, ON M6J 1X4
Phone: (647) 346-1386

#212
Umbra Store
Category: Home Decor
Average price: Expensive
Area: Downtown Core
Address: 165 John Street
Toronto, ON M5T 1X3
Phone: (416) 599-0088

#213
Felichia Bridal
Category: Bridal
Average price: Modest
Area: Little Italy, Bickford Park
Address: 601 College Street
Toronto, ON M6G 1B5
Phone: (647) 350-5559

#214
The Kitchen and Glass Place
Category: Kitchen & Bath
Average price: Modest
Area: Yorkville
Address: 840 Yonge Street
Toronto, ON M4W 2H1
Phone: (416) 927-9925

#215
Cry If I Want To
Category: Event Planning, Home Decor
Average price: Modest
Area: Leslieville
Address: 1175 Queen St. East
Toronto, ON M4M 1L5
Phone: (416) 466-2797

#216
Bumbleberry Kids
Category: Baby Gear & Furniture
Average price: Inexpensive
Area: Leslieville
Address: 1584 Queen Street E
Toronto, ON M4L 1G1
Phone: (416) 691-5556

#217
Canon Blanc
Category: Women's Clothing, Men's Clothing, Accessories
Average price: Expensive
Area: Niagara, West Queen West, Trinity Bellwoods
Address: 679 Queen Street W
Toronto, ON M6J 1E6
Phone: (647) 346-5060

#218
Ransack The Universe
Category: Used, Vintage, Consignment, Arts & Crafts
Average price: Inexpensive
Area: Brockton Village, Bloordale Village, Wallace Emerson
Address: 1207 Bloor Street W
Toronto, ON M6H 1N4
Phone: (647) 703-6675

#219
William Ashley China
Category: Kitchen & Bath, Home Decor
Average price: Expensive
Area: Yorkville, Downtown Core
Address: 55 Bloor St W
Toronto, ON M4W 3V1
Phone: (416) 964-2900

#220
Sephora
Category: Cosmetics & Beauty Supply
Average price: Expensive
Area: Discovery District, Yorkville
Address: 131 Bloor St W
Toronto, ON M5S 1P7
Phone: (416) 513-1100

#221
The Papery
Category: Cards & Stationery
Average price: Expensive
Area: Yonge and St. Clair, Deer Park
Address: 1424 Yonge Street
Toronto, ON M4T 1Y5
Phone: (416) 968-0706

#222
MAC Cosmetics
Category: Cosmetics & Beauty Supply
Average price: Modest
Area: Discovery District, Yorkville
Address: 91 Bloor St. West
Toronto, ON M5S 1M1
Phone: (416) 929-7555

#223
Lilliput Hats
Category: Accessories
Average price: Expensive
Area: Palmerston
Address: 462 College Street
Toronto, ON M6G 1A1
Phone: (416) 536-5933

#224
Bang-On
Category: Accessories
Average price: Modest
Area: Alexandra Park, Queen Street West
Address: 489 Queen Street W
Toronto, ON M5V 2B4
Phone: (416) 596-8443

#225
401 Games Toys & Sportscards
Category: Toy Store
Average price: Modest
Area: Downtown Core
Address: 518 Yonge Street
Toronto, ON M4Y 1X9
Phone: (416) 599-6446

#226
Burberry
Category: Fashion
Average price: Exclusive
Area: Yorkville, Downtown Core
Address: 144 Bloor St W
Toronto, ON M5S
Phone: (416) 920-7717

#227
The Runners Shop
Category: Sporting Goods, Shoe Store
Average price: Modest
Area: The Annex, Downtown Core
Address: 180 Bloor St W
Toronto, ON M5S 2V6
Phone: (416) 923-9702

#228
Girl Friday Clothing
Category: Accessories, Women's Clothing
Average price: Modest
Area: Little Italy, Bickford Park
Address: 776 College Street
Toronto, ON M6G 1C6
Phone: (416) 531-1036

#229
Davenport Garden Centre
Category: Nursery, Gardening
Average price: Expensive
Area: The Annex
Address: 368 Davenport Rd
Toronto, ON M5R 1K6
Phone: (416) 929-7222

#230
Jonathan+Olivia
Category: Women's Clothing, Men's Clothing, Shoe Store, Jewelry
Average price: Expensive
Area: Ossington Strip, Trinity Bellwoods, Beaconsfield Village
Address: 49 Ossington Avenue
Toronto, ON M6J 2Y9
Phone: (416) 849-5956

#231
G & S Dye & Accessories
Category: Fabric Store
Average price: Expensive
Area: Downtown Core
Address: 250 Dundas St W
Toronto, ON M5T 2Z5
Phone: (416) 596-0550

#232
Common Sort
Category: Thrift Store, Used, Vintage, Consignment
Average price: Modest
Area: Parkdale
Address: 1414 Queen Street W
Toronto, ON M6K 1L9
Phone: (416) 463-7678

#233
El Pipil
Category: Shopping
Average price: Expensive
Area: Riverdale
Address: 267 Danforth Ave
Toronto, ON M4K 1N2
Phone: (416) 465-9625

#234
Dragon City
Category: Shopping Center
Average price: Modest
Area: Alexandra Park, Chinatown, Downtown Core
Address: 280 Spadina Avenue
Toronto, ON M5T 3A5
Phone: (416) 979-7777

#235
Wong's Camera
Category: Photography Store
Average price: Inexpensive
Area: Riverdale
Address: 110 Danforth Avenue
Toronto, ON M4K 1N1
Phone: (416) 469-9909

#236
69 Vintage Collective
Category: Thrift Store, Used, Vintage, Consignment
Average price: Modest
Area: Brockton Village, Bloordale Village, Wallace Emerson
Address: 1207 Bloor St W
Toronto, ON M6H
Phone: (416) 516-1234

#237
Flower Creations
Category: Florist
Average price: Modest
Area: Financial District, Downtown Core
Address: 121 King Street W
Toronto, ON M5H 3T9
Phone: (416) 364-2395

#238
The Film Buff East
Category: Videos, Video Game Rental
Average price: Inexpensive
Area: Leslieville
Address: 1380 Queen Street E
Toronto, ON M4L 1C9
Phone: (416) 465-4324

#239
Velotique
Category: Bikes
Average price: Modest
Area: Leslieville
Address: 1592 Queen Street E
Toronto, ON M4L 1G1
Phone: (416) 466-3171

#240
Romni Wool
Category: Knitting Supplies
Average price: Expensive
Area: Niagara, West Queen West, Trinity Bellwoods
Address: 658 Queen St W
Toronto, ON M6J 1E5
Phone: (416) 703-0202

#241
New Era
Category: Accessories, Men's Clothing
Average price: Expensive
Area: Entertainment District, Queen Street West, Downtown Core
Address: 202 Queen St W
Toronto, ON M5V 1Z2
Phone: (416) 597-2277

#242
Telegramme Prints and Custom Framing
Category: Cards & Stationery, Framing
Average price: Modest
Area: Little Portugal, Ossington Strip
Address: 194 Ossington Avenue
Toronto, ON M6J 2Z7
Phone: (647) 351-8998

#243
Victoria's Secret
Category: Lingerie
Average price: Modest
Area: Downtown Core
Address: 220 Yonge St
Toronto, ON M5B 2H1
Phone: (416) 205-1222

#244
Holy Cow
Category: Home Decor
Average price: Modest
Area: Leslieville
Address: 1100 Queen St E
Toronto, ON M4M 1K8
Phone: (416) 778-6555

#245
Kops Records
Category: Antiques, Vinyl Records
Average price: Exclusive
Area: Entertainment District, Queen Street West, Downtown Core
Address: 229 Queen Street W
Toronto, ON M5V 1Z4
Phone: (416) 593-8523

#246
H & M
Category: Men's Clothing, Women's Clothing
Average price: Modest
Area: Yorkville, Downtown Core
Address: 13-15 Bloor St W
Toronto, ON M4W 1A3
Phone: (416) 920-4029

#247
BMV Books
Category: Bookstore, Newspapers, Magazines, Music & DVDs
Average price: Inexpensive
Area: Downtown Core
Address: 10 Edward St
Toronto, ON M5G 1C9
Phone: (416) 977-3087

#248
The Detox Market
Category: Cosmetics & Beauty Supply
Average price: Expensive
Area: Entertainment District
Address: 367 King Street W
Toronto, ON M5V 1K1
Phone: (416) 548-9879

#249
Lettuce Knit
Category: Knitting Supplies
Average price: Expensive
Area: Kensington Market
Address: 86 Nassau Street
Toronto, ON M5T 1M5
Phone: (416) 203-9970

#250
GravityPope
Category: Shoe Store, Women's Clothing, Men's Clothing
Average price: Expensive
Area: Ossington Strip, West Queen West, Beaconsfield Village
Address: 1010 Queen Street W
Toronto, ON M6J 1H7
Phone: (647) 748-5155

#251
Sydney's
Category: Sewing & Alterations, Men's Clothing
Average price: Expensive
Area: West Queen West
Address: 682 Queen St W
Toronto, ON M6J 1E5
Phone: (416) 603-3369

#252
Magpie Design
Category: Accessories, Women's Clothing
Average price: Expensive
Area: Niagara, West Queen West
Address: 884 Queen St W
Toronto, ON M6J 1G3
Phone: (416) 536-6158

#253
Bungalow
Category: Antiques, Used, Vintage, Consignment
Average price: Expensive
Area: Kensington Market
Address: 273 Av Augusta
Toronto, ON M5T 2M1
Phone: (416) 598-0204

#254
DLR Clothing & Accessories
Category: Women's Clothing, Accessories
Average price: Expensive
Area: Wychwood
Address: 52 Vaughan Rd
Toronto, ON M6C 1A1
Phone: (416) 652-5512

#255
The Cashmere Shop
Category: Fashion
Average price: Expensive
Area: Yorkville
Address: 24 Bellair Street
Toronto, ON M5R 2C7
Phone: (416) 925-0831

#256
The Centre Shop
Category: Arts & Crafts, Accessories
Average price: Expensive
Area: Harbourfront
Address: 235 Queens Quay W
Toronto, ON M5J 2G8
Phone: (416) 973-4993

#257
Lady Mosquito
Category: Jewelry, Accessories
Average price: Modest
Area: Ossington Strip, West Queen West, Beaconsfield Village
Address: 1022 Queen St W
Toronto, ON M6J 1H6
Phone: (647) 344-3266

#258
Jacob
Category: Lingerie, Accessories, Women's Clothing
Average price: Modest
Area: Yorkville, Downtown Core
Address: 55 Bloor St W
Toronto, ON M4W 1A5
Phone: (416) 925-9488

#259
Watch It
Category: Watches, Eyewear & Opticians, Accessories
Average price: Modest
Area: Ryerson, Downtown Core
Address: 317 Yonge Street
Toronto, ON M5B
Phone: (416) 597-2929

#260
Urban Barn
Category: Home Decor, Furniture Store
Average price: Modest
Area: Corktown
Address: 275 King Street E
Toronto, ON M5A 1K2
Phone: (416) 214-4970

#261
Winners
Category: Department Store, Men's Clothing, Women's Clothing
Average price: Modest
Area: Alexandra Park, Queen Street West
Address: 585 Queen St W
Toronto, ON M5V 2B7
Phone: (416) 203-1694

#262
Annie Aime
Category: Fashion
Average price: Expensive
Area: Ossington Strip, Trinity Bellwoods, Beaconsfield Village
Address: 42 Ossington Avenue
Toronto, ON M6J 2Y7
Phone: (416) 840-5227

#263
Ginger Flower Studio
Category: Florist
Average price: Modest
Area: Yonge and St. Clair, Deer Park
Address: 50 St Clair Ave E
Toronto, ON M4T 1M9
Phone: (416) 925-1135

#264
Gussied Up
Category: Women's Clothing
Average price: Modest
Area: The Annex, Seaton Village
Address: 1090 Bathurst St
Toronto, ON M5R 1W5
Phone: (647) 352-7587

#265
AAA Army Surplus
Category: Thrift Store, Used, Vintage, Consignment
Average price: Modest
Area: Kensington Market
Address: 199 Baldwin Street
Toronto, ON M5T 1M1
Phone: (416) 597-9592

#266
Raindrops
Category: Accessories, Women's Clothing, Children's Clothing
Average price: Modest
Area: Yorkville, Downtown Core
Address: 50 Bloor Street W
Toronto, ON M4W 3L8
Phone: (416) 203-7246

#267
Ez-Vape Toronto
Category: Tobacco Shop
Average price: Modest
Area: Downtown Core
Address: 634 Yonge Street
Toronto, ON M4Y 1Z8
Phone: (647) 979-3244

#268
The Labyrinth Bookstore
Category: Comic Books, Bookstore
Average price: Modest
Area: The Annex
Address: 386 Bloor Street W
Toronto, ON M5S 1X4
Phone: (416) 840-4506

#269
The Accessory Bar
Category: Watches, Accessories, Eyewear & Opticians
Average price: Expensive
Area: Ryerson, Downtown Core
Address: 350 Yonge Street
Toronto, ON M5B 1S5
Phone: (416) 792-0882

#270
House of Vintage
Category: Used, Vintage, Consignment, Accessories
Average price: Expensive
Area: Parkdale
Address: 1239 Queen St W
Toronto, ON M6K 1L5
Phone: (416) 535-2142

#271
Pharma Plus
Category: Drugstore
Average price: Modest
Area: Church-Wellesley Village, Downtown Core
Address: 63 Wellesley Street E
Toronto, ON M4Y 1G7
Phone: (416) 924-7760

#272
Frame It On Bloor
Category: Art Gallery, Framing
Average price: Expensive
Area: High Park
Address: 1610 Bloor St W
Toronto, ON M6P 1A7
Phone: (416) 588-4226

#273
The Elegant Garage Sale
Category: Furniture Store, Antiques
Average price: Modest
Area: Mount Pleasant and Davisville
Address: 1588 Bayview Ave
Toronto, ON M4G 3B7
Phone: (416) 322-9744

#274
Roots
Category: Sports Wear, Men's Clothing, Women's Clothing
Average price: Modest
Area: Downtown Core
Address: Toronto Eaton Centre
Toronto, ON M5B 2H1
Phone: (416) 593-9640

#275
Apple Store - Eaton Centre
Category: Computers, IT Service, Computer Repair
Average price: Expensive
Area: Downtown Core
Address: 220 Yonge Street
Toronto, ON M5B 2H1
Phone: (647) 258-0801

#276
Ewanika
Category: Women's Clothing
Average price: Expensive
Area: Little Italy, Palmerston
Address: 490 College St
Toronto, ON M6G 1A4
Phone: (416) 927-9699

#277
Cube Works Studio
Category: Art Gallery
Average price: Modest
Area: Distillery District
Address: 55 Mill St
Toronto, ON M5A
Phone: (416) 879-4259

#278
Club Monaco
Category: Men's Clothing, Women's Clothing
Average price: Modest
Area: Downtown Core
Address: 220 Yonge St
Toronto, ON M5B 2H1
Phone: (416) 977-2064

#279
The Chief Salvage
Category: Home Decor
Average price: Modest
Area: Brockton Village
Address: 1493 Dundas St W
Toronto, ON M6K 1T5
Phone: (647) 352-1983

#280
Sasmart - Smart Wear
Category: Thrift Store, Kitchen & Bath
Average price: Inexpensive
Area: Kensington Market
Address: 6 Denison Square
Toronto, ON M5T 1K8
Phone: (416) 593-9694

#281
Gotstyle Distillery
Category: Men's Clothing, Women's Clothing
Average price: Expensive
Area: Distillery District, West Don Lands
Address: 21 Trinity Street
Toronto, ON M5A 3C4
Phone: (416) 260-9696

#282
Trap Door Boutique
Category: Women's Clothing
Average price: Modest
Area: The Junction
Address: 2993 Dundas Street W
Toronto, ON M6P 1Z4
Phone: (647) 827-6994

#283
Tom's Place
Category: Accessories, Men's Clothing, Formal Wear
Average price: Modest
Area: Kensington Market
Address: 190 Baldwin Street
Toronto, ON M5T 1L8
Phone: (416) 596-0297

#284
Off the Cuff Resale Designer Menswear
Category: Formal Wear, Men's Clothing
Average price: Expensive
Area: Mount Pleasant and Davisville
Address: 5 Avenue Broadway
Toronto, ON M4P 1T7
Phone: (416) 489-4248

#285
Floorplaysocks
Category: Accessories, Women's Clothing
Average price: Modest
Area: West Queen West
Address: 762 Queen Street W
Toronto, ON M6J 1E9
Phone: (416) 606-2492

#286
Carte Blanche
Category: Fashion
Average price: Modest
Area: Niagara, West Queen West
Address: 758 Queen St W
Toronto, ON M6J 1E9
Phone: (416) 532-0347

#287
King West Flowers
Category: Florist
Average price: Modest
Area: Niagara
Address: 720 King St W
Toronto, ON M5V 2T3
Phone: (416) 203-1258

#288
Next Door Clothing
Category: Women's Clothing, Men's Clothing
Average price: Expensive
Area: Entertainment District
Address: 433 Queen St. West
Toronto, ON M5V 1A1
Phone: (416) 593-6267

#289
Kali Vintage
Category: Used, Vintage, Consignment
Average price: Modest
Area: Alexandra Park, Chinatown, Kensington Market
Address: 2 Kensington Avenue
Toronto, ON M5T 2J9
Phone: (416) 340-1778

#290
Davids Footwear
Category: Shoe Store
Average price: Exclusive
Area: Discovery District, Yorkville
Address: 66 Bloor Street W
Toronto, ON M5S 1L9
Phone: (416) 920-1000

#291
The Future Of Frances Watson
Category: Women's Clothing, Men's Clothing
Average price: Expensive
Area: Parkdale
Address: 1390 Queen Street W
Toronto, ON M6K 1L7
Phone: (416) 531-8892

#292
The Embellished Room
Category: Women's Clothing
Average price: Inexpensive
Area: The Beach
Address: 1978 Queen St E
Toronto, ON M4L 1H9
Phone: (416) 546-5164

#293
The Brides' Project
Category: Bridal
Average price: Modest
Area: Riverdale
Address: 431 Broadview Ave
Toronto, ON M4K 2N1
Phone: (416) 469-6777

#294
Dueling Grounds
Category: Hobby Shop
Average price: Expensive
Area: Brockton Village, Bloordale Village
Address: 1193 Bloor Street W
Toronto, ON M6H 1N4
Phone: (416) 534-3835

#295
The Make Den
Category: Arts & Crafts
Average price: Modest
Area: Brockton Village, Bloordale Village
Address: 1244 Bloor Street W
Toronto, ON M6H 1N4
Phone: (415) 705-6925

#296
High Times
Category: Tobacco Shop
Average price: Inexpensive
Area: Koreatown, Bickford Park, Seaton Village
Address: 714 Bloor Street W
Toronto, ON M6G 1L5
Phone: (647) 347-8004

#297
Dollarama
Category: Discount Store
Average price: Inexpensive
Area: Parkdale
Address: 1337 Queen St W
Toronto, ON M6K 1L8
Phone: (416) 531-4809

#298
Distill
Category: Art Gallery
Average price: Expensive
Area: Distillery District
Address: 24 Tank House Lane
Toronto, ON M5A 3C4
Phone: (416) 304-0033

#299
Antiques At The St-Lawrence
Category: Antiques
Average price: Modest
Area: St. Lawrence, Downtown Core
Address: 92 Front Street E
Toronto, ON M5E 1C4
Phone: (416) 350-8865

#300
The Bay
Category: Department Store
Average price: Expensive
Area: Downtown Core
Address: 44 Bloor Street E
Toronto, ON M4W 3H7
Phone: (416) 972-3333

#301
Lululemon Athletica
Category: Sports Wear, Women's Clothing, Yoga
Average price: Expensive
Area: Downtown Core
Address: 218 Yonge St
Toronto, ON M5B 2H1
Phone: (416) 597-0422

#302
Refried Beats
Category: Music & DVDs
Average price: Inexpensive
Area: Downtown Core
Address: 599 Yonge Street
Toronto, ON M4Y 1Z4
Phone: (416) 920-2417

#303
Alligator Party
Category: Party & Event Planning
Average price: Inexpensive
Area: Seaton Village
Address: 505 Dupont St
Toronto, ON M6G 1Y6
Phone: (416) 532-1162

#304
Above Ground Art Supplies
Category: Art Supplies
Average price: Modest
Area: Downtown Core
Address: 74 McCaul Street
Toronto, ON M5T 3K2
Phone: (416) 591-1601

#305
Kitchen Stuff Plus
Category: Department Store
Average price: Modest
Area: Liberty Village
Address: 1A - 75 Hanna Avenue
Toronto, ON M6K 3N7
Phone: (416) 532-5500

#306
Australian Boot Company
Category: Shoe Store
Average price: Expensive
Area: West Queen West, Trinity Bellwoods
Address: 698 Queen St W
Toronto, ON M6J 1E7
Phone: (416) 504-2411

#307
Fresh Collective
Category: Accessories, Women's Clothing
Average price: Modest
Area: Kensington Market
Address: 274 Augusta Avenue
Toronto, ON M5T 2L9
Phone: (416) 966-0123

#308
Bed Bath and Beyond
Category: Kitchen & Bath, Home Decor
Average price: Modest
Area: Ryerson, Downtown Core
Address: 382 Yonge Street
Toronto, ON M5B 1S8
Phone: (416) 205-9653

#309
Gap
Category: Women's Clothing, Men's Clothing, Children's Clothing
Average price: Modest
Area: Downtown Core
Address: 260 Yonge St - E1
Toronto, ON M5B 2L9
Phone: (416) 599-8802

#310
Zara
Category: Accessories, Women's Clothing, Men's Clothing
Average price: Modest
Area: Yorkville
Address: 50 Bloor St W
Toronto, ON M4W 3L8
Phone: (416) 916-2401

#311
Hero Video Games & Collectables
Category: Videos, Video Game Rental
Average price: Inexpensive
Area: Little Italy, Trinity Bellwoods
Address: 870 Dundas Street W
Toronto, ON M6J 1V7
Phone: (647) 556-4307

#312
Surmesur
Category: Men's Clothing
Average price: Modest
Area: Corktown, Downtown Core
Address: 108 Queen Street E
Toronto, ON M5C 1S6
Phone: (416) 214-2840

#313
Spring Shoes
Category: Shoe Store
Average price: Inexpensive
Area: Downtown Core
Address: 220 Yonge St
Toronto, ON M4W 1A7
Phone: (416) 340-2563

#314
Queen Video
Category: Videos, Video Game Rental
Average price: Inexpensive
Area: Bickford Park
Address: 688 College Street
Toronto, ON M6G 1C1
Phone: (416) 532-0555

#315
HMV
Category: Music & DVDs
Average price: Expensive
Area: Yorkville
Address: 50 Bloor Street W
Toronto, ON M4W 3L8
Phone: (416) 324-9979

#316
Village by the Grange
Category: Shopping Center
Average price: Inexpensive
Area: Downtown Core
Address: 53 McCaul Street
Toronto, ON M5T 2W9
Phone: (416) 599-5797

#317
Bridal Fashion Fraire
Category: Bridal
Average price: Modest
Area: Entertainment District, Downtown Core
Address: 123 Spadina Avenue
Toronto, ON M5V 2K8
Phone: (416) 598-3174

#318
Forever XXI
Category: Women's Clothing, Accessories, Men's Clothing
Average price: Inexpensive
Area: Ryerson, Downtown Core
Address: 302 Yonge St
Toronto, ON M5B 1R4
Phone: (416) 260-9019

#319
Flashback 2
Category: Used, Vintage, Consignment
Average price: Expensive
Area: Kensington Market
Address: 25 Kensington Avenue
Toronto, ON M5T
Phone: (647) 343-5569

#320
Crown Flora Studio
Category: Flowers & Gifts, Home Decor
Average price: Modest
Area: Parkdale, Roncesvalles
Address: 1537 Queen Street W
Toronto, ON M6R 1B2
Phone: (647) 861-5799

#321
Sandpipers Sports & Funwear
Category: Sporting Goods, Accessories, Women's Clothing
Average price: Exclusive
Area: Yorkville
Address: 87 Yorkville Avenue
Toronto, ON M5R 1C1
Phone: (416) 921-2376

#322
Galleria Shopping Centre
Category: Shopping Center
Average price: Inexpensive
Area: Wallace Emerson
Address: 1245 Dupont Street
Toronto, ON M6H 2A6
Phone: (416) 533-2317

#323
Harry Rosen
Category: Men's Clothing
Average price: Expensive
Area: Financial District, Downtown Core
Address: 100 King Street W
Toronto, ON M5X 1E2
Phone: (416) 981-9097

#324
Shopper's Drug Mart
Category: Cosmetics & Beauty Supply
Average price: Modest
Area: Downtown Core
Address: 465 Yonge St
Toronto, ON M4Y 1X4
Phone: (416) 408-4000

#325
Optika
Category: Eyewear & Opticians
Average price: Modest
Area: Yonge and Eglinton
Address: 2300 Yonge St
Toronto, ON M4P 1E4
Phone: (416) 483-5571

#326
Toronto Sculpture Garden
Category: Art Gallery, Park
Average price: Modest
Area: Corktown, St. Lawrence, Downtown Core
Address: 115 King St E
Toronto, ON M5C
Phone: (416) 515-9658

#327
Hideaway Antiques
Category: Antiques, Furniture Store
Average price: Expensive
Area: Parkdale, Roncesvalles
Address: 1605 Queen Street W
Toronto, ON M6R 1A9
Phone: (416) 539-0833

#328
Playful Minds
Category: Toy Store
Average price: Modest
Area: Wychwood
Address: 657 Street Clair Avenue W
Toronto, ON M6C 1A7
Phone: (416) 651-4028

#329
Charlie's Bike Shop
Category: Bikes
Average price: Inexpensive
Area: Corktown
Address: 242.5 Queen Street E
Toronto, ON M5A 1S5
Phone: (416) 546-2200

#330
Celebration Shoes
Category: Shoe Store
Average price: Expensive
Area: Yorkville
Address: 106 Yorkville Avenue
Toronto, ON M5R 1B9
Phone: (416) 703-2789

#331
Common Sort
Category: Thrift Store, Used, Vintage, Consignment
Average price: Modest
Area: Riverdale
Address: 804 Queen St E
Toronto, ON M4M
Phone: (416) 463-7678

#332
The 100-Mile Child
Category: Toy Store, Baby Gear & Furniture
Average price: Expensive
Area: The Danforth
Address: 348 Danforth Avenue
Toronto, ON M4K 1N7
Phone: (416) 254-0150

#333
Neohome Houseware
Category: Houseware
Average price: Inexpensive
Area: Alexandra Park, Chinatown, Downtown Core
Address: 251 Spadina Ave
Toronto, ON M5T 2E2
Phone: (416) 597-8288

#334
Walmart
Category: Department Store
Average price: Inexpensive
Area: Brockton Village
Address: 900 Dufferin Street
Toronto, ON M6H 4A9
Phone: (416) 537-2561

#335
Dancing Days
Category: Accessories, Women's Clothing
Average price: Modest
Area: Kensington Market
Address: 17 Kensington Avenue
Toronto, ON M5T 2J8
Phone: (416) 599-9827

#336
Second Nature Boutique
Category: Women's Clothing
Average price: Expensive
Area: Mount Pleasant and Davisville
Address: 514 Mt Pleasant Road
Toronto, ON M4S 2M2
Phone: (416) 481-4924

#337
Adina Photo
Category: Home Decor, Photographers
Average price: Modest
Area: Downtown Core
Address: 3 Grosvenor Street
Toronto, ON M4Y 1A9
Phone: (416) 960-9252

#338
Paperboy Cards & Gifts
Category: Cards & Stationery
Average price: Expensive
Area: Yonge and St. Clair, Deer Park
Address: 7 Pleasant Blvd
Toronto, ON M4T 1K2
Phone: (416) 926-8622

#339
Zara
Category: Men's Clothing, Women's Clothing
Average price: Modest
Area: Downtown Core
Address: 220 Yonge St
Toronto, ON M5B 2H1
Phone: (647) 288-0333

#340
Diamonds For Less
Category: Jewelry
Average price: Modest
Area: Downtown Core
Address: 5 Shuter St
Toronto, ON M5B 2H8
Phone: (416) 362-9944

#341
Merit Decorating Centre
Category: Hardware Store
Average price: Modest
Area: Bickford Park
Address: 700 College St
Toronto, ON M6G 1C1
Phone: (416) 534-6337

#342
Sash & Bustle
Category: Bridal
Average price: Modest
Area: Leslieville
Address: 233 Carlaw Avenue
Toronto, ON M4M 3N6
Phone: (647) 340-5850

#343
Livestock
Category: Shoe Store, Men's Clothing
Average price: Expensive
Area: Entertainment District, Downtown Core
Address: 116 Spadina Ave
Toronto, ON M5V 2K6
Phone: (416) 360-5483

#344
Specchio Shoes
Category: Shoe Store, Women's Clothing
Average price: Exclusive
Area: Yorkville
Address: 1240 Bay St
Toronto, ON M5R 2A7
Phone: (416) 961-7989

#345
I Miss You
Category: Thrift Store
Average price: Expensive
Area: Ossington Strip, Trinity Bellwoods
Address: 63 Ossington Ave
Toronto, ON M6J 2Z2
Phone: (416) 916-7021

#346
Fabulous Frames
Category: Eyewear & Opticians
Average price: Modest
Area: Corktown
Address: 185 Queen Street E
Toronto, ON M5A 1S2
Phone: (647) 352-5010

#347
Open Air Books & Maps
Category: Bookstore
Average price: Modest
Area: Downtown Core
Address: 25 Toronto St
Toronto, ON M5C 2R1
Phone: (416) 363-0719

#348
Golf Town Canada
Category: Sporting Goods, Golf
Average price: Modest
Area: Entertainment District
Address: 266 King Street W
Toronto, ON M5V 1H8
Phone: (416) 977-4733

#349
Syllogy Incorporated
Category: Home Decor, Art Gallery
Average price: Modest
Area: Riverdale
Address: 217 Danforth Avenue
Toronto, ON M4K 1N2
Phone: (416) 916-8673

#350
Avenue Flower
Category: Florist
Average price: Modest
Area: Roncesvalles
Address: 163 Roncesvalles Avenue
Toronto, ON M6R 2L3
Phone: (416) 922-0348

#351
Perfect Pitch Downtown
Category: Musical Instruments
Average price: Inexpensive
Area: City Place, Entertainment District,
Address: 361 Front Street W
Toronto, ON M5V 3R5
Phone: (647) 448-7723

#352
Just You Sarah & Tom
Category: Toy Store, Gift Shop
Average price: Modest
Area: Downtown Core
Address: 686 Yonge Street
Toronto, ON M4Y 2A6
Phone: (416) 962-4619

#353
Belo Fashions Boutique
Category: Bridal, Women's Clothing
Average price: Modest
Area: High Park, Roncesvalles
Address: 420 Roncesvalles Ave
Toronto, ON M6R 2N2
Phone: (647) 349-8822

#354
Balfour Books
Category: Bookstore
Average price: Modest
Area: Palmerston
Address: 468 College St
Toronto, ON M6G 1B5
Phone: (416) 531-9911

#355
Anice Jewellery
Category: Gift Shop, Hobby Shop
Average price: Modest
Area: Kensington Market
Address: 167 Augusta Avenue
Toronto, ON M5T 2L4
Phone: (647) 501-5526

#356
Rapp Optical Limited
Category: Eyewear & Opticians
Average price: Expensive
Area: Little Italy, Bickford Park
Address: 788 College St
Toronto, ON M6G 1C6
Phone: (416) 537-6590

#357
Cheers Smoke & Gift Shop
Category: Tobacco Shop
Average price: Modest
Area: Downtown Core
Address: 170 McCaul Street
Toronto, ON M5T 1W4
Phone: (416) 348-9524

#358
Zebuu
Category: Interior Design, Art Gallery
Average price: Expensive
Area: Brockton Village, Bloordale Village, Wallace Emerson
Address: 1265 Bloor Street W
Toronto, ON M6H 1N7
Phone: (647) 748-1265

#359
Metropolis Living
Category: Antiques, Furniture Store, Art Gallery
Average price: Expensive
Area: The Junction
Address: 2989 Dundas St W
Toronto, ON M6P 1Z4
Phone: (647) 343-6900

#360
Eat Your Words
Category: Bookstore
Average price: Expensive
Area: Bloor-West Village
Address: 778 Annette Street
Toronto, ON M6S 2E2
Phone: (416) 604-2665

#361
Trixie
Category: Accessories, Women's Clothing
Average price: Expensive
Area: Bloor-West Village, Swansea
Address: 2313 Bloor St W
Toronto, ON M6S 1P1
Phone: (416) 762-0084

#362
Old Navy
Category: Fashion
Average price: Modest
Area: Downtown Core
Address: 220 Yonge St
Toronto, ON M5B 2L7
Phone: (416) 593-0065

#363
Casalife
Category: Furniture Store
Average price: Expensive
Area: Liberty Village
Address: 171 E Liberty St
Toronto, ON M6K 3P6
Phone: (416) 922-2785

#364
MetroCycleTO
Category: Bike Rentals, Bikes
Average price: Inexpensive
Area: Parkdale
Address: 74 Springhurst Avenue
Toronto, ON M6K 2V2
Phone: (647) 771-1650

#365
Club Monaco
Category: Accessories, Women's Clothing
Average price: Expensive
Area: Entertainment District, Queen Street West, Downtown Core
Address: 403 Queen Street W
Toronto, ON M5V 2A5
Phone: (416) 979-5633

#366
Sunrise Records
Category: Music & DVDs
Average price: Modest
Area: Yorkville, Downtown Core
Address: 784 Yonge St
Toronto, ON M4Y
Phone: (416) 920-9390

#367
4 Your Hair Extensions
Category: Cosmetics & Beauty Supply
Average price: Expensive
Area: Parkdale
Address: 1368 Queen St W
Toronto, ON M6K 1L7
Phone: (416) 530-4001

#368
Periwinkle
Category: Arts & Crafts, Jewelry, Accessories
Average price: Modest
Area: Bloor-West Village, Swansea
Address: 2137 Bloor St W
Toronto, ON M6S 1N2
Phone: (416) 551-2553

#369
Rent Frock Repeat
Category: Women's Clothing
Average price: Expensive
Area: Roncesvalles
Address: 35 Golden Avenue
Toronto, ON M6R 2J5
Phone: (416) 269-6374

#370
Ivory Parade
Category: Hobby Shop, Cards & Stationery
Average price: Modest
Area: Little Italy, Bickford Park
Address: 760 College St
Toronto, ON M6G 1C4
Phone: (416) 533-4144

#371
Value Village
Category: Thrift Store
Average price: Inexpensive
Area: The Danforth
Address: 2119 Danforth Ave
Toronto, ON M4C 1J9
Phone: (416) 698-0621

#372
Anime Xtreme
Category: Bookstore, Comic Books
Average price: Modest
Area: Chinatown, Kensington Market
Address: 315 Spadina Ave
Toronto, ON M5T 2E9
Phone: (416) 979-0399

#373
Joe Fresh
Category: Fashion
Average price: Modest
Area: Alexandra Park
Address: 589 Queen Street West
Toronto, ON M5V 2B7
Phone: (416) 361-6342

#374
Shoppers Drug Mart
Category: Cosmetics & Beauty Supply, Drugstore, Photography Store
Average price: Modest
Area: The Annex
Address: 292 Dupont Street
Toronto, ON M5R 1V9
Phone: (416) 972-0232

#375
Grassroots Environmental
Category: Cosmetics & Beauty Supply, Home & Garden, Baby Gear & Furniture
Average price: Modest
Area: Riverdale
Address: 372 Danforth Ave
Toronto, ON M4K 1N8
Phone: (416) 466-2841

#376
Grand & Toy
Category: Office Equipment
Average price: Modest
Area: The Annex, Downtown Core
Address: 180 Bloor Street W
Toronto, ON M5S 2V6
Phone: (416) 928-0213

#377
Guerlain Canada
Category: Cosmetics & Beauty Supply
Average price: Expensive
Area: Yorkville
Address: 110 Bloor Street W
Toronto, ON M5S 2W7
Phone: (416) 929-6114

#378
Chanel Boutique
Category: Accessories, Women's Clothing, Cosmetics & Beauty Supply
Average price: Exclusive
Area: Discovery District, Yorkville
Address: 131 Bloor Street W
Toronto, ON M5S 1R1
Phone: (416) 925-2577

#379
DeSerres
Category: Art Supplies
Average price: Modest
Area: Entertainment District, Downtown Core
Address: 130 Spadina Ave
Toronto, ON M5V 2K8
Phone: (416) 703-4748

#380
Dots Gift Boutique
Category: Gift Shop, Toy Store
Average price: Expensive
Area: Downtown Core
Address: 613 Yonge Street
Toronto, ON M4Y 1Z5
Phone: (416) 929-3687

#381
China Town Dollar Mart
Category: Shopping
Average price: Inexpensive
Area: Chinatown, Downtown Core
Address: 490 Dundas St W
Toronto, ON M5T 1G9
Phone: (416) 977-6362

#382
Alternative Thinking
Category: Bookstore, Venues, Event Space
Average price: Modest
Area: Palmerston
Address: 758 Bathurst Street
Toronto, ON M5S 2R6
Phone: (647) 932-8311

#383
Oliver Spencer
Category: Women's Clothing, Men's Clothing, Leather Goods
Average price: Expensive
Area: West Queen West, Trinity Bellwoods
Address: 962 Queen Street W
Toronto, ON M6J 1G6
Phone: (647) 348-7673

#384
Marty Millionaire
Category: Furniture Store
Average price: Modest
Area: Corktown
Address: 345 Queen Street East
Toronto, ON M5A 1S9
Phone: (416) 366-6433

#385
The Rock Store
Category: Jewelry
Average price: Expensive
Area: Koreatown, Palmerston
Address: 602 Markham St
Toronto, ON M6G 2L7
Phone: (416) 516-2191

#386
L'occitane En Provence
Category: Cosmetics & Beauty Supply
Average price: Expensive
Area: Yorkville, Downtown Core
Address: 150 Bloor Street W
Toronto, ON M5S 2X9
Phone: (416) 413-4899

#387
Shoppers Drug Mart
Category: Drugstore
Average price: Modest
Area: Dovercourt
Address: 958 Bloor Street W
Toronto, ON M6H 1L6
Phone: (416) 538-0105

#388
Gloria Fashion & Gift
Category: Accessories, Cosmetics & Beauty Supply
Average price: Modest
Area: Koreatown, Palmerston, Seaton Village
Address: 654 Bloor Street W
Toronto, ON M6G 1K9
Phone: (416) 533-8110

#389
Yonge Pharmacy
Category: Drugstore
Average price: Modest
Area: Downtown Core
Address: 159 Yonge Street
Toronto, ON M5C 1X7
Phone: (416) 603-4888

#390
Mama Loves You Vintage
Category: Used, Vintage, Consignment
Average price: Modest
Area: Alexandra Park, Queen Street West
Address: 541 Queen St, W
Toronto, ON M6K 1T5
Phone: (416) 603-4747

#391
Bloor Dovercourt Appliances
Category: Appliances
Average price: Modest
Area: Dovercourt, Dufferin Grove
Address: 959 Bloor Street W
Toronto, ON M6H 1L7
Phone: (416) 534-4207

#392
Swipe Design
Category: Bookstore, Toy Store
Average price: Expensive
Area: Entertainment District, Downtown Core
Address: 401 Richmond Street W
Toronto, ON M5V 3E7
Phone: (416) 363-1332

#393
House Of Rinka
Category: Women's Clothing
Average price: Modest
Area: Koreatown, Palmerston, Seaton Village
Address: 605 Bloor Street W
Toronto, ON M6G 1K6
Phone: (416) 516-8878

#394
Ultra Lighting
Category: Home Decor
Average price: Modest
Area: Entertainment District, Downtown Core
Address: 129 Spadina Avenue
Toronto, ON M5R 2T1
Phone: (416) 868-9606

#395
Envelop
Category: Men's Clothing, Women's Clothing
Average price: Expensive
Area: Riverdale
Address: 311 Av Danforth
Toronto, ON M4K 1N7
Phone: (416) 405-9993

#396
Williams-Sonoma
Category: Kitchen & Bath
Average price: Expensive
Area: Discovery District, Yorkville, Downtown Core
Address: 100 Bloor Street W
Toronto, ON M5S 1M4
Phone: (416) 962-9455

#397
Clearly Contacts
Category: Eyewear & Opticians
Average price: Modest
Area: Entertainment District
Address: 317 Queen Street W
Toronto, ON M5V 2A4
Phone: (416) 205-9161

#398
Ziliotto Design
Category: Women's Clothing
Average price: Modest
Area: West Queen West, Trinity Bellwoods
Address: 764 Queen St W
Toronto, ON M6J
Phone: (416) 867-1632

#399
Lemur
Category: Flowers & Gifts
Average price: Expensive
Area: The Danforth
Address: 900 Danforth Ave
Toronto, ON M4J
Phone: (416) 465-1413

#400
Ends
Category: Women's Clothing, Home Decor, Men's Clothing
Average price: Modest
Area: The Beach
Address: 1930 Queen St E
Toronto, ON M4L 1H6
Phone: (416) 699-2271

#401
Huh
Category: Women's Clothing, Accessories
Average price: Expensive
Area: Niagara, West Queen West, Trinity Bellwoods
Address: 847 Queen Street W
Toronto, ON M6J 1G4
Phone: (416) 645-1702

#402
Sporting Life Bikes & Boards
Category: Bikes
Average price: Expensive
Area: Mount Pleasant and Davisville, Yonge and Eglinton
Address: 2454 Yonge St
Toronto, ON M4P 2H5
Phone: (416) 485-4440

#403
Bikes On Wheels
Category: Bikes
Average price: Modest
Area: Kensington Market
Address: 309 Augusta Ave
Toronto, ON M5T 2M2
Phone: (416) 966-2453

#404
Fine Shoe Sales & Repair
Category: Shoe Repair, Shoe Store
Average price: Modest
Area: Greektown, Riverdale
Address: 845 Av Danforth
Toronto, ON M4J 1L2
Phone: (416) 463-5085

#405
Accufix Appliance
Category: Appliances, Appliances & Repair
Average price: Modest
Area: East York
Address: 1167 Woodbine Ave
Toronto, ON M4C 4C6
Phone: (416) 467-6494

#406
HMV
Category: Music & DVDs
Average price: Modest
Area: Ryerson, Downtown Core
Address: 333 Yonge Street
Toronto, ON M5B 1R7
Phone: (416) 596-0333

#407
Leigh and Harlow
Category: Fashion
Average price: Modest
Area: Niagara, West Queen West, Trinity Bellwoods
Address: 634 Queen Street W
Toronto, ON M6J 1E4
Phone: (647) 430-7774

#408
Kind Exchange
Category: Used, Vintage, Consignment
Average price: Inexpensive
Area: Alexandra Park, Queen Street West
Address: 611 Queen Street W
Toronto, ON M5V 2B7
Phone: (647) 349-5463

#409
Soho Art Custom Framing
Category: Framing
Average price: Modest
Area: Roncesvalles
Address: 77 Roncesvalles Avenue
Toronto, ON M6R 2K6
Phone: (416) 531-2047

#410
CB2
Category: Home & Garden
Average price: Modest
Area: Alexandra Park,
Queen Street West
Address: 651 Queen Street West
Toronto, ON M5V 2B7
Phone: (416) 366-2828

#411
The Cat's Meow
Category: Used, Vintage, Consignment
Average price: Expensive
Area: The Annex, Summer Hill
Address: 180 Avenue Road
Toronto, ON M5R 2J1
Phone: (647) 435-5875

#412
Kid Icarus
Category: Cards & Stationery,
Screen Printing, Gift Shop
Average price: Exclusive
Area: Kensington Market
Address: 205 Augusta Avenue
Toronto, ON M5T 2L4
Phone: (416) 977-7236

#413
Shoppers Drug Mart
Category: Drugstore
Average price: Modest
Area: Downtown Core
Address: 728 Yonge Street
Toronto, ON M4Y
Phone: (416) 920-0098

#414
Book City
Category: Bookstore
Average price: Modest
Area: Yonge and St. Clair, Deer Park
Address: 1430 Yonge Street
Toronto, ON M4T 1Y6
Phone: (416) 926-0749

#415
Neat
Category: Home Decor
Average price: Expensive
Area: West Queen West,
Trinity Bellwoods
Address: 628 Queen Street West
Toronto, ON M6J 1E4
Phone: (416) 368-6328

#416
Shoppers Drug Mart
Category: Cosmetics & Beauty Supply,
Drugstore, Grocery
Average price: Modest
Area: Entertainment District,
Downtown Core
Address: 388 King St W
Toronto, ON M5V 1K2
Phone: (416) 597-6550

#417
Curry's Art Store
Category: Art Supplies
Average price: Modest
Area: West Queen West
Address: 1153 Queen Street W
Toronto, ON M6J 1J4
Phone: (416) 536-7878

#418
Jacob & Sebastian
Category: Cosmetics & Beauty Supply
Average price: Expensive
Area: Distillery District
Address: 27 Tank House Lane
Toronto, ON M5A 3C4
Phone: (416) 360-7750

#419
Phila Optical
Category: Eyewear & Opticians
Average price: Modest
Area: High Park, Roncesvalles
Address: 359 Roncesvalles Avenue
Toronto, ON M6R 2M8
Phone: (416) 538-8580

#420
Serpentine
Category: Men's Clothing
Average price: Expensive
Area: Yorkville
Address: 18 Hazelton Avenue
Toronto, ON M5R 2E2
Phone: (416) 513-1818

#421
Exile
Category: Accessories, Women's Clothing
Average price: Expensive
Area: Kensington Market
Address: 22 Kensington Avenue
Toronto, ON M5T 2J7
Phone: (416) 596-0827

#422
Kazuo Fashion
Category: Men's Clothing, Women's Clothing
Average price: Modest
Area: Entertainment District, Queen Street West, Downtown Core
Address: 371 Queen St W
Toronto, ON M5V 2A4
Phone: (416) 408-3366

#423
Creatron
Category: Electronics
Average price: Modest
Area: Chinatown, University of Toronto
Address: 255 College Street
Toronto, ON M5T 1R5
Phone: (416) 977-9258

#424
Studio Gang
Category: Shopping
Average price: Modest
Area: Ossington Strip, Trinity Bellwoods, Beaconsfield Village
Address: 112 Ossington Avenue
Toronto, ON M6J 2Z4
Phone: (416) 536-4264

#425
Little Burgundy
Category: Shoe Store, Accessories
Average price: Expensive
Area: Entertainment District, Queen Street West, Downtown Core
Address: 393 Queen Street W
Toronto, ON M5V 2A5
Phone: (416) 593-4794

#426
Fabric Fabric
Category: Home Decor, Fabric Store
Average price: Expensive
Area: The Junction
Address: 530 Keele St
Toronto, ON M6N 3C9
Phone: (416) 595-0001

#427
Origo Books
Category: Bookstore, Art Gallery
Average price: Modest
Area: St. Lawrence
Address: 49 Lower Jarvis Street
Toronto, ON M5E 1R8
Phone: (416) 703-3535

#428
Town Shoes
Category: Shoe Store
Average price: Expensive
Area: Mount Pleasant and Davisville, Yonge and Eglinton
Address: 2283 Yonge Street
Toronto, ON M4P 2C6
Phone: (416) 489-7474

#429
Town Shoes
Category: Shoe Store
Average price: Modest
Area: Downtown Core
Address: 220 Yonge St
Toronto, ON M4K 3Y3
Phone: (416) 979-9914

#430
Hashtag Gallery
Category: Art Gallery
Average price: Modest
Area: Trinity Bellwoods
Address: 801 Dundas Street W
Toronto, ON M6J 1V2
Phone: (416) 861-1866

#431
Vintage Depot
Category: Used, Vintage, Consignment
Average price: Modest
Area: Brockton Village, Bloordale Village, Wallace Emerson
Address: 1271 Bloor St W
Toronto, ON M6H
Phone: (416) 588-6513

#432
Laywine's
Category: Office Equipment, Cards & Stationery
Average price: Expensive
Area: Yorkville
Address: 25 Bellair St
Toronto, ON M5R 3L3
Phone: (416) 921-7131

#433
Gerrard Square Shopping Centre
Category: Shopping Center
Average price: Modest
Area: Leslieville
Address: 1000 Gerrard Street E
Toronto, ON M4M 3G6
Phone: (416) 461-0964

#434
Trade Secrets
Category: Cosmetics & Beauty Supply
Average price: Modest
Area: Downtown Core
Address: 260 Yonge Street
Toronto, ON M5B 2L9
Phone: (416) 595-7304

#435
Gallant Bicycles
Category: Bikes
Average price: Expensive
Area: Koreatown, Palmerston, Bickford Park, Seaton Village
Address: 678 Bloor Street W
Toronto, ON M6G 1L2
Phone: (416) 572-2593

#436
Kimberley Jackson
Category: Furniture Store
Average price: Modest
Area: Riverdale
Address: 700 Queen Street E
Toronto, ON M4M 1H1
Phone: (416) 690-8787

#437
Future Shop
Category: Office Equipment, Electronics
Average price: Expensive
Area: Ryerson, Downtown Core
Address: 325 Yonge Street
Toronto, ON M5B 1S1
Phone: (416) 971-5377

#438
Neurotica Records and CDs
Category: Music & DVDs
Average price: Modest
Area: West Queen West, Trinity Bellwoods
Address: 642 Queen Street W
Toronto, ON M6J 1E4
Phone: (416) 603-7796

#439
Ace Gifts Plus
Category: Cosmetics & Beauty Supply
Average price: Inexpensive
Area: Chinatown, Kensington Market, Downtown Core
Address: 367 Spadina Avenue
Toronto, ON M5T 2G3
Phone: (416) 977-6181

#440
Shoe Room at The National Ballet School
Category: Sporting Goods
Average price: Modest
Area: Church-Wellesley Village, Downtown Core
Address: 400 Jarvis Street
Toronto, ON M4Y 2G6
Phone: (416) 964-5100

#441
Vogue Sposa Bridal Boutique
Category: Bridal
Average price: Expensive
Area: The Danforth
Address: 304 Danforth Ave
Toronto, ON M4K 1N6
Phone: (416) 466-8884

#442
Annex Photo & Digital Imaging
Category: Photography Store
Average price: Expensive
Area: The Annex
Address: 362 Bloor St W
Toronto, ON M5S 1X2
Phone: (416) 922-0920

#443
Badlands Vintage
Category: Used, Vintage, Consignment
Average price: Modest
Area: Trinity Bellwoods
Address: 104 Ossington Ave
Toronto, ON M6J
Phone: (416) 553-5871

#444
The Engine Gallery
Category: Art Gallery
Average price: Exclusive
Area: West Queen West, Beaconsfield Village
Address: 1112 Queen Street W
Toronto, ON M6J 1H9
Phone: (416) 531-9905

#445
Ziggy's At Home
Category: Home Decor, Furniture Store
Average price: Modest
Area: Little Italy, Bickford Park
Address: 794 College St
Toronto, ON M6G 1C6
Phone: (416) 535-8728

#446
The Home Depot
Category: Nursery, Gardening, Hardware Store, Department Store
Average price: Modest
Area: Leslieville
Address: 1000 Gerrard Street E
Toronto, ON M4M 3G6
Phone: (416) 462-6270

#447
Snowdon Pharmacy
Category: Drugstore, Women's Clothing
Average price: Modest
Area: The Annex, Downtown Core
Address: 264 Bloor St W
Toronto, ON M5S 1V8
Phone: (416) 922-2156

#448
Another Story Bookshop
Category: Bookstore
Average price: Modest
Area: High Park, Roncesvalles
Address: 315 Av Roncesvalles
Toronto, ON M6R 2M6
Phone: (416) 462-1104

#449
Poppies
Category: Florist
Average price: Modest
Area: West Queen West, Beaconsfield Village
Address: 1094 Queen Street W
Toronto, ON M6J 1H9
Phone: (416) 538-2497

#450
Bath & Body Works
Category: Cosmetics & Beauty Supply
Average price: Inexpensive
Area: Downtown Core
Address: 220 Yonge St
Toronto, ON M5B 2L7
Phone: (416) 598-1561

#451
Atlas Machinery
Category: Hardware Store
Average price: Inexpensive
Area: Entertainment District, Queen Street West, Downtown Core
Address: 233 Queen Street W
Toronto, ON M5V 1Z4
Phone: (416) 598-3553

#452
Yang's Fruit & Flower Market
Category: Florist, Fruits & Veggies
Average price: Modest
Area: The Annex
Address: 132 Avenue Road
Toronto, ON M5R 2H6
Phone: (416) 413-9195

#453
Secrett Jewel Salon
Category: Jewelry
Average price: Modest
Area: Yorkville
Address: 162 Cumberland Street
Toronto, ON M5R 3N5
Phone: (416) 967-7500

#454
H&M
Category: Women's Clothing, Men's Clothing
Average price: Modest
Area: Downtown Core
Address: 1 Dundas Street W
Toronto, ON M5G 1Z3
Phone: (416) 593-0064

#455
Remenyi House of Music
Category: Musical Instruments
Average price: Modest
Area: The Annex, Downtown Core
Address: 210 Bloor Street W
Toronto, ON M5S 1T8
Phone: (416) 961-3111

#456
Photo 123
Category: Hobby Shop, Photographers, Photography Store
Average price: Modest
Area: Yorkville, Downtown Core
Address: 730 Yonge Street
Toronto, ON M4Y 2B7
Phone: (416) 920-3844

#457
Flowers and More
Category: Florist
Average price: Modest
Area: Bloor-West Village
Address: 379 Jane Street
Toronto, ON M6S
Phone: (416) 762-0154

#458
Uppity
Category: Antiques
Average price: Modest
Area: Leslieville
Address: 1124 Queen Street E
Toronto, ON M4M 1K8
Phone: (647) 436-0661

#459
Mendocino
Category: Women's Clothing
Average price: Expensive
Area: Discovery District, Yorkville, Downtown Core
Address: 131 Bloor St W
Toronto, ON M5S 1P7
Phone: (416) 927-8618

#460
Pottery Barn
Category: Shopping
Average price: Modest
Area: Discovery District, Yorkville, Downtown Core
Address: 100 Bloor Street W
Toronto, ON M5S 3L3
Phone: (416) 962-2276

#461
Espinosa Master Tailor
Category: Sewing & Alterations, Men's Clothing
Average price: Expensive
Area: Yorkville
Address: 50 Cumberland St
Toronto, ON M4W 1J5
Phone: (416) 921-9931

#462
Glad Day Bookshop
Category: Bookstore
Average price: Modest
Area: Downtown Core
Address: 598 Yonge Street
Toronto, ON M4Y 1Z3
Phone: (416) 961-4161

#463
Presse Internationale Shope
Category: Newspapers, Magazines, Bookstore
Average price: Modest
Area: The Annex
Address: 537 Bloor Street W
Toronto, ON M5S 1Y5
Phone: (416) 531-5008

#464
Ten Editions Books
Category: Bookstore
Average price: Modest
Area: University of Toronto, Downtown Core
Address: 698 Spadina Avenue
Toronto, ON M5S 2J2
Phone: (416) 964-3803

#465
Over the Rainbow
Category: Accessories, Men's Clothing, Women's Clothing
Average price: Expensive
Area: Yorkville
Address: 101 Yorkville Avenue
Toronto, ON M5R 1C1
Phone: (416) 967-7448

#466
East West Futons
Category: Furniture Store, Mattresses
Average price: Modest
Area: The Annex
Address: 464 Bloor Street W
Toronto, ON M5S 1X8
Phone: (416) 588-1391

#467
Re: Reading Used Books
Category: Bookstore
Average price: Inexpensive
Area: Greektown, Riverdale
Address: 548 Danforth Avenue
Toronto, ON M4K 1P8
Phone: (647) 347-8733

#468
David Mirvish Books on Art
Category: Bookstore
Average price: Modest
Area: Palmerston
Address: 596 Markham Street
Toronto, ON M6G 2L8
Phone: (416) 531-9975

#469
The Green Iguana Glassworks
Category: Art Gallery
Average price: Modest
Area: Palmerston
Address: 589 Markham Street
Toronto, ON M6G 2L7
Phone: (416) 536-8655

#470
Lululemon Athletica
Category: Sports Wear, Women's Clothing, Yoga
Average price: Expensive
Area: Yonge and Eglinton
Address: 2558 Yonge Street
Toronto, ON M4P 2J2
Phone: (416) 487-1390

#471
Paradise Bound
Category: Vinyl Records, Art Gallery
Average price: Modest
Area: Kensington Market
Address: 270 Augusta Avenue
Toronto, ON M5T 2L9
Phone: (416) 916-7770

#472
Aritzia
Category: Accessories, Women's Clothing
Average price: Expensive
Area: Yorkville
Address: 50 Bloor St W
Toronto, ON M4W 3L8
Phone: (416) 934-0935

#473
Axiom Ladies Boutique
Category: Women's Clothing
Average price: Inexpensive
Area: Church-Wellesley Village, Downtown Core
Address: 592 Yonge Street
Toronto, ON M4Y 1Z3
Phone: (416) 598-9393

#474
Staples
Category: Office Equipment
Average price: Inexpensive
Area: Downtown Core
Address: 375 University Avenue
Toronto, ON M5G 2J5
Phone: (416) 598-4818

#475
Foundery
Category: Art Gallery, Venues, Event Space
Average price: Inexpensive
Area: Little Italy
Address: 376 Bathurst Street
Toronto, ON M5T 2S6
Phone: (416) 938-1229

#476
Foamite Danforth
Category: Mattresses
Average price: Modest
Area: The Danforth
Address: 1494 Danforth Avenue
Toronto, ON M4J 1N4
Phone: (416) 463-9880

#477
Guess
Category: Fashion
Average price: Exclusive
Area: Ryerson, Downtown Core
Address: 306 Yonge Street
Toronto, ON M5B 1R4
Phone: (416) 506-8882

#478
Lacoste Boutique
Category: Women's Clothing, Men's Clothing
Average price: Expensive
Area: Ryerson, Downtown Core
Address: 220 Yonge St
Toronto, ON M5B
Phone: (416) 593-0001

#479
The Claddagh House
Category: Jewelry
Average price: Expensive
Area: Downtown Core
Address: 211 Yonge Street
Toronto, ON M5B 1M4
Phone: (416) 366-1247

#480
Spoiled Baby
Category: Children's Clothing, Baby Gear & Furniture
Average price: Expensive
Area: Mount Pleasant and Davisville
Address: 2 Av Davisville
Toronto, ON M4S 1E8
Phone: (416) 484-0470

#481
Musideum
Category: Musical Instruments
Average price: Inexpensive
Area: Entertainment District
Address: 401 Richmond Street W
Toronto, ON M5V 3A8
Phone: (416) 599-7323

#482
Snug As A Bug
Category: Children's Clothing, Baby Gear & Furniture
Average price: Expensive
Area: The Junction
Address: 3022 Dundas Street W
Toronto, ON M6P 1Z3
Phone: (416) 534-6881

#483
Corktown Designs Jewellery
Category: Jewelry
Average price: Expensive
Area: Distillery District
Address: 55 Mill Street
Toronto, ON M5A 3C4
Phone: (416) 861-3020

#484
Broadview Flower Market
Category: Florist
Average price: Modest
Area: Riverdale
Address: 737 Av Broadview
Toronto, ON M4K 2P6
Phone: (416) 778-0288

#485
Baldwin Naturals-Organic Food Market
Category: Shopping, Health Market, Fruits & Veggies
Average price: Modest
Area: Downtown Core
Address: 16 Baldwin Street
Toronto, ON M5T 1L2
Phone: (416) 979-1777

#486
Dutil Denim
Category: Men's Clothing, Women's Clothing
Average price: Expensive
Area: West Queen West
Address: 704 Queen Street W
Toronto, ON M6J 1E7
Phone: (647) 352-2560

#487
Zoinks Music & Books
Category: Books, Mags, Music & Video
Average price: Inexpensive
Area: Dovercourt, Dufferin Grove
Address: 1019 Bloor Street W
Toronto, ON M6H 1M1
Phone: (416) 913-8827

#488
Winners
Category: Department Store
Average price: Modest
Area: Entertainment District, Downtown Core
Address: 57 Spadina Avenue
Toronto, ON M4W 1A7
Phone: (416) 585-2052

#489
Auto Grotto
Category: Hobby Shop
Average price: Expensive
Area: Distillery District
Address: 55 Mill Street
Toronto, ON M5A 3C4
Phone: (416) 304-0005

#490
Anne Sportun
Category: Jewelry
Average price: Expensive
Area: West Queen West, Trinity Bellwoods
Address: 742 Queen Street W
Toronto, ON M6J 1E9
Phone: (416) 363-4114

#491
Robber
Category: Shopping
Average price: Expensive
Area: Niagara, West Queen West, Trinity Bellwoods
Address: 863 Queen St W
Toronto, ON M6J 1G4
Phone: (647) 351-0724

#492
Fawn
Category: Women's Clothing
Average price: Expensive
Area: Niagara, West Queen West, Trinity Bellwoods
Address: 967 Queen St W
Toronto, ON M6J 1G9
Phone: (647) 344-4703

#493
Dr. Martens
Category: Shoe Store
Average price: Expensive
Area: Entertainment District, Queen Street West, Downtown Core
Address: 391 Queen St W
Toronto, ON M5V
Phone: (416) 585-9595

#494
Freshly Baked Tees
Category: Screen Printing, Men's Clothing
Average price: Modest
Area: Alexandra Park, Queen Street West
Address: 557 Queen Street W
Toronto, ON M5V 2B4
Phone: (416) 907-3575

#495
Cyclemotive
Category: Bikes
Average price: Expensive
Area: Niagara
Address: 156 Bathurst Street
Toronto, ON M5V 2R3
Phone: (416) 916-5551

#496
Axis Gear Company
Category: Shopping
Average price: Modest
Area: Brockton Village
Address: 1541 Dundas Street W
Toronto, ON M6K 1T6
Phone: (416) 537-9229

#497
The Lifestyle Shop
Category: Furniture Store
Average price: Modest
Area: Downtown Core
Address: 64 Av Spadina
Toronto, ON M5V 2H8
Phone: (416) 599-5433

#498
Museum of Contemporary Canadian Art
Category: Art Gallery
Average price: Inexpensive
Area: West Queen West, Trinity Bellwoods
Address: 952 Queen St W
Toronto, ON M6J 1G8
Phone: (416) 395-0067

#499
Brandy Melville Toronto
Category: Women's Clothing
Average price: Modest
Area: Queen Street West, Downtown Core
Address: 326 Queen Street W
Toronto, ON M5V 2A4
Phone: (647) 351-2611

#500
Little Peeps
Category: Children's Clothing
Average price: Modest
Area: Riverdale
Address: 768 Queen St E
Toronto, ON M4M 1H4
Phone: (416) 406-5437

TOP 500 RESTAURANTS

The Most Recommended by Locals & Trevelers

(From #1 to #500)

#1
Under The Table Restaurant
Cuisines: Comfort Food
Average price: $11-$30
Area: Cabbagetown
Address: 568 Parliament Street
Toronto, ON M4X 1P8
Phone: (647) 351-1533

#2
Black Hoof
Cuisines: Gastropub, Cocktail Bar
Average price: $31-$60
Area: Little Italy
Address: 928 Dundas Street W
Toronto, ON M6J 1W3
Phone: (416) 551-8854

#3
Khao San Road
Cuisines: Thai
Average price: $11-$30
Area: Entertainment District, Downtown Core
Address: 326 Adelaide Street W
Toronto, ON M5V 1R3
Phone: (647) 352-5773

#4
Ruby Watchco
Cuisines: Canadian
Average price: $31-$60
Area: Riverdale
Address: 730 Queen Street E
Toronto, ON M4M 1H2
Phone: (416) 465-0100

#5
Seven Lives Tacos Y Mariscos
Cuisines: Mexican, Seafood
Average price: Under $10
Area: Kensington Market
Address: 69 Kensington Avenue
Toronto, ON M5T 2L6
Phone: (416) 393-4636

#6
Black Camel
Cuisines: Sandwiches
Average price: Under $10
Area: Rosedale
Address: 4 Crescent Road
Toronto, ON M4W 1S9
Phone: (416) 929-7518

#7
Bar Isabel
Cuisines: Spanish, Tapas Bar
Average price: $31-$60
Area: Little Italy, Bickford Park
Address: 797 College Street
Toronto, ON M6G 1C6
Phone: (416) 532-2222

#8
Guu Izakaya
Cuisines: Japanese, Tapas
Average price: $11-$30
Area: Downtown Core
Address: 398 Church Street
Toronto, ON M5B
Phone: (416) 977-0999

#9
The Gabardine
Cuisines: Canadian
Average price: $11-$30
Area: Financial District, Downtown Core
Address: 372 Bay St
Toronto, ON M5H 3W1
Phone: (647) 352-3211

#10
Scaramouche Restaurant Pasta Bar & Grill
Cuisines: French
Average price: Above $61
Area: South Hill
Address: 1 Benvenuto Pl
Toronto, ON M4V 2L1
Phone: (416) 961-8011

#11
Eat Fresh Be Healthy
Cuisines: Italian
Average price: $11-$30
Area: Discovery District, Downtown Core
Address: 185 Dundas Street W
Toronto, ON M5G 1C7
Phone: (647) 258-8808

#12
The Stockyards
Cuisines: American, Southern
Average price: $11-$30
Area: Wychwood
Address: 699 St Clair Avenue W
Toronto, ON M6C 1B2
Phone: (416) 658-9666

#13
Kaiju
Cuisines: Japanese, Malaysian
Average price: Under $10
Area: Ryerson, Downtown Core
Address: 384 Yonge Street
Toronto, ON M5B
Phone: (647) 748-6338

#14
Lo Zingaro
Cuisines: Italian
Average price: $11-$30
Area: Queen Street West
Address: 571 Queen Street West
Toronto, ON M5V 2B6
Phone: (416) 361-6154

#15
Mystic Muffin
Cuisines: Sandwiches, Middle Eastern
Average price: Under $10
Area: Corktown, Downtown Core
Address: 113 Jarvis Street
Toronto, ON M5C 2H4
Phone: (416) 941-1474

#16
Fabarnak Restaurant & Catering
Cuisines: Soup, Sandwiches, Canadian
Average price: $11-$30
Area: Church-Wellesley Village, Downtown Core
Address: 519 Church Street
Toronto, ON M4Y 2C9
Phone: (416) 355-6781

#17
Café Polonez
Cuisines: Polish
Average price: $11-$30
Area: High Park, Roncesvalles
Address: 195 Roncesvalles Avenue
Toronto, ON M6R 2L5
Phone: (416) 532-8432

#18
The Emerson
Cuisines: Canadian
Average price: $31-$60
Area: Brockton Village, Bloordale Village
Address: 1279 Bloor Street W
Toronto, ON M6H 1N7
Phone: (416) 532-1717

#19
The Hole In the Wall
Cuisines: Pub, Canadian
Average price: $11-$30
Area: The Junction
Address: 2867 Dundas Street W
Toronto, ON M6P 1Y9
Phone: (647) 350-3564

#20
Schnitzel Queen
Cuisines: Sandwiches, German
Average price: Under $10
Area: Corktown
Address: 237 Queen Street E
Toronto, ON M5A 1S5
Phone: (416) 363-9176

#21
Ravi Soups
Cuisines: Sandwiches, Soup
Average price: $11-$30
Area: Entertainment District, Downtown Core
Address: 322 Adelaide Street W
Toronto, ON M5V 1R1
Phone: (647) 435-8365

#22
Fresco's Fish & Chips
Cuisines: Fish & Chips, Food Delivery Service, American
Average price: $11-$30
Area: Kensington Market
Address: 213 Augusta Avenue
Toronto, ON M5T 2L4
Phone: (416) 546-4557

#23
Hibiscus
Cuisines: Vegan, Vegetarian, Gluten-Free
Average price: Under $10
Area: Kensington Market
Address: 238 Augusta Avenue
Toronto, ON M5T 2L7
Phone: (416) 364-6183

#24
Canoe
Cuisines: Canadian
Average price: Above $61
Area: Financial District, Downtown Core
Address: 66 Wellington Street W
Toronto, ON M5K 1H6
Phone: (416) 364-0054

#25
Dance Mac
Cuisines: Comfort Food
Average price: Under $10
Area: Entertainment District, Queen Street West, Downtown Core
Address: 238 Queen Street W
Toronto, ON M5V 1Z9
Phone: (647) 351-8500

#26
The Fish Store & Sandwiches
Cuisines: Sandwiches, Seafood
Average price: Under $10
Area: Little Italy, Bickford Park
Address: 657 College St
Toronto, ON M6G 1B7
Phone: (416) 533-2822

#27
Beerbistro
Cuisines: Canadian, Pub
Average price: $11-$30
Area: Downtown Core
Address: 18 King Street E
Toronto, ON M5C 1C4
Phone: (416) 861-9872

#28
Wow Sushi
Cuisines: Sushi Bar
Average price: $11-$30
Area: Downtown Core
Address: 11 Charles Street W
Toronto, ON M4Y 1R4
Phone: (416) 923-1888

#29
Joso's
Cuisines: Seafood
Average price: $31-$60
Area: Summer Hill, Yorkville
Address: 202 Davenport Rd
Toronto, ON M5R 1J2
Phone: (416) 925-1903

#30
Grand Electric
Cuisines: Bar, Mexican
Average price: $11-$30
Area: Parkdale
Address: 1330 Queen Street W
Toronto, ON M6K 1L4
Phone: (416) 627-3459

#31
Pai Northen Thai Kitchen
Cuisines: Thai
Average price: $11-$30
Area: Entertainment District, Downtown Core
Address: 18 Duncan Street
Toronto, ON M5H 3G6
Phone: (416) 901-4724

#33
George
Cuisines: Canadian
Average price: Above $61
Area: Corktown, Downtown Core
Address: 111 Queen St E
Toronto, ON M5C 1S2
Phone: (416) 863-6006

#32
The Caledonian
Cuisines: Pub, Scottish
Average price: $11-$30
Area: Dufferin Grove
Address: 856 College Street
Toronto, ON M6H 1A1
Phone: (647) 547-9827

#34
Manpuku Japanese Eatery
Cuisines: Japanese
Average price: Under $10
Area: Downtown Core
Address: 105 McCaul St
Toronto, ON M5T 2X4
Phone: (416) 979-6763

#35
Buk Chang Dong Soon Tofu
Cuisines: Korean
Average price: Under $10
Area: Koreatown, Palmerston, Bickford Park
Address: 691 Bloor Street W
Toronto, ON M6G 1L3
Phone: (416) 537-0972

#36
Richmond Station
Cuisines: Canadian
Average price: $31-$60
Area: Downtown Core
Address: 1 Richmond Street W
Toronto, ON M5H 1W2
Phone: (647) 748-1444

#37
The Senator
Cuisines: Coffee & Tea
Average price: $11-$30
Area: Downtown Core
Address: 249 Victoria St
Toronto, ON M5B 1T8
Phone: (416) 364-7517

#38
Museum Tavern
Cuisines: American
Average price: $11-$30
Area: The Annex, Downtown Core
Address: 208 Bloor Street W
Toronto, ON M5S 1W2
Phone: (416) 920-0110

#39
Playa Cabana
Cuisines: Mexican, Bar
Average price: $11-$30
Area: The Annex
Address: 111 Dupont St
Toronto, ON M5R 1V4
Phone: (416) 929-3911

#40
Barque Smokehouse
Cuisines: Barbeque
Average price: $11-$30
Area: High Park, Roncesvalles
Address: 299 Roncesvalles Avenue
Toronto, ON M6R 2M3
Phone: (416) 532-7700

#41
Northwood
Cuisines: Bar, Cafe
Average price: $11-$30
Area: Bickford Park
Address: 815 W Bloor Street
Toronto, ON M6G 1M1
Phone: (416) 846-8324

#42
Bach Yen
Cuisines: Vietnamese
Average price: Under $10
Area: Riverdale
Address: 738 Gerrard Street E
Toronto, ON M4M 1Y3
Phone: (647) 347-8160

#43
Yuzu No Hana
Cuisines: Sushi Bar, Japanese
Average price: $31-$60
Area: Entertainment District, Downtown Core
Address: 236 Adelaide Street W
Toronto, ON M5H 1W7
Phone: (416) 205-9808

#44
White Brick Kitchen
Cuisines: Comfort Food
Average price: $11-$30
Area: Koreatown, Palmerston, Seaton Village
Address: 641 Bloor Street W
Toronto, ON M6G 1L1
Phone: (647) 347-9188

#45
Aft Kitchen & Bar
Cuisines: Bar, American, Barbeque
Average price: $11-$30
Area: Riverdale
Address: 686 Queen Street E
Toronto, ON M4M 1H1
Phone: (647) 346-1541

#46
Beast
Cuisines: Canadian, Breakfast & Brunch, Tapas
Average price: $11-$30
Area: Niagara
Address: 96 Tecumseth Street
Toronto, ON M6J 2H1
Phone: (647) 352-6000

#47
The Fuzz Box
Cuisines: Sandwiches, Donairs
Average price: Under $10
Area: The Danforth
Address: 1246 Danforth Avenue
Toronto, ON M4J 1M6
Phone: (416) 769-1432

#48
Fanny Chadwick's
Cuisines: Canadian, Comfort Food
Average price: $11-$30
Area: The Annex
Address: 268 Howland Avenue
Toronto, ON M5R 3B6
Phone: (416) 944-1606

#49
Como En Casa
Cuisines: Mexican
Average price: Under $10
Area: Church-Wellesley Village, Downtown Core
Address: 565 Yonge Street
Toronto, ON M4Y 1Z2
Phone: (647) 748-6666

#50
Santouka
Cuisines: Japanese
Average price: $11-$30
Area: Ryerson, Downtown Core
Address: 91 Dundas Street E
Toronto, ON M5B 1E1
Phone: (647) 748-1717

#51
Banh Mi Boys
Cuisines: Vietnamese, Asian Fusion
Average price: Under $10
Area: Ryerson, Downtown Core
Address: 399 Yonge Street
Toronto, ON M5B
Phone: (416) 979-0303

#52
Frank's Kitchen
Cuisines: French
Average price: $31-$60
Area: Little Italy, Palmerston, Bickford Park
Address: 588 College Street
Toronto, ON M6G 1B3
Phone: (416) 516-5861

#53
416 Snack Bar
Cuisines: Tapas, Bar
Average price: $11-$30
Area: Alexandra Park, Queen Street West, West Queen West, Trinity Bellwoods
Address: 181 Bathurst St
Toronto, ON M5T
Phone: (416) 364-9320

#54
Japango
Cuisines: Sushi Bar
Average price: $11-$30
Area: Downtown Core
Address: 122 Elizabeth Street
Toronto, ON M5G 1P5
Phone: (416) 599-5557

#55
Scheffler's Delicatessen
Cuisines: Deli, Cheese Shop
Average price: $11-$30
Area: St. Lawrence, Downtown Core
Address: 93 Front St E
Toronto, ON M5E 1C3
Phone: (416) 364-2806

#56
barVolo
Cuisines: Bar, Brasserie, Canadian
Average price: $11-$30
Area: Church-Wellesley Village, Downtown Core
Address: 587 Yonge St
Toronto, ON M4Y 1Z4
Phone: (416) 928-0008

#57
Sidecar
Cuisines: European, Canadian
Average price: $31-$60
Area: Little Italy, Palmerston, Bickford Park
Address: 577 College St
Toronto, ON M6G 1B2
Phone: (416) 536-7000

#58
Byblos
Cuisines: Mediterranean
Average price: $31-$60
Area: Entertainment District, Downtown Core
Address: 11 Duncan Street
Toronto, ON M5V 3M2
Phone: (647) 660-0909

#59
Millie Creperie
Cuisines: Creperies, Desserts, Japanese
Average price: Under $10
Area: Kensington Market
Address: 161 Baldwin Street
Toronto, ON M5T 1L8
Phone: (416) 977-1922

#60
La Palette
Cuisines: French
Average price: $31-$60
Area: Alexandra Park, Queen Street West
Address: 492 Queen Street West
Toronto, ON M5V 2B3
Phone: (416) 929-4900

#61
Little Coxwell Vietnamese & Thai
Cuisines: Vietnamese, Thai
Average price: $11-$30
Area: East York
Address: 986 Coxwell Avenue
Toronto, ON M4C 3G5
Phone: (416) 916-2565

#62
Lola's Kitchen
Cuisines: Breakfast & Brunch, Vegan, Gluten-Free
Average price: $11-$30
Area: Church-Wellesley Village, Downtown Core
Address: 634 Church Street
Toronto, ON M4Y 2G3
Phone: (416) 966-3991

#63
Campagnolo
Cuisines: Tapas, Italian
Average price: $31-$60
Area: Little Italy
Address: 832 Dundas Street W
Toronto, ON M6J 1V3
Phone: (416) 364-4785

#64
Sansotei Ramen
Cuisines: Ramen
Average price: $11-$30
Area: Downtown Core
Address: 179 Dundas Street W
Toronto, ON M5G 1Z8
Phone: (647) 748-3833

#65
Asada Mexican Grill
Cuisines: Mexican
Average price: Under $10
Area: Wychwood
Address: 809 Saint Clair Avenue W
Toronto, ON M6G 3P7
Phone: (416) 654-9488

#66
Kekou Gelato House
Cuisines: Cafe
Average price: Under $10
Area: Downtown Core
Address: 13 Baldwin Street
Toronto, ON M5T 1L1
Phone: (416) 792-8858

#67
Salad Days
Cuisines: Salads
Average price: Under $10
Area: Yorkville, Downtown Core
Address: 2 Bloor Street W
Toronto, ON M4W 1A1
Phone: (647) 436-9472

#68
Sotto Sotto Restaurant
Cuisines: Italian
Average price: Above $61
Area: The Annex
Address: 116a Avenue Rd
Toronto, ON M5R 2H4
Phone: (416) 962-0011

#69
Burrito Boyz
Cuisines: Mexican
Average price: Under $10
Area: Entertainment District, Downtown Core
Address: 218 Adelaide Street W
Toronto, ON M5H 1W7
Phone: (647) 439-4065

#70
Seor Ak San
Cuisines: Korean
Average price: Under $10
Area: Chinatown, Kensington Market, Downtown Core
Address: 357 Spadina Avenue
Toronto, ON M5T
Phone: (416) 977-2788

#71
Estiatorio VOLOS
Cuisines: Seafood, Greek, Mediterranean
Average price: $31-$60
Area: Financial District, Downtown Core
Address: 133 Richmond Street W
Toronto, ON M5H 2L3
Phone: (416) 861-1211

#72
La Carnita
Cuisines: Mexican
Average price: $11-$30
Area: Little Italy, Palmerston
Address: 501 College Street
Toronto, ON M5S 2K2
Phone: (416) 964-1555

#73
Karelia Kitchen
Cuisines: Scandinavian, Sandwiches
Average price: $11-$30
Area: Brockton Village, Bloordale Village
Address: 1194 Bloor Street W
Toronto, ON M6H 1N2
Phone: (647) 748-1194

#74
Enoteca Sociale
Cuisines: Italian
Average price: $31-$60
Area: Little Portugal, Beaconsfield Village
Address: 1288 Dundas St W
Toronto, ON M6J 1X7
Phone: (416) 534-1200

#75
Capitano Burgers & Gelato
Cuisines: Ice Cream, Burgers
Average price: Under $10
Area: Church-Wellesley Village, Downtown Core
Address: 645 Yonge Street
Toronto, ON M4Y 1Z9
Phone: (647) 350-0555

#76
Agio
Cuisines: Italian
Average price: $11-$30
Area: Corso Italia
Address: 1351 St Clair Avenue W
Toronto, ON M6E 1C5
Phone: (647) 348-4814

#77
Harbour Sixty
Cuisines: Steakhouse, Seafood
Average price: Above $61
Area: Harbourfront
Address: 60 Harbour Street
Toronto, ON M5J 1B7
Phone: (416) 777-2111

#78
The Wren
Cuisines: Bar, American
Average price: $11-$30
Area: The Danforth
Address: 1382 Danforth Avenue
Toronto, ON M4J 1M9
Phone: (647) 748-1382

#79
FIKA
Cuisines: Coffee & Tea, Sandwiches
Average price: Under $10
Area: Kensington Market
Address: 28 Kensington Avenue
Toronto, ON M5T 2K1
Phone: (416) 994-7669

#80
The Queen & Beaver Pub
Cuisines: Pub, British, Sports Bar
Average price: $11-$30
Area: Downtown Core
Address: 35 Elm St
Toronto, ON M5G 1H1
Phone: (647) 347-2712

#81
Pizzeria Libretto
Cuisines: Pizza, Italian
Average price: $11-$30
Area: The Danforth, Greektown
Address: 550 Danforth Avenue
Toronto, ON M4K 1P7
Phone: (416) 466-0400

#82
Porchetta & Co
Cuisines: Sandwiches
Average price: Under $10
Area: Trinity Bellwoods
Address: 825 Dundas Street W
Toronto, ON M6J
Phone: (647) 352-6611

#83
L'Avenue Bistro
Cuisines: French
Average price: $31-$60
Area: Mount Pleasant and Davisville
Address: 1568 Bayview Avenue
Toronto, ON M4S 1T3
Phone: (416) 485-1568

#84
Grazie Ristorante
Cuisines: Italian
Average price: $11-$30
Area: Mount Pleasant and Davisville, Yonge and Eglinton
Address: 2373 Yonge St
Toronto, ON M4P 2C8
Phone: (416) 488-0822

#85
Hair Of The Dog
Cuisines: Pub, Comfort Food, Breakfast & Brunch
Average price: $11-$30
Area: Church-Wellesley Village, Downtown Core
Address: 425 Church Street
Toronto, ON M4Y 2C3
Phone: (416) 964-2708

#86
Union
Cuisines: French, Wine Bar
Average price: $31-$60
Area: Ossington Strip, Trinity Bellwoods
Address: 72A Ossington Avenue
Toronto, ON M6J 2Y7
Phone: (416) 850-0093

#87
Red Cranberries Restaurant
Cuisines: Bar
Average price: $11-$30
Area: Cabbagetown
Address: 601 Parliament St
Toronto, ON M4X 1P9
Phone: (416) 925-6330

#88
Dumpling House Restaurant
Cuisines: Chinese
Average price: Under $10
Area: Chinatown, Kensington Market, Downtown Core
Address: 328 Spadina Ave
Toronto, ON M5T 2E7
Phone: (416) 596-8898

#89
Sabai Sabai Kitchen and Bar
Cuisines: Thai, Bar, Vegan
Average price: $11-$30
Area: Downtown Core
Address: 225 Church Street
Toronto, ON M5B 1Y7
Phone: (647) 748-4225

#90
Yummy Korean Restaurant
Cuisines: Korean
Average price: Under $10
Area: Koreatown, Palmerston, Seaton Village
Address: 620 Bloor Street W
Toronto, ON M6G 1K8
Phone: (647) 345-6588

#91
Farmhouse Tavern
Cuisines: Canadian
Average price: $31-$60
Area: The Junction
Address: 1627 Dupont Street
Toronto, ON M6P
Phone: (416) 561-9114

#92
Pizzeria Libretto
Cuisines: Pizza, Italian
Average price: $11-$30
Area: Little Portugal, Ossington Strip, Trinity Bellwoods, Beaconsfield Village
Address: 221 Ossington Ave
Toronto, ON M6J 2Z8
Phone: (416) 532-8000

#93
Korean Village Restaurant
Cuisines: Korean
Average price: $11-$30
Area: Koreatown, Palmerston, Seaton Village
Address: 628 Bloor Street W
Toronto, ON M6G 1K7
Phone: (416) 536-0290

#94
Pantheon Restaurant
Cuisines: Greek, Mediterranean
Average price: $11-$30
Area: Greektown, Riverdale
Address: 407 Danforth Avenue
Toronto, ON M4K 1P1
Phone: (416) 778-1929

#95
Weezie's
Cuisines: Canadian
Average price: $31-$60
Area: Corktown
Address: 354 King St E
Toronto, ON M5A 1K9
Phone: (416) 777-9339

#96
Mangia & Bevi
Cuisines: Italian, Pizza
Average price: $11-$30
Area: Corktown
Address: 260 King Street East
Toronto, ON M5R 4L5
Phone: (416) 203-1635

#97
Restaurant Chantecler
Cuisines: Canadian
Average price: $11-$30
Area: Parkdale
Address: 1320 Queen Street W
Toronto, ON M6K 1L4
Phone: (416) 628-3586

#98
Gio Rana's Really Really Nice Restaurant
Cuisines: Italian, Tapas
Average price: $31-$60
Area: Leslieville
Address: 1220 Queen Street E
Toronto, ON M4M 1L7
Phone: (416) 469-5225

#99
Hudson Kitchen
Cuisines: Canadian
Average price: $11-$30
Area: Little Italy, Trinity Bellwoods
Address: 800 Dundas St W
Toronto, ON M6J 1V1
Phone: (416) 644-8839

#100
Etsu Restaurant
Cuisines: Japanese, Korean
Average price: $11-$30
Area: Downtown Core
Address: 45 Baldwin Street
Toronto, ON M5T 1L3
Phone: (416) 599-4200

#101
The Burger's Priest
Cuisines: Burgers
Average price: $11-$30
Area: Alexandra Park, Queen Street West
Address: 463 Queen Street W
Toronto, ON M5V 2A9
Phone: (647) 748-8108

#102
Jumbo Empanadas
Cuisines: Latin American
Average price: Under $10
Area: Kensington Market
Address: 245 Augusta Avenue
Toronto, ON M5T 1M5
Phone: (416) 977-0056

#103
House of Gourmet
Cuisines: Chinese
Average price: $11-$30
Area: Chinatown, Downtown Core
Address: 484 Dundas St W
Toronto, ON M5T 1G9
Phone: (416) 217-0167

#104
Luma
Cuisines: Canadian
Average price: $31-$60
Area: Entertainment District, Downtown Core
Address: 350 King Street W
Toronto, ON M5V 3X2
Phone: (647) 288-4715

#105
Xtreme Taste
Cuisines: Middle Eastern
Average price: Under $10
Area: Yorkville
Address: 6 Cumberland Street
Toronto, ON M4W 1J5
Phone: (647) 347-3618

#106
Clubhouse Sandwich Shop
Cuisines: Sandwiches
Average price: Under $10
Area: Chinatown, University of Toronto
Address: 455 Spadina Avenue
Toronto, ON M5S 2G7
Phone: (647) 502-1291

#107
Chino Locos Original
Cuisines: Mexican
Average price: Under $10
Area: Leslieville
Address: 4 Greenwood Avenue
Toronto, ON M4L 2P4
Phone: (647) 345-5626

#108
Mengrai Gourmet Thai
Cuisines: Thai
Average price: $31-$60
Area: Corktown
Address: 82 Ontario Street
Toronto, ON M5A 2V3
Phone: (416) 840-2759

#109
Electric Mud BBQ
Cuisines: Barbeque
Average price: $11-$30
Area: Parkdale
Address: 5 Brock Avenue
Toronto, ON M6K 1L4
Phone: (416) 516-8286

#110
Hey Meatball
Cuisines: Bar, Canadian
Average price: $11-$30
Area: Little Italy, Bickford Park
Address: 719 College Street
Toronto, ON M6G
Phone: (416) 546-1483

#111
The Monk's Table
Cuisines: Pub, British
Average price: $11-$30
Area: Summer Hill
Address: 1276 Yonge Street
Toronto, ON M4T 1W5
Phone: (416) 920-9074

#112
La Bella Managua
Cuisines: Latin American
Average price: $11-$30
Area: Christie Pits, Bickford Park
Address: 872 Bloor Street W
Toronto, ON M6G 1M5
Phone: (416) 913-4227

#113
Earl's Kitchen & Bar
Cuisines: American, Bar
Average price: $11-$30
Area: Financial District, Downtown Core
Address: 150 King Street W
Toronto, ON M5H 2B6
Phone: (416) 916-0227

#114
Utopia Café & Grill
Cuisines: Tex-Mex, Burgers
Average price: $11-$30
Area: Little Italy, Palmerston, Bickford Park
Address: 586 College St
Toronto, ON M6G 1B3
Phone: (416) 534-7751

#115
Cantanhede O Bairradino
Cuisines: Portuguese
Average price: Under $10
Area: Wallace Emerson
Address: 662 Lansdowne Avenue
Toronto, ON M6H 3Y8
Phone: (416) 531-6912

#116
Fusaro's
Cuisines: Italian, Pizza
Average price: $11-$30
Area: Corktown
Address: 294 Richmond St E
Toronto, ON M5A 4S7
Phone: (647) 347-3309

#117
Est West Cafe
Cuisines: Sandwiches
Average price: Under $10
Area: Downtown Core
Address: 700 University Ave
Toronto, ON M5G 1Z5
Phone: (416) 506-0777

#118
Bannock
Cuisines: Canadian
Average price: $11-$30
Area: Downtown Core
Address: 401 Bay Street
Toronto, ON M5H 2Y4
Phone: (416) 861-6996

#119
Maizal
Cuisines: Mexican
Average price: $11-$30
Area: Liberty Village
Address: 133 Jefferson Avenue
Toronto, ON M6K 3E4
Phone: (647) 351-0133

#120
Rose and Sons
Cuisines: Comfort Food
Average price: $11-$30
Area: The Annex
Address: 176 Dupont Street
Toronto, ON M5R 2E6
Phone: (647) 748-3287

#121
This End Up
Cuisines: Sandwiches, Bar
Average price: $11-$30
Area: Dufferin Grove, Little Portugal, Beaconsfield Village
Address: 1454 Dundas Street W
Toronto, ON M6J 1Y6
Phone: (647) 347-8700

#122
Rashers
Cuisines: Sandwiches, Comfort Food, Breakfast & Brunch
Average price: Under $10
Area: Leslieville
Address: 948 Queen Street E
Toronto, ON M4M 1J7
Phone: (416) 710-8220

#123
Woodlot Bakery & Restaurant
Cuisines: Vegetarian, Canadian, Comfort Food
Average price: $31-$60
Area: Little Italy, Palmerston
Address: 293 Palmerston Avenue
Toronto, ON M6J 2J3
Phone: (647) 342-6307

#124
El Trompo Taco Bar
Cuisines: Mexican
Average price: $11-$30
Area: Kensington Market
Address: 277 Augusta Ave
Toronto, ON M5T 2M1
Phone: (416) 260-0097

#125
Fieramosca
Cuisines: Italian
Average price: $31-$60
Area: The Annex
Address: 36A Prince Arthur Avenue
Toronto, ON M5R 1A9
Phone: (416) 323-0636

#126
Five Doors North
Cuisines: Italian
Average price: $31-$60
Area: Mount Pleasant and Davisville
Address: 2088 Yonge Street
Toronto, ON M4S 2A3
Phone: (416) 480-6234

#127
L'Unita
Cuisines: Italian
Average price: $31-$60
Area: The Annex
Address: 134 Avenue Road
Toronto, ON M5R 2H6
Phone: (416) 964-8686

#128
Nguyen Huong Food
Cuisines: Bakery, Vietnamese
Average price: Under $10
Area: Chinatown, Kensington Market, Downtown Core
Address: 322 Spadina Avenue
Toronto, ON M5T 2G2
Phone: (416) 599-4625

#129
Amore Fine Foods
Cuisines: Caterer, Sandwiches
Average price: Under $10
Area: Seaton Village
Address: 934 Manning Avenue
Toronto, ON M6G 2X4
Phone: (416) 579-3701

#130
Yummy Yummy Dumplings
Cuisines: Chinese
Average price: Under $10
Area: Downtown Core
Address: 79 Huron Street
Toronto, ON M5T 2A8
Phone: (647) 859-8998

#131
The Burger's Priest
Cuisines: Burgers
Average price: $11-$30
Area: Upper Beach
Address: 1636 Queen Street E
Toronto, ON M4L 1G3
Phone: (647) 346-0617

#132
Annona Resturant
Cuisines: Canadian
Average price: $11-$30
Area: The Annex, Downtown Core
Address: 4 Avenue Road
Toronto, ON M5R 2E8
Phone: (416) 324-1567

#133
The Ace
Cuisines: Diner, Comfort Food, Breakfast & Brunch, Canadian
Average price: $11-$30
Area: High Park, Roncesvalles
Address: 231A Roncesvalles Avenue
Toronto, ON M6R 2L6
Phone: (416) 792-7729

#134
The Carbon Bar
Cuisines: Bar, Canadian
Average price: $31-$60
Area: Corktown, Downtown Core
Address: 99 Queen St E
Toronto, ON M5C 1S2
Phone: (416) 947-7000

#135
Tacos El Asador
Cuisines: Mexican, Latin American
Average price: Under $10
Area: Koreatown, Palmerston, Bickford Park, Seaton Village
Address: 690 Bloor Street W
Toronto, ON M6G 1L2
Phone: (416) 538-9747

#136
Hodo Kwaja
Cuisines: Bakery, Korean
Average price: Under $10
Area: Koreatown, Palmerston, Seaton Village
Address: 656 Bloor Street W
Toronto, ON M6G 1K9
Phone: (416) 538-1208

#137
Ramen Isshin
Cuisines: Japanese
Average price: $11-$30
Area: Kensington Market
Address: 421 College Street
Toronto, ON M5T 1T1
Phone: (416) 367-4013

#138
Cava
Cuisines: Tapas Bar
Average price: $31-$60
Area: Yonge and St. Clair, Deer Park
Address: 1560 Yonge St
Toronto, ON M4T 2S9
Phone: (416) 979-9918

#139
Brick Street Bakery
Cuisines: Bakery, Sandwiches
Average price: Under $10
Area: Distillery District
Address: 55 Mill St
Toronto, ON M5A 3C4
Phone: (416) 214-4949

#140
Lady Marmalade
Cuisines: Breakfast & Brunch, Mexican
Average price: $11-$30
Area: Leslieville
Address: 898 Queen Street E
Toronto, ON M4M 1J3
Phone: (647) 351-7645

#141
Gushi
Cuisines: Street Vendor, Japanese
Average price: Under $10
Area: Alexandra Park
Address: 707 Dundas Street W
Toronto, ON M5T 2W6
Phone: (416) 525-7351

#142
Falasca
Cuisines: Italian
Average price: $11-$30
Area: Mount Pleasant and Davisville
Address: 2059 Yonge St
Toronto, ON M4S 2A2
Phone: (647) 352-5155

#143
Prohibition Gastrohouse
Cuisines: Pub, Gastropub, Sports Bar
Average price: $11-$30
Area: Riverdale
Address: 696 Queen Street E
Toronto, ON M4M 1G9
Phone: (416) 406-2669

#144
Southern Accent Restaurant
Cuisines: Cajun/Creole, Southern
Average price: $11-$30
Area: Palmerston
Address: 595 Markham Street
Toronto, ON M6G 2L7
Phone: (416) 536-3211

#145
Arepa Café
Cuisines: Latin American
Average price: $11-$30
Area: Alexandra Park, Queen Street West
Address: 490 Queen Street W
Toronto, ON M5V 2B3
Phone: (416) 362-4111

#146
Sorrel
Cuisines: French, Mediterranean
Average price: $31-$60
Area: Yorkville
Address: 84 Yorkville
Toronto, ON M5R
Phone: (416) 926-1010

#147
Gandhi Cuisine
Cuisines: Indian
Average price: $11-$30
Area: Alexandra Park, Queen Street West
Address: 554 Queen Street W
Toronto, ON M5V 2B5
Phone: (416) 504-8155

#148
Kingyo
Cuisines: Japanese
Average price: $31-$60
Area: Cabbagetown
Address: 51B Winchester Street
Toronto, ON M4X 1R7
Phone: (647) 748-2121

#149
The Comrade
Cuisines: Lounge, Canadian
Average price: $11-$30
Area: Riverdale
Address: 758 Queen Street E
Toronto, ON M4M 1H4
Phone: (416) 778-9449

#150
California Sandwiches
Cuisines: Sandwiches
Average price: Under $10
Area: Little Italy
Address: 244 Claremont Street
Toronto, ON M6J 2N2
Phone: (416) 603-3317

#151
Hopgood's Foodliner
Cuisines: Canadian
Average price: $31-$60
Area: High Park, Roncesvalles
Address: 325 Roncesvalles Avenue
Toronto, ON M6R 2M6
Phone: (416) 533-2723

#152
Mercatto
Cuisines: Italian
Average price: $11-$30
Area: Downtown Core
Address: 15 Toronto Street
Toronto, ON M5C 2E3
Phone: (416) 366-4567

#153
Adega Restaurante
Cuisines: Portuguese, Spanish
Average price: $31-$60
Area: Downtown Core
Address: 33 Elm St
Toronto, ON M5G 1H1
Phone: (416) 977-4338

#154
Frankie's Bar and Cafe
Cuisines: Breakfast & Brunch, Diner
Average price: Under $10
Area: Ossington Strip, West Queen West, Trinity Bellwoods
Address: 994 Queen Street W
Toronto, ON M6J 1H1
Phone: (416) 588-1936

#155
Burrito Bandidos
Cuisines: Tex-Mex
Average price: Under $10
Area: Downtown Core
Address: 496 Yonge St
Toronto, ON M4Y 1X9
Phone: (647) 352-4770

#156
Buster's Sea Cove
Cuisines: Seafood
Average price: $11-$30
Area: St. Lawrence, Downtown Core
Address: 93 Front Street E
Toronto, ON M5E 1C3
Phone: (416) 369-9048

#157
North of Brooklyn Pizzeria
Cuisines: Pizza
Average price: Under $10
Area: West Queen West, Trinity Bellwoods
Address: 650 1/2 Queen Street W
Toronto, ON M6J
Phone: (647) 352-5700

#158
Skin+Bones
Cuisines: Canadian
Average price: $31-$60
Area: Leslieville
Address: 980 Queen Street E
Toronto, ON M4M 1K1
Phone: (416) 524-5209

#159
Messini Authentic Gyros
Cuisines: Greek, Mediterranean
Average price: Under $10
Area: Greektown, Riverdale
Address: 445 Danforth Ave
Toronto, ON M4K 1P1
Phone: (416) 778-4861

#160
Caffe Di Portici
Cuisines: Italian, Pizza, Cafe
Average price: $11-$30
Area: Yorkville
Address: 6 Scollard Street
Toronto, ON M5R 3K8
Phone: (647) 351-2235

#161
The County General
Cuisines: Bar, Canadian
Average price: $11-$30
Area: Niagara, West Queen West, Trinity Bellwoods
Address: 936 Queen St W
Toronto, ON M6J 1G9
Phone: (416) 531-4447

#162
Bazara Asian Cuisine
Cuisines: Asian Fusion, Sushi Bar
Average price: $11-$30
Area: Little Portugal, Ossington Strip, Beaconsfield Village
Address: 188 Ossington Avenue
Toronto, ON M6J 2Z7
Phone: (647) 748-0288

#163
Mezes
Cuisines: Greek, Mediterranean
Average price: $11-$30
Area: Greektown, Riverdale
Address: 456 Danforth Ave
Toronto, ON M4K 1P4
Phone: (416) 778-5150

#164
Le Ti Colibri
Cuisines: Caribbean
Average price: Under $10
Area: Kensington Market
Address: 291 Augusta Avenue
Toronto, ON M5T 1N9
Phone: (416) 925-2223

#165
C'est What?
Cuisines: Brewery, Music Venues, Canadian
Average price: $11-$30
Area: St. Lawrence, Downtown Core
Address: 67 Front Street E
Toronto, ON M5E 1B5
Phone: (416) 867-9499

#166
Victor
Cuisines: French
Average price: Above $61
Area: Entertainment District, Downtown Core
Address: 30 Mercer St
Toronto, ON M5V
Phone: (416) 883-3431

#167
Tokyo Kitchen
Cuisines: Japanese
Average price: $11-$30
Area: Church-Wellesley Village, Downtown Core
Address: 20 Charles St E
Toronto, ON M4Y 1T1
Phone: (416) 515-0387

#168
King's Tacos
Cuisines: Mexican
Average price: $11-$30
Area: Corso Italia
Address: 1216 Saint Clair Avenue W
Toronto, ON M6E
Phone: (647) 342-0262

#169
Big House Pizza
Cuisines: Pizza
Average price: Under $10
Area: The Danforth
Address: 962 Danforth Avenue
Toronto, ON M4J 1L8
Phone: (416) 759-8484

#170
Nota Bene
Cuisines: Canadian
Average price: $31-$60
Area: Entertainment District, Queen Street West, Downtown Core
Address: 180 Queen St W
Toronto, ON M5V 3X3
Phone: (416) 977-6400

#171
Jang Su Chon
Cuisines: Korean
Average price: Under $10
Area: Chinatown, Kensington Market, Downtown Core
Address: 6 St Andrew St
Toronto, ON M5T 2K2
Phone: (416) 596-8388

#172
Burrito Bandidos
Cuisines: Tex-Mex
Average price: Under $10
Area: Entertainment District
Address: 120 Peter St
Toronto, ON M5V 2G7
Phone: (416) 593-9191

#173
SCADDABUSH Italian Kitchen & Bar
Cuisines: Wine Bar, Italian, Beer
Average price: $11-$30
Area: Downtown Core
Address: 382 Yonge Street
Toronto, ON M5B 1S8
Phone: (416) 597-8838

#174
Yours Truly
Cuisines: Canadian
Average price: Above $61
Area: Little Portugal, Ossington Strip, Trinity Bellwoods, Beaconsfield Village
Address: 229 Ossington Avenue
Toronto, ON M6J 2Z9
Phone: (416) 533-2243

#175
Tabülè Middle Eastern Cuisine
Cuisines: Middle Eastern
Average price: $11-$30
Area: Riverdale
Address: 810 Queen Street E
Toronto, ON M4M 1H7
Phone: (416) 465-2500

#176
Darbar Persian Grill
Cuisines: Persian/Iranian
Average price: $11-$30
Area: Yonge and Eglinton
Address: 288 Eglinton West & Avenue Road, Toronto, ON M4R 1B2
Phone: (416) 519-4545

#177
Live Organic Food Bar
Cuisines: Vegan, Live/Raw Food, Organic Store
Average price: $11-$30
Area: The Annex
Address: 264 Dupont St
Toronto, ON M5R 1V7
Phone: (416) 515-2002

#178
The Grilled Cheese
Cuisines: American, Sandwiches
Average price: Under $10
Area: Kensington Market
Address: 66 1/2 Nassau Street
Toronto, ON M5T
Phone: (416) 868-9669

#179
Brock Sandwich
Cuisines: Salad, Fast Food, Sandwiches
Average price: $11-$30
Area: Brockton Village, Bloordale Village, Wallace Emerson
Address: 1260 Bloor Street W
Toronto, ON M6H 1N5
Phone: (647) 748-1260

#180
The Grove
Cuisines: Canadian
Average price: $31-$60
Area: Dufferin Grove, Little Portugal, Beaconsfield Village
Address: 1214 Dundas Street W
Toronto, ON M6J
Phone: (416) 588-2299

#181
Tokyo Sushi House
Cuisines: Sushi Bar
Average price: $11-$30
Area: Downtown Core
Address: 33 St Joseph Street
Toronto, ON M4Y 1J8
Phone: (416) 513-0002

#182
Starving Artist
Cuisines: Breakfast & Brunch
Average price: $11-$30
Area: Wallace Emerson
Address: 584 Lansdowne Avenue
Toronto, ON M6H 3
Phone: (647) 342-5058

#183
Bestellen
Cuisines: European
Average price: $31-$60
Area: Dufferin Grove
Address: 972 College St
Toronto, ON M6H 1A5
Phone: (647) 341-6769

#184
Karine's
Cuisines: Vegan, Vegetarian, Breakfast & Brunch
Average price: Under $10
Area: Downtown Core
Address: 109 McCaul Street
Toronto, ON M5T 3K5
Phone: (416) 591-0863

#185
Foxley Bistro and Bar
Cuisines: Asian Fusion, Tapas Bar
Average price: $31-$60
Area: Little Portugal, Ossington Strip, Trinity Bellwoods, Beaconsfield Village
Address: 207 Ossington Avenue
Toronto, ON M6J 2Z8
Phone: (416) 534-8520

#186
Earth Rosedale
Cuisines: Canadian
Average price: $31-$60
Area: Rosedale
Address: 1055 Yonge Street
Toronto, ON M4W 2L2
Phone: (416) 551-9890

#187
Koyoi Restaurant & Bar
Cuisines: Japanese
Average price: $11-$30
Area: Downtown Core
Address: 2 Irwin Ave
Toronto, ON M4Y 1K9
Phone: (647) 351-5128

#188
Merryberry
Cuisines: Canadian
Average price: $11-$30
Area: Cabbagetown
Address: 559 Parliament St
Toronto, ON M4X 1P7
Phone: (647) 348-0411

#189
The P&L Burger
Cuisines: Burgers
Average price: $11-$30
Area: Alexandra Park, Queen Street West
Address: 507 Queen Street W
Toronto, ON M5V
Phone: (416) 603-9919

#190
Kinton Ramen
Cuisines: Ramen
Average price: $11-$30
Area: Downtown Core
Address: 51 Baldwin Street
Toronto, ON M5T 1Y9
Phone: (647) 748-8900

#191
La Vecchia
Cuisines: Italian
Average price: $11-$30
Area: Mount Pleasant and Davisville, Yonge and Eglinton
Address: 2405 Yonge St
Toronto, ON M4P 2E7
Phone: (416) 489-0630

#192
Corned Beef House
Cuisines: Sandwiches, Canadian
Average price: $11-$30
Area: Entertainment District, Downtown Core
Address: 270 Adelaide St W
Toronto, ON M5H 1X6
Phone: (416) 977-2333

#193
Banh Mi Boys
Cuisines: Vietnamese, Asian Fusion
Average price: Under $10
Area: Alexandra Park, Queen Street West
Address: 392 Queen Street W
Toronto, ON M5V 2A9
Phone: (416) 363-0588

#194
Cool Runnings Restaurant
Cuisines: Caribbean
Average price: Under $10
Area: Upper Beach
Address: 146 Main Street
Toronto, ON M4E 2V8
Phone: (416) 693-8724

#195
Solo Sushi Bekkan
Cuisines: Japanese
Average price: $11-$30
Area: Downtown Core
Address: 3 Grosvenor Street
Toronto, ON M4Y 1A9
Phone: (416) 925-3388

#196
Holy Chuck
Cuisines: Burgers
Average price: $11-$30
Area: Yonge and St. Clair, Deer Park
Address: 1450 Yonge Street
Toronto, ON M4T 1Y7
Phone: (416) 962-4825

#197
Oyster Boy
Cuisines: Seafood
Average price: $31-$60
Area: Niagara, West Queen West, Trinity Bellwoods
Address: 872 Queen Street W
Toronto, ON M6J 1G3
Phone: (416) 534-3432

#198
Fat Louie's BBQ
Cuisines: Southern, Food Truck
Average price: Under $10
Area: The Junction
Address: 110 W Toronto Street
Toronto, ON M6N 3E4
Phone: (416) 655-0246

#199
Bonjour Brioche
Cuisines: Breakfast & Brunch, French
Average price: $11-$30
Area: Riverdale
Address: 812 Queen Street E
Toronto, ON M4M 1H7
Phone: (416) 406-1250

#200
Dimmi Bar & Trattoria
Cuisines: Italian
Average price: $11-$30
Area: Yorkville
Address: 140 Cumberland St
Toronto, ON M5R 1A8
Phone: (416) 975-1100

#201
Utsav
Cuisines: Food Delivery Service, Indian
Average price: $11-$30
Area: Yorkville
Address: 69 Yorkville Ave
Toronto, ON M5R 1B8
Phone: (416) 961-8349

#202
Keeffaa Ethiopian
Cuisines: Ethiopian
Average price: $11-$30
Area: Corktown
Address: 368 Queen Street E
Toronto, ON M5A
Phone: (647) 349-0900

#203
Bitondo's Pizzeria
Cuisines: Pizza, Italian
Average price: Under $10
Area: Little Italy
Address: 11 Clinton Street
Toronto, ON M6J 2N7
Phone: (416) 533-4101

#204
Mr Jerk
Cuisines: Caribbean, Seafood, Ethnic Food
Average price: Under $10
Area: Cabbagetown
Address: 209 Wellesley Street E
Toronto, ON M4X 1G1
Phone: (416) 961-8913

#205
I Went To Philly
Cuisines: Diner
Average price: $11-$30
Area: Downtown Core
Address: 462 Yonge Street
Toronto, ON M4Y 1S9
Phone: (416) 927-9090

#206
Positano Restaurant
Cuisines: Pizza, Italian
Average price: $11-$30
Area: Mount Pleasant and Davisville
Address: 633 Mount Pleasant Rd
Toronto, ON M4S 2M9
Phone: (416) 932-3982

#207
Mexico Lindo
Cuisines: Mexican
Average price: $11-$30
Area: Mount Pleasant and Davisville
Address: 1618 Bayview Ave
Toronto, ON M4S 1T3
Phone: (647) 436-4340

#208
Swan Restaurant
Cuisines: Diner, Breakfast & Brunch
Average price: $11-$30
Area: Niagara, West Queen West, Trinity Bellwoods
Address: 892 Queen Street W
Toronto, ON M6J 1G3
Phone: (416) 532-0452

#209
Rhum Corner
Cuisines: Caribbean, Salad, Cocktail Bar
Average price: $11-$30
Area: Little Italy, Trinity Bellwoods
Address: 926 Dundas Street W
Toronto, ON M6J 1W3
Phone: (647) 346-9356

#210
Le Paradis Brasserie Bistro
Cuisines: French, Breakfast & Brunch
Average price: $11-$30
Area: The Annex
Address: 166 Bedford Road
Toronto, ON M5R 2K9
Phone: (416) 921-0995

#211
Leslie Jones
Cuisines: Canadian
Average price: $31-$60
Area: Leslieville
Address: 1182 Queen Street E
Toronto, ON M4M 1L4
Phone: (416) 463-5663

#212
The Combine Eatery
Cuisines: Canadian
Average price: $11-$30
Area: Riverdale
Address: 162 Danforth Avenue
Toronto, ON M4K 1N2
Phone: (416) 792-8088

#213
The Westerly
Cuisines: American
Average price: $11-$30
Area: High Park, Roncesvalles
Address: 413 Roncesvalles Avenue
Toronto, ON M6R 2N1
Phone: (416) 551-6660

#214
The Depanneur
Cuisines: Breakfast & Brunch
Average price: $11-$30
Area: Dufferin Grove
Address: 1033A College Street
Toronto, ON M6H 1A8
Phone: (416) 828-1990

#215
Sneaky Dee's
Cuisines: Tex-Mex, Dive Bar
Average price: $11-$30
Area: Kensington Market
Address: 431 College Street
Toronto, ON M5T 1T1
Phone: (416) 603-3090

#216
Hot Beans
Cuisines: Vegan, Mexican
Average price: Under $10
Area: Kensington Market
Address: 160 Baldwin Street
Toronto, ON M5T 3K7
Phone: (647) 352-7581

#217
Negroni
Cuisines: Sandwiches, Italian
Average price: $11-$30
Area: Palmerston
Address: 492 College Street
Toronto, ON M6G 1A4
Phone: (416) 413-0005

#218
Noodle King
Cuisines: Chinese
Average price: Under $10
Area: Downtown Core
Address: 123 Queen Street W
Toronto, ON M5H 3M9
Phone: (416) 861-9398

#219
Fresh
Cuisines: Vegetarian
Average price: $11-$30
Area: The Annex, University of Toronto
Address: 326 Bloor St W
Toronto, ON M5S 1W5
Phone: (416) 531-2635

#220
Nazareth Restaurant
Cuisines: Ethiopian, Vegetarian
Average price: Under $10
Area: Dovercourt, Dufferin Grove
Address: 969 Bloor Street W
Toronto, ON M6H 1L7
Phone: (416) 535-0797

#221
Blu Ristorante
Cuisines: Italian, Lounge
Average price: $31-$60
Area: Yorkville
Address: 17 Yorkville Avenue
Toronto, ON M4W 1L1
Phone: (416) 921-1471

#222
Kalendar
Cuisines: Italian, French,
Breakfast & Brunch
Average price: $11-$30
Area: Palmerston
Address: 546 College Street
Toronto, ON M6G 1B1
Phone: (416) 923-4138

#223
Dumpling House
Cuisines: Chinese
Average price: Under $10
Area: Riverdale
Address: 619 Gerrard Street E
Toronto, ON M4M 1Y2
Phone: (416) 901-0288

#224
La Société
Cuisines: French
Average price: $31-$60
Area: Discovery District, Yorkville,
Downtown Core
Address: 131 Bloor Street W
Toronto, ON M5S 3L7
Phone: (416) 551-9929

#225
The Annex HodgePodge
Cuisines: Vegan, Deli, Sandwiches
Average price: Under $10
Area: The Annex
Address: 258 Dupont Avenue
Toronto, ON M5R
Phone: (416) 513-1333

#226
Ja Bistro
Cuisines: Japanese
Average price: $31-$60
Area: Entertainment District,
Downtown Core
Address: 222 Richmond Street W
Toronto, ON M5V 1W4
Phone: (647) 748-0222

#227
Kupfert & Kim
Cuisines: Vegetarian, Vegan,
Gluten-Free
Average price: $11-$30
Area: Financial District, Downtown Core
Address: 100 King Street West
Toronto, ON M5X 1C7
Phone: (416) 504-1233

#228
Barberian's Steak House
Cuisines: Steakhouse
Average price: Above $61
Area: Downtown Core
Address: 7 Elm Street
Toronto, ON M5G 1H1
Phone: (416) 597-0335

#229
Qi Sushi
Cuisines: Japanese, Sushi Bar
Average price: $11-$30
Area: Cabbagetown
Address: 358 Gerrard Street E
Toronto, ON M5A 2H4
Phone: (416) 929-8989

#230
Queen Mother Cafe
Cuisines: Asian Fusion, Thai
Average price: $11-$30
Area: Entertainment District, Queen Street West, Downtown Core
Address: 206 Queen St W
Toronto, ON M5V 1Z2
Phone: (416) 598-4719

#231
Crêpe It Up
Cuisines: Creperies, Breakfast & Brunch
Average price: Under $10
Area: Church-Wellesley Village, Downtown Core
Address: 507 Church St
Toronto, ON M4Y 2C9
Phone: (416) 916-3558

#232
Bero restaurant
Cuisines: Spanish, European, Mediterranean
Average price: Above $61
Area: Leslieville
Address: 889 Queen Street E
Toronto, ON M4M 1J6
Phone: (416) 477-3393

#233
Ascari Enoteca
Cuisines: Italian, Bar
Average price: $31-$60
Area: Leslieville
Address: 1111 Queen Street E
Toronto, ON M4M
Phone: (416) 792-4157

#234
Shangrila
Cuisines: Himalayan/Nepalese, Asian Fusion, Diner
Average price: Under $10
Area: Parkdale, Roncesvalles
Address: 1600 Queen Street W
Toronto, ON M6R 1A8
Phone: (416) 588-1100

#235
Mezzetta Cafe Restaurant
Cuisines: Mediterranean, Tapas Bar
Average price: $11-$30
Area: Wychwood
Address: 681 St Clair Ave W
Toronto, ON M6C 1A7
Phone: (416) 658-5687

#236
Delica Kitchen
Cuisines: Salad, Cafe, Sandwiches
Average price: $11-$30
Area: Yonge and St. Clair, Deer Park
Address: 1440 Yonge Street
Toronto, ON M4T 1Y5
Phone: (416) 546-5408

#237
Superfood Eateries
Cuisines: Vegan, Vegetarian, Juice Bar& Smoothies
Average price: $11-$30
Area: Entertainment District, Downtown Core
Address: 268 Adelaide Street W
Toronto, ON M5H 1X6
Phone: (647) 827-9656

#238
The Lakeview
Cuisines: Diner, Canadian
Average price: $11-$30
Area: Little Italy, Little Portugal, Ossington Strip, Trinity Bellwoods
Address: 1132 Dundas Street W
Toronto, ON M6J 1X2
Phone: (416) 850-8886

#239
The Burgernator
Cuisines: Burgers
Average price: $11-$30
Area: Kensington Market
Address: 269 Augusta Avenue
Toronto, ON M5T 1M5
Phone: (647) 748-0990

#240
AAA Bar
Cuisines: Barbeque, Pub
Average price: $11-$30
Area: Corktown, Downtown Core
Address: 138 Adelaide Street E
Toronto, ON M5C 1K9
Phone: (416) 850-2726

#241
7 West Cafe
Cuisines: Italian, Breakfast & Brunch
Average price: $11-$30
Area: Downtown Core
Address: 7 Charles St W
Toronto, ON M4Y 1R4
Phone: (416) 928-9041

#242
The Rebel House
Cuisines: Pub, Gastropub
Average price: $11-$30
Area: Summer Hill
Address: 1068 Yonge Street
Toronto, ON M4W 2L4
Phone: (416) 927-0704

#243
Chatime
Cuisines: Coffee & Tea,
Tea Rooms, Chinese
Average price: Under $10
Area: Discovery District, Downtown Core
Address: 132 Dundas Street W
Toronto, ON M5G 1C3
Phone: (647) 340-8406

#244
Coquine Restaurant
Cuisines: French
Average price: $31-$60
Area: Mount Pleasant and Davisville
Address: 2075 Yonge St
Toronto, ON M4S 2A4
Phone: (416) 322-6767

#245
Mt Fuji Restaurant
Cuisines: Japanese
Average price: $11-$30
Area: Discovery District, Downtown Core
Address: 72 Gerrard St W
Toronto, ON M5G 1J5
Phone: (416) 971-5882

#246
Mildred's Temple Kitchen
Cuisines: Breakfast & Brunch, Canadian
Average price: $11-$30
Area: Liberty Village
Address: 85 Hanna Avenue
Toronto, ON M6K 3S3
Phone: (416) 588-5695

#247
Copacabana Brazilian Steak House
Cuisines: Brazilian, Steakhouse
Average price: $31-$60
Area: Mount Pleasant and Davisville,
Yonge and Eglinton
Address: 150 Eglinton Avenue E
Toronto, ON M4P 1E8
Phone: (416) 916-2099

#248
King's Noodle Restaurant
Cuisines: Chinese
Average price: Under $10
Area: Chinatown, Kensington Market,
Downtown Core
Address: 296 Spadina Avenue
Toronto, ON M5T 2E7
Phone: (416) 598-1817

#249
Mean Bao
Cuisines: Chinese
Average price: Under $10
Area: Downtown Core
Address: 275 Dundas Street W
Toronto, ON M5T 3K1
Phone: (416) 850-5616

#250
Sky Blue Sky Sandwiches
Cuisines: Sandwiches
Average price: Under $10
Area: Koreatown, Palmerston,
Seaton Village
Address: 605 Bloor Street W
Toronto, ON M6G 1K5
Phone: (647) 351-7945

#251
Donatello Restaurant
Cuisines: Italian, Seafood
Average price: $31-$60
Area: Downtown Core
Address: 37 Elm Street
Toronto, ON M5G 1H1
Phone: (416) 595-5001

#252
Opus Restaurant
Cuisines: Canadian
Average price: Above $61
Area: The Annex
Address: 37 Prince Arthur Ave
Toronto, ON M5R 1B2
Phone: (416) 921-3105

#253
Caplansky's Delicatessen
Cuisines: Deli, Sandwiches, Caterer
Average price: $11-$30
Area: Little Italy
Address: 356 College St
Toronto, ON M5T 1S6
Phone: (416) 500-3852

#254
Bosk
Cuisines: Canadian
Average price: Above $61
Area: Financial District, Downtown Core
Address: 188 University Avenue
Toronto, ON M5H 0A3
Phone: (647) 788-8294

#255
Mill Street Brew Pub
Cuisines: Bar, Brasserie
Average price: $11-$30
Area: Distillery District
Address: 55 Mill St
Toronto, ON M5A 3C4
Phone: (416) 681-0338

#256
Terroni
Cuisines: Italian
Average price: $31-$60
Area: Niagara, West Queen West, Trinity Bellwoods
Address: 720 Queen Street W
Toronto, ON M6J 1E8
Phone: (416) 504-0320

#257
The Keg Steakhouse + Bar
Cuisines: Steakhouse, Bar, Seafood
Average price: $31-$60
Area: St. Lawrence
Address: 26 The Esplanade
Toronto, ON M5E 1A7
Phone: (416) 367-0685

#258
Citizenry
Cuisines: Shopping, Cafe
Average price: Under $10
Area: West Queen West, Trinity Bellwoods
Address: 982 Queen Street W
Toronto, ON M6J 1H1
Phone: (647) 458-6672

#259
Green Eggplant Restaurant
Cuisines: Mediterranean
Average price: $11-$30
Area: The Beach
Address: 1968 Queen St E
Toronto, ON M4L 1H8
Phone: (416) 913-3361

#260
Table 17
Cuisines: French, European
Average price: $31-$60
Area: Riverdale
Address: 782 Queen St E
Toronto, ON M4M 1H4
Phone: (416) 519-1851

#261
Vinny's Panini
Cuisines: Sandwiches
Average price: Under $10
Area: Christie Pits
Address: 787 Dupont St
Toronto, ON M6G 1Z5
Phone: (416) 531-9454

#262
URSA
Cuisines: Canadian
Average price: Above $61
Area: West Queen West, Trinity Bellwoods
Address: 924 Queen Street W
Toronto, ON M6J
Phone: (416) 536-8963

#263
Wallflower
Cuisines: Canadian, Bar
Average price: $11-$30
Area: Brockton Village
Address: 1665 Dundas Street W
Toronto, ON M6K
Phone: (647) 352-5605

#264
Byzantium
Cuisines: Gay Bar, Canadian
Average price: $31-$60
Area: Church-Wellesley Village, Downtown Core
Address: 499 Church St
Toronto, ON M4Y 2C6
Phone: (416) 922-3859

#265
Le Neuf Café
Cuisines: Coffee & Tea, French
Average price: $11-$30
Area: Entertainment District, Downtown Core
Address: 9 Clarence Square
Toronto, ON M5V
Phone: (647) 351-6855

#266
Burro Burrito
Cuisines: Mexican
Average price: Under $10
Area: Entertainment District, Downtown Core
Address: 388 Richmond Street W
Toronto, ON M5V 3P1
Phone: (647) 349-6688

#267
FOUR
Cuisines: Gluten-Free
Average price: $11-$30
Area: Financial District, Downtown Core
Address: 188 Bay Street
Toronto, ON M5L 1G6
Phone: (416) 368-1444

#268
Indie Ale House
Cuisines: Brewery, Gastropub, Pizza
Average price: $11-$30
Area: The Junction
Address: 2876 Dundas Street W
Toronto, ON M6P 1Y9
Phone: (416) 760-9691

#269
Alexandros Take-Out
Cuisines: Greek
Average price: Under $10
Area: Harbourfront
Address: 5 Queens Quay W
Toronto, ON M5J 2H1
Phone: (416) 367-0633

#270
Bent
Cuisines: Asian Fusion
Average price: $31-$60
Area: Trinity Bellwoods
Address: 777 Dundas Street W
Toronto, ON M6J 1V1
Phone: (647) 352-0092

#271
Ka Ka Lucky Seafood B B Q
Cuisines: Seafood
Average price: Under $10
Area: Riverdale
Address: 349 Broadview Ave
Toronto, ON M4M 2H1
Phone: (416) 461-3811

#272
Agave Y Aguacate
Cuisines: Mexican
Average price: $31-$60
Area: Downtown Core
Address: 35 Baldwin Street
Toronto, ON M5T 1L1
Phone: (647) 748-6448

#273
Tabule Restaurant
Cuisines: Middle Eastern, Vegan, Vegetarian
Average price: $11-$30
Area: Mount Pleasant and Davisville
Address: 2009 Yonge Street
Toronto, ON M4S 1Z8
Phone: (416) 483-3747

#274
Ka Chi
Cuisines: Korean
Average price: Under $10
Area: Kensington Market
Address: 8 St. Andrews Street
Toronto, ON M5T 2G4
Phone: (416) 597-1999

#275
iQ Food Co.
Cuisines: Salad, Fast Food, Gluten-Free
Average price: $11-$30
Area: Downtown Core
Address: 181 Bay Street
Toronto, ON M5J 2T3
Phone: (647) 346-0792

#276
Okonomi House Restaurant
Cuisines: Japanese
Average price: Under $10
Area: Downtown Core
Address: 23 Charles Street W
Toronto, ON M4Y 2R4
Phone: (416) 925-6176

#277
Reposado Bar & Lounge
Cuisines: Lounge, Tapas, Mexican
Average price: $31-$60
Area: Ossington Strip, Trinity Bellwoods, Beaconsfield Village
Address: 136 Ossington Avenue
Toronto, ON M6J 2Z5
Phone: (416) 532-6474

#278
The Beaconsfield
Cuisines: Pub, Canadian
Average price: $11-$30
Area: West Queen West, Beaconsfield Village
Address: 1154 Queen St W
Toronto, ON M6J 1J5
Phone: (416) 516-2550

#279
School Restaurant
Cuisines: Bakery, Canadian, Breakfast & Brunch
Average price: $11-$30
Area: Liberty Village
Address: 70 Fraser Ave
Toronto, ON M6K 3E1
Phone: (416) 588-0005

#280
Terroni
Cuisines: Italian
Average price: $11-$30
Area: Downtown Core
Address: 57A Adelaide Street E
Toronto, ON M5C 1K6
Phone: (416) 203-3093

#281
Playa Cabana Cantina
Cuisines: Mexican
Average price: $11-$30
Area: The Junction
Address: 2883 Dundas Street W
Toronto, ON M6P 1Y9
Phone: (647) 352-7767

#282
The Keg Steakhouse + Bar
Cuisines: Steakhouse, Bar, Seafood
Average price: $31-$60
Area: Financial District, Downtown Core
Address: 165 York Street
Toronto, ON M5H 3R8
Phone: (416) 703-1773

#283
San Francesco Foods
Cuisines: Italian, Sandwiches, Pizza
Average price: Under $10
Area: Little Italy
Address: 10 Clinton Street
Toronto, ON M6J
Phone: (416) 534-7867

#284
Tommaso's Trattoria
Cuisines: Italian
Average price: $11-$30
Area: Riverdale
Address: 400 Eastern Ave
Toronto, ON M4M 1B9
Phone: (416) 466-0988

#285
Café Boulud
Cuisines: Cafe, Desserts
Average price: Above $61
Area: Yorkville
Address: 60 Yorkville Avenue
Toronto, ON M3C 2K8
Phone: (416) 963-6000

#286
Le Petit Déjeuner
Cuisines: Breakfast & Brunch, Belgian
Average price: $11-$30
Area: Corktown
Address: 191 King St E
Toronto, ON M5A 1J5
Phone: (416) 703-1560

#287
The Saint Tavern
Cuisines: Bar, Gastropub
Average price: $31-$60
Area: Little Portugal, Ossington Strip, Trinity Bellwoods, Beaconsfield Village
Address: 227 Ossington Ave
Toronto, ON M6J 3A1
Phone: (647) 350-2100

#288
Union Social Eatery
Cuisines: American, Canadian
Average price: $11-$30
Area: Yonge and St. Clair, Deer Park
Address: 21 St. Clair W
Toronto, ON M4T 1L9
Phone: (416) 901-3456

#289
Fusaro's Kitchen
Cuisines: Italian, Pizza
Average price: $11-$30
Area: Entertainment District, Downtown Core
Address: 147 Spadina Avenue
Toronto, ON M5V 2L7
Phone: (416) 260-8414

#290
Old York Bar & Grill
Cuisines: Pub, Breakfast & Brunch
Average price: $11-$30
Area: Niagara
Address: 167 Niagara St
Toronto, ON M5V 1C9
Phone: (416) 703-9675

#291
East Thirty-Six
Cuisines: Restaurants, Cocktail Bar
Average price: $11-$30
Area: St. Lawrence, Downtown Core
Address: 36 Wellington Street E
Toronto, ON M5E 1C7
Phone: (647) 350-3636

#292
Folia Grill
Cuisines: Fast Food, Greek
Average price: Under $10
Area: East York
Address: 1031 Pape Avenue
Toronto, ON M4K 3W1
Phone: (416) 424-2800

#293
Coach House Restaurant
Cuisines: Diner
Average price: Under $10
Area: Downtown Core
Address: 574 Yonge St
Toronto, ON M4Y 1Z3
Phone: (416) 922-5551

#294
Smoque N' Bones
Cuisines: Barbeque
Average price: $11-$30
Area: Niagara, West Queen West, Trinity Bellwoods
Address: 869 Queen Street W
Toronto, ON M6J
Phone: (647) 341-5730

#295
Kawa Sushi
Cuisines: Sushi Bar
Average price: $11-$30
Area: Church-Wellesley Village, Downtown Core
Address: 451 Church St
Toronto, ON M4Y 2C5
Phone: (416) 921-2888

#296
TOCA
Cuisines: Canadian
Average price: Above $61
Area: Entertainment District, Downtown Core
Address: 181 Wellington Street W
Toronto, ON M5V 3G7
Phone: (416) 572-8008

#297
Island Foods
Cuisines: Caribbean
Average price: Under $10
Area: Liberty Village
Address: 1182 King Street W
Toronto, ON M6K 1E6
Phone: (416) 532-6298

#298
Matagali Restaurant
Cuisines: Indian
Average price: $11-$30
Area: Discovery District, Downtown Core
Address: 69 Elm Street
Toronto, ON M5G 1H2
Phone: (416) 599-9994

#299
Grasslands
Cuisines: Vegan, Lounge, European
Average price: $11-$30
Area: Alexandra Park, Queen Street West
Address: 478 Queen Street W
Toronto, ON M5V 2B4
Phone: (416) 504-5127

#300
Shibui Robata Bar
Cuisines: Japanese, Bar
Average price: $31-$60
Area: Entertainment District, Downtown Core
Address: 230 Adelaide Street W
Toronto, ON M5H
Phone: (647) 748-3211

#301
Hank's
Cuisines: Breakfast & Brunch, Cafe
Average price: $11-$30
Area: St. Lawrence
Address: 9 1/2 Church Street
Toronto, ON M5E 1M2
Phone: (416) 504-2657

#302
Daddyo's Pasta & Salads
Cuisines: Italian
Average price: $11-$30
Area: University of Toronto, Downtown Core
Address: 673 Spadina Avenue
Toronto, ON M5S 2H9
Phone: (416) 598-5522

#303
Boar
Cuisines: Sandwiches
Average price: $11-$30
Area: Mount Pleasant and Davisville
Address: 3 Glebe Road E
Toronto, ON M4S 1N6
Phone: (416) 482-1616

#304
The Chase
Cuisines: Canadian
Average price: Above $61
Area: Downtown Core
Address: 10 Temperance Street
Toronto, ON M5H 1Y4
Phone: (647) 348-7000

#305
Tofu Village House of Soon Tofu
Cuisines: Korean
Average price: Under $10
Area: Koreatown, Palmerston, Bickford Park, Seaton Village
Address: 681 Bloor Street West
Toronto, ON M6G 4B9
Phone: (647) 345-3836

#306
Mother's Dumplings
Cuisines: Chinese
Average price: $11-$30
Area: Chinatown, Downtown Core
Address: 421 Spadina Ave
Toronto, ON M5T 2A8
Phone: (416) 217-2008

#307
Portico Restaurant
Cuisines: Canadian
Average price: $31-$60
Area: Downtown Core
Address: 15 Richmond Street E
Toronto, ON M5C
Phone: (416) 601-3774

#308
Pho Linh
Cuisines: Vietnamese
Average price: Under $10
Area: Brockton Village
Address: 1156 College Street W
Toronto, ON M6H 1B6
Phone: (416) 516-3891

#309
Casa Di Giorgios
Cuisines: Italian, Pizza
Average price: $11-$30
Area: Upper Beach
Address: 1646 Queen St E
Toronto, ON M4L 1G3
Phone: (416) 686-7066

#310
Kokoro Sushi
Cuisines: Sushi Bar
Average price: $11-$30
Area: Harbourfront
Address: 16 Yonge St
Toronto, ON M5M 3G5
Phone: (416) 363-9379

#311
Hapa Izakaya
Cuisines: Japanese
Average price: $31-$60
Area: Bickford Park
Address: 602 College Street
Toronto, ON M6G
Phone: (647) 748-4272

#312
Local Kitchen & Winebar
Cuisines: Wine Bar, Canadian, Italian
Average price: $31-$60
Area: Parkdale, Roncesvalles
Address: 1710 Queen Street W
Toronto, ON M6N
Phone: (416) 534-6700

#313

Rock Lobster Food Co

Cuisines: Seafood
Average price: $11-$30
Area: Alexandra Park, Queen Street West
Address: 538 Queen Street W Toronto, ON M5V 2B7
Phone: (416) 203-6623

#314

The Roxton

Cuisines: Pub, Canadian
Average price: $11-$30
Area: Bickford Park
Address: 379 Harbord Street Toronto, ON M6G 1H8
Phone: (416) 535-8181

#315

Lisa Marie

Cuisines: Canadian
Average price: $11-$30
Area: West Queen West, Trinity Bellwoods
Address: 638 Queen Street W Toronto, ON M6J 1E3
Phone: (647) 748-6822

#316

Me Va Me Kitchen Express

Cuisines: Mediterranean
Average price: $11-$30
Area: Entertainment District, Queen Street West, Downtown Core
Address: 240 Queen Street West Toronto, ON M5V 1Z7
Phone: (416) 546-3770

#317

Nove Trattoria

Cuisines: Italian
Average price: $11-$30
Area: Yonge and St. Clair, Deer Park
Address: 1406 Yonge St Toronto, ON M4T 1Y5
Phone: (647) 345-5848

#318

Me&Mine

Cuisines: Canadian
Average price: $11-$30
Area: Brockton Village
Address: 1144 College Street Toronto, ON M6H 1B6
Phone: (416) 535-5858

#319

Asuka Japanese Restaurant

Cuisines: Japanese, Sushi Bar
Average price: $11-$30
Area: Yorkville
Address: 108 Yorkville Ave Toronto, ON M5R 1B9
Phone: (416) 975-9084

#320

Pizza Pide

Cuisines: Pizza, Turkish
Average price: Under $10
Area: Leslieville
Address: 949 Gerrard Street E Toronto, ON M4M 1Z1
Phone: (416) 462-9666

#321

Habits Gastropub

Cuisines: Gastropub
Average price: $11-$30
Area: Dufferin Grove
Address: 928 College Street Toronto, ON M6H 1A4
Phone: (416) 533-7272

#322

Smoke's Poutinerie

Cuisines: Fast Food, Poutineries
Average price: Under $10
Area: Entertainment District, Downtown Core
Address: 218 Adelaide St W Toronto, ON M5H 1W7
Phone: (416) 599-2873

#323

La Forchetta

Cuisines: Italian
Average price: $31-$60
Area: Little Italy, Bickford Park
Address: 613 College Street Toronto, ON M6G
Phone: (416) 534-3100

#324

The Innis Cafe

Cuisines: Cafe
Average price: Under $10
Area: University of Toronto, Downtown Core
Address: 2 Sussex Ave Toronto, ON M5S 1J5
Phone: (416) 977-7434

#325
Daio Japanese Restaurant
Cuisines: Japanese
Average price: $11-$30
Area: Church-Wellesley Village, Downtown Core
Address: 45 Carlton Street
Toronto, ON M5B 2H9
Phone: (416) 260-2116

#326
No One Writes To The Colonel
Cuisines: Bar, Italian
Average price: $11-$30
Area: Little Italy, Palmerston
Address: 460 College Street
Toronto, ON M6G 1A4
Phone: (416) 551-7647

#327
Mad Mexican
Cuisines: Mexican
Average price: $11-$30
Area: Bloor-West Village
Address: 383 Jane Street
Toronto, ON M6S 3Z3
Phone: (416) 907-5787

#328
Sushi 930
Cuisines: Sushi Bar
Average price: $11-$30
Area: Niagara
Address: 930 King Street W
Toronto, ON M5V 1P5
Phone: (416) 603-9992

#329
Bindia Indian Bistro
Cuisines: Canadian, Indian
Average price: $11-$30
Area: St. Lawrence, Downtown Core
Address: 16 Market Street
Toronto, ON M5E
Phone: (416) 863-0000

#330
Blowfish on Bay
Cuisines: Asian Fusion
Average price: $31-$60
Area: Financial District, Downtown Core
Address: 333 Bay St
Toronto, ON M5H 2T4
Phone: (416) 860-0606

#331
La Cubana
Cuisines: Cuban
Average price: $11-$30
Area: High Park, Roncesvalles
Address: 392 Roncesvalles Avenue
Toronto, ON M6R 2M9
Phone: (416) 538-7500

#332
The Happy Hooker
Cuisines: Seafood
Average price: $11-$30
Area: Trinity Bellwoods
Address: 887 Dundas Street W
Toronto, ON M6J 2P8
Phone: (416) 603-4665

#333
Gilead Cafe and Bistro
Cuisines: Cafe, Canadian
Average price: $11-$30
Area: Corktown
Address: 4 Gilead Place
Toronto, ON M5A 3C9
Phone: (647) 288-0680

#334
The Shore Club
Cuisines: Seafood, Steakhouse
Average price: $31-$60
Area: Entertainment District, Downtown Core
Address: 155 Wellington St W
Toronto, ON M5V 3K2
Phone: (416) 351-3311

#335
Joe Mamas
Cuisines: Cajun/Creole
Average price: $11-$30
Area: Entertainment District, Downtown Core
Address: 317 King St W
Toronto, ON M5V 1J5
Phone: (416) 340-6469

#336
Factory Girl
Cuisines: Pizza, Italian
Average price: $11-$30
Area: Riverdale
Address: 193 Danforth Avenue
Toronto, ON M4K 1N2
Phone: (647) 352-2799

#337
Origin
Cuisines: Tapas, Asian Fusion
Average price: $31-$60
Area: St. Lawrence, Downtown Core
Address: 109 King Street E
Toronto, ON M5C 1G6
Phone: (416) 603-8009

#338
El Catrin
Cuisines: Tapas, Mexican
Average price: $31-$60
Area: Distillery District
Address: 18 Tank House Lane
Toronto, ON M5A 3C4
Phone: (416) 203-2121

#339
Woods Restaurant & Bar
Cuisines: Canadian
Average price: $31-$60
Area: St. Lawrence, Downtown Core
Address: 45 Colborne Street
Toronto, ON M5E 1E3
Phone: (416) 214-9918

#340
Bryden's
Cuisines: Pub, Sandwiches
Average price: $11-$30
Area: Swansea
Address: 2455 Bloor Street W
Toronto, ON M6S 1P7
Phone: (416) 760-8069

#341
Trattoria Nervosa
Cuisines: Italian, Coffee & Tea
Average price: $31-$60
Area: Yorkville
Address: 75 Yorkville Ave
Toronto, ON M5R
Phone: (416) 961-4642

#342
Pamier Kabob
Cuisines: Afghan
Average price: $11-$30
Area: Entertainment District, Downtown Core
Address: 119 Spadina Avenue
Toronto, ON M5V 2L1
Phone: (647) 352-2623

#343
Chacho's Fine Mexican Dining
Cuisines: Mexican
Average price: $11-$30
Area: Mount Pleasant and Davisville
Address: 234 Merton Street
Toronto, ON M4S 1A1
Phone: (416) 932-2434

#344
Kit Kat Italian Bar & Grill
Cuisines: Italian, Mediterranean
Average price: $11-$30
Area: Entertainment District, Downtown Core
Address: 297 King Street W
Toronto, ON M5V 1J5
Phone: (416) 977-4461

#345
The 420 Smokehouse
Cuisines: Barbeque
Average price: $11-$30
Area: Cabbagetown
Address: 420 Parliament Street
Toronto, ON M5A 3A1
Phone: (416) 924-5858

#346
L'Ouvrier
Cuisines: Breakfast & Brunch, Canadian
Average price: $31-$60
Area: Trinity Bellwoods
Address: 791 Dundas St W
Toronto, ON M6J 1V1
Phone: (416) 901-9581

#347
Off The Hook Gourmet Fish N Chips
Cuisines: Gluten-Free, Fish & Chips, Comfort Food
Average price: $11-$30
Area: Riverdale
Address: 749 Broadview Avenue
Toronto, ON M4J 3R3
Phone: (416) 465-4356

#348
Black Skirt
Cuisines: Italian
Average price: $11-$30
Area: Dufferin Grove
Address: 974 College Street
Toronto, ON M6H 1A5
Phone: (416) 532-7424

#349
Pasta Pantry Fine Foods
Cuisines: Italian
Average price: $11-$30
Area: Mount Pleasant and Davisville
Address: 1997 Yonge St
Toronto, ON M4S 1Z8
Phone: (416) 482-4848

#350
Sushi Place
Cuisines: Sushi Bar
Average price: $11-$30
Area: High Park
Address: 1730 Bloor Street W
Toronto, ON M6P 1B3
Phone: (416) 766-6688

#351
Bodega
Cuisines: French
Average price: $31-$60
Area: Downtown Core
Address: 30 Baldwin Street
Toronto, ON M5T 1L3
Phone: (416) 977-1287

#352
Mi-Ne Sushi
Cuisines: Japanese
Average price: $11-$30
Area: City Place, Entertainment District
Address: 325 Bremner Boulevard
Toronto, ON M5V
Phone: (416) 623-1975

#353
El Fogón
Cuisines: Peruvian
Average price: $11-$30
Area: Wychwood
Address: 543 St Clair Avenue W
Toronto, ON M6C 1A3
Phone: (416) 850-8041

#354
Sorn Thai Restaurant
Cuisines: Thai
Average price: $11-$30
Area: Yonge and Eglinton
Address: 2550 Yonge Street
Toronto, ON M4P 2J2
Phone: (416) 322-3563

#355
Smoke Bourbon Bar-B-Q House
Cuisines: Barbeque
Average price: $11-$30
Area: Palmerston, Bickford Park
Address: 291 Harbord Street
Toronto, ON M6G 1G5
Phone: (647) 342-1840

#356
Victory Café
Cuisines: Pub, Canadian
Average price: $11-$30
Area: Palmerston
Address: 581 Markham St
Toronto, ON M6G 2L7
Phone: (416) 516-5787

#357
Bacchus Roti Shop
Cuisines: Caribbean, Indian
Average price: Under $10
Area: Parkdale
Address: 1376 Queen Street W
Toronto, ON M6K 1L7
Phone: (416) 532-8191

#358
Lan Sushi
Cuisines: Japanese, Sushi Bar
Average price: $11-$30
Area: The Junction
Address: 2982 Dundas Street W
Toronto, ON M6P 1Z4
Phone: (647) 342-1244

#359
Donair Kebab House
Cuisines: Turkish
Average price: Under $10
Area: Ryerson, Downtown Core
Address: 391 Yonge Street
Toronto, ON M5B 1S1
Phone: (416) 593-6914

#360
Simone's Caribbean Restaurant
Cuisines: Caribbean
Average price: $11-$30
Area: The Danforth, Greektown
Address: 596 Danforth Avenue
Toronto, ON M4K 1R1
Phone: (416) 792-5252

#361
Mercatto
Cuisines: Italian
Average price: $11-$30
Area: Discovery District, Downtown Core
Address: 101 College St
Toronto, ON M5G 1L7
Phone: (416) 595-5625

#362
El Arepazo
Cuisines: Canadian, Venezuelan
Average price: Under $10
Area: Kensington Market
Address: 214 Augusta Avenue
Toronto, ON M5T 2L6
Phone: (647) 472-1011

#363
Patty and Franks Gourmet Burgers and Hot Dogs
Cuisines: Hot Dogs, Fast Food, Burgers
Average price: Under $10
Area: Greektown, Riverdale
Address: 467 Danforth Avenue
Toronto, ON M4K 1P4
Phone: (416) 792-1467

#364
Porzia Restaurant
Cuisines: Canadian
Average price: $31-$60
Area: Parkdale
Address: 1314 Queen Street W
Toronto, ON M6K 1L4
Phone: (647) 342-5776

#365
ND Sushi & Grill
Cuisines: Japanese, Sushi Bar
Average price: $11-$30
Area: Downtown Core
Address: 3 Baldwin Street
Toronto, ON M5T 1L1
Phone: (416) 551-6362

#366
Allen's
Cuisines: Irish, Pub
Average price: $11-$30
Area: Riverdale
Address: 143 Danforth Avenue
Toronto, ON M4K 1N2
Phone: (416) 463-3086

#367
Raijin Ramen
Cuisines: Japanese
Average price: $11-$30
Area: Ryerson, Downtown Core
Address: 3 Gerrard Street E
Toronto, ON M5B 2P3
Phone: (647) 748-1500

#368
JOEY Eaton Centre
Cuisines: Canadian, Sports Bar
Average price: $31-$60
Area: Downtown Core
Address: 1 Dundas St W
Toronto, ON M5G 1Z3
Phone: (647) 352-5639

#369
Arisu
Cuisines: Japanese, Korean
Average price: $11-$30
Area: Koreatown, Palmerston, Seaton Village
Address: 584 Bloor Street W
Toronto, ON M6G 1K4
Phone: (416) 533-8104

#370
Brazil Esfiha House
Cuisines: Brazilian
Average price: $11-$30
Area: Church-Wellesley Village, Downtown Core
Address: 7 Maitland Street
Toronto, ON M4Y 1Y5
Phone: (416) 920-0101

#371
Cardinal Rule
Cuisines: Diner
Average price: $11-$30
Area: Parkdale, Roncesvalles
Address: 5 Roncesvalles Avenue
Toronto, ON M6R 2K2
Phone: (647) 352-0202

#372
Bivy
Cuisines: Cafe
Average price: $11-$30
Area: Brockton Village
Address: 1600 Dundas Street W
Toronto, ON M6K 1T5
Phone: (416) 534-8800

#373
Bread & Butter
Cuisines: German, Deli
Average price: Under $10
Area: Mount Pleasant and Davisville
Address: 507 Mount Pleasant Rd
Toronto, ON M4S 2L9
Phone: (416) 488-0036

#374
The Grapefruit Moon
Cuisines: Breakfast & Brunch, Burgers, Vegetarian
Average price: $11-$30
Area: Seaton Village
Address: 968 Bathurst Street
Toronto, ON M5R 3G6
Phone: (416) 534-9056

#375
Beach Hill Restaurant
Cuisines: Caribbean, Breakfast & Brunch
Average price: $11-$30
Area: Upper Beach
Address: 1917 Gerrard Street E
Toronto, ON M4L 2B8
Phone: (416) 465-8002

#376
Caffino Ristorante
Cuisines: Italian
Average price: $11-$30
Area: Liberty Village
Address: 1185 King St W
Toronto, ON M6K 3C5
Phone: (416) 588-9010

#377
Reds Midtown Tavern
Cuisines: Wine Bar, Seafood, Breakfast & Brunch
Average price: $11-$30
Area: Downtown Core
Address: 382 Yonge Street
Toronto, ON M5B 1S8
Phone: (416) 598-3535

#378
Slab Burgers
Cuisines: Burgers
Average price: Under $10
Area: Downtown Core
Address: 47 Charles Street W
Toronto, ON M4Y 2R4
Phone: (647) 350-5883

#379
Kibo Sushi House
Cuisines: Japanese, Sushi Bar
Average price: $11-$30
Area: Cabbagetown
Address: 533 Parliament Street
Toronto, ON M4X 1P3
Phone: (647) 352-3788

#380
TALLBOYS - Craft Beer House
Cuisines: Pub, Canadian
Average price: $11-$30
Area: Christie Pits, Bickford Park
Address: 838 Bloor Street W
Toronto, ON M6G 1M2
Phone: (416) 535-7486

#381
Via Mercanti
Cuisines: Pizza, Italian
Average price: $11-$30
Area: Kensington Market
Address: 188 Augusta Avenue
Toronto, ON M5T 1M1
Phone: (647) 343-6647

#382
Quinta Restaurant
Cuisines: Iberian, French, Breakfast & Brunch
Average price: $11-$30
Area: Dufferin Grove, Little Portugal, Beaconsfield Village
Address: 1282 Dundas Street W
Toronto, ON M6J 1X7
Phone: (416) 534-0407

#383
Hey Lucy
Cuisines: Bar, Italian, Pizza
Average price: $11-$30
Area: Entertainment District, Downtown Core
Address: 295 King Street W
Toronto, ON M5V 1J5
Phone: (416) 979-1010

#384
Urban Eatery at the Eaton Centre
Cuisines: Fast Food
Average price: $11-$30
Area: Downtown Core
Address: 220 Yonge St, Ste 110
Toronto, ON M5B 2L7
Phone: (416) 598-8560

#385
Hawthorne Food and Drink
Cuisines: Canadian, Gastropub
Average price: $11-$30
Area: Downtown Core
Address: 60 Richmond Street E
Toronto, ON M5C 1N8
Phone: (647) 930-9517

#386
Ryoji Ramen & Izakaya
Cuisines: Japanese, Tapas Bar
Average price: $11-$30
Area: Bickford Park
Address: 690 College Street
Toronto, ON M6G 1C1
Phone: (416) 533-8083

#387
Nirvana
Cuisines: Asian Fusion, Bar
Average price: $11-$30
Area: Kensington Market
Address: 434 College St
Toronto, ON M4W 1A7
Phone: (416) 927-8885

#388
Ginger
Cuisines: Vietnamese
Average price: Under $10
Area: Church-Wellesley Village, Downtown Core
Address: 695 Yonge Street
Toronto, ON M4Y 2B2
Phone: (416) 966-2424

#389
Caribbean Bistro
Cuisines: Caribbean
Average price: $11-$30
Area: Mount Pleasant and Davisville, Yonge and Eglinton
Address: 2439A Yonge Street
Toronto, ON M4P 1A1
Phone: (416) 480-1581

#390
Carmen Cocina Española
Cuisines: Spanish
Average price: $11-$30
Area: West Queen West, Trinity Bellwoods
Address: 922 Queen Street W
Toronto, ON M5T 2L9
Phone: (416) 535-0404

#391
The Host
Cuisines: Indian
Average price: $11-$30
Area: The Annex
Address: 14 Prince Arthur Ave
Toronto, ON M5R 1A9
Phone: (416) 962-4678

#392
Emporium Latino
Cuisines: Latin American, Ethnic Food
Average price: Under $10
Area: Kensington Market
Address: 243 Augusta Ave
Toronto, ON M5T 2L8
Phone: (416) 351-9646

#393
Churrasco Villa Toronto's Original
Cuisines: Portuguese
Average price: $11-$30
Area: Mount Pleasant and Davisville, Yonge and Eglinton
Address: 254 Eglinton Ave E
Toronto, ON M4P 1K2
Phone: (416) 487-7070

#394
FuZen
Cuisines: Sushi Bar, Japanese
Average price: $11-$30
Area: Corktown
Address: 132 Front Street E
Toronto, ON M5A 1E1
Phone: (416) 363-0202

#395
Harlem Restaurant
Cuisines: Southern, Cajun/Creole
Average price: $11-$30
Area: Corktown, Downtown Core
Address: 67 Richmond Street E
Toronto, ON M5C 1N9
Phone: (416) 368-1920

#396
Toma Burger Addiction
Cuisines: Burgers, Canadian
Average price: $11-$30
Area: Niagara, West Queen West, Trinity Bellwoods
Address: 712 Queen Street W
Toronto, ON M6J 1E8
Phone: (416) 901-1027

#397
Cluny Bistro & Boulangerie
Cuisines: French
Average price: $31-$60
Area: Distillery District
Address: 35 Tank House Lane
Toronto, ON M5A 3C4
Phone: (416) 203-2632

#398
Real Thailand Restaurant
Cuisines: Thai
Average price: $11-$30
Area: The Annex
Address: 350 Bloor St W
Toronto, ON M5S 1W9
Phone: (416) 924-7444

#399
Paramount Fine Foods
Cuisines: Middle Eastern
Average price: $11-$30
Area: Downtown Core
Address: 253 Yonge St
Toronto, ON M7A 2H1
Phone: (416) 366-3600

#400
Kintaro Izakaya
Cuisines: Japanese
Average price: $11-$30
Area: Church-Wellesley Village, Downtown Core
Address: 459 Church Street
Toronto, ON M4Y 2C8
Phone: (647) 560-5335

#401
Urban Herbivore
Cuisines: Vegan, Sandwiches
Average price: $11-$30
Area: Kensington Market
Address: 64 Oxford Street
Toronto, ON M5T 1P1
Phone: (416) 927-1231

#402
Tappo Wine Bar & Restaurant
Cuisines: Wine Bar, Canadian
Average price: $31-$60
Area: Distillery District
Address: 55 Mill Street
Toronto, ON M5A 3C4
Phone: (647) 430-1111

#403
Mitzi's Café
Cuisines: Breakfast & Brunch
Average price: $11-$30
Area: Roncesvalles
Address: 100 Sorauren Avenue
Toronto, ON M6R 2E2
Phone: (416) 588-1234

#404
Sukho Thai
Cuisines: Thai
Average price: $11-$30
Area: St. Lawrence, Downtown Core
Address: 52 Wellington Street E
Toronto, ON M5E 1C9
Phone: (647) 351-4612

#405
Epicure Cafe & Grill
Cuisines: Italian, Canadian
Average price: $11-$30
Area: Alexandra Park, Queen Street West
Address: 502 Queen St W
Toronto, ON M5V 2B3
Phone: (416) 504-8942

#406
Piola
Cuisines: Pizza, Italian
Average price: $11-$30
Area: West Queen West
Address: 1165 Queen Street W
Toronto, ON M6J 1J6
Phone: (416) 477-4652

#407
Trattoria Mercatto
Cuisines: Italian
Average price: $11-$30
Area: Downtown Core
Address: 220 Yonge Street
Toronto, ON M5B 2H1
Phone: (647) 352-3390

#408
Freshwest Grill
Cuisines: Tex-Mex
Average price: Under $10
Area: Financial District, Downtown Core
Address: 100 Wellington St W
Toronto, ON M5K 1N9
Phone: (416) 861-8163

#409
Apalla
Cuisines: Indian
Average price: $11-$30
Area: Niagara, West Queen West, Trinity Bellwoods
Address: 811 Queen St W
Toronto, ON M6J
Phone: (647) 428-7119

#410
Strada 241
Cuisines: Italian, Cafe, Coffee & Tea
Average price: $11-$30
Area: Alexandra Park, Chinatown, Downtown Core
Address: 241 Spadina Avenue
Toronto, ON M5T
Phone: (647) 351-1200

#411
Burrito Bandidos
Cuisines: Tex-Mex
Average price: Under $10
Area: The Annex
Address: 362 Bloor St W
Toronto, ON M5S 1X2
Phone: (416) 944-9061

#412
Mazz Sushi
Cuisines: Japanese, Sushi Bar
Average price: $11-$30
Area: Dovercourt, Dufferin Grove
Address: 993 Bloor Street W
Toronto, ON M6H 1M1
Phone: (416) 536-7631

#413
Templeton's
Cuisines: Canadian
Average price: $11-$30
Area: Kensington Market
Address: 319 Augusta Avenue
Toronto, ON M5T 1N9
Phone: (416) 922-7423

#414
Somethin' 2 Talk About
Cuisines: Sandwiches, French, Middle Eastern
Average price: Under $10
Area: Discovery District, Downtown Core
Address: 78 Gerrard Street W
Toronto, ON M5G 1J5
Phone: (416) 260-1752

#415
Jaipur Grille
Cuisines: Indian
Average price: $11-$30
Area: Mount Pleasant and Davisville
Address: 2066 Yonge Street
Toronto, ON M4S 2A3
Phone: (416) 322-5678

#416
Mr Pide
Cuisines: Pizza
Average price: Under $10
Area: The Danforth, Greektown
Address: 800 Danforth Ave
Toronto, ON M4J 1L2
Phone: (647) 351-7433

#417
Bolet's Burrito
Cuisines: Mexican
Average price: Under $10
Area: Corktown, St. Lawrence
Address: 134 Lower Sherbourne
Toronto, ON M5A 1K5
Phone: (416) 364-5811

#418
Fresh
Cuisines: Vegetarian, Vegan
Average price: $11-$30
Area: Entertainment District, Downtown Core
Address: 147 Spadina Avenue
Toronto, ON M5V 2L7
Phone: (416) 599-4442

#419
Pho Pasteur
Cuisines: Vietnamese
Average price: $11-$30
Area: Alexandra Park, Chinatown, Kensington Market
Address: 525 Dundas St W
Toronto, ON M5T 1H4
Phone: (416) 351-7188

#420
Golden Thai Restaurant
Cuisines: Thai
Average price: $11-$30
Area: Corktown, Downtown Core
Address: 105 Church Street
Toronto, ON M5C 2G3
Phone: (416) 868-6668

#421
Pizzeria Defina
Cuisines: Pizza, Italian
Average price: $11-$30
Area: High Park, Roncesvalles
Address: 321 Roncesvalles Ave
Toronto, ON M6R 2M6
Phone: (416) 534-4414

#422
Silk
Cuisines: Thai
Average price: $11-$30
Area: The Junction
Address: 2907 Dundas St W
Toronto, ON M6P 1Z1
Phone: (416) 368-1368

#423
The Library Bar
Cuisines: Lounge, Canadian, Diner
Average price: $31-$60
Area: Financial District, Downtown Core
Address: 100 Front Street W
Toronto, ON M5J 1E3
Phone: (416) 368-2511

#424
Ravi Soups
Cuisines: Soup
Average price: $11-$30
Area: West Queen West, Beaconsfield Village
Address: 1128 Queen Street W
Toronto, ON M6J 1J3
Phone: (416) 538-7284

#425
Arriba Restaurant
Cuisines: Breakfast & Brunch, Canadian
Average price: $11-$30
Area: Entertainment District
Address: 1 Blue Jays Way
Toronto, ON M5V
Phone: (416) 341-5045

#426
Farmer's Daughter Eatery
Cuisines: Cocktail Bar, Seafood, Breakfast & Brunch
Average price: $11-$30
Area: The Junction
Address: 1558 Dupont Street
Toronto, ON M6P 3S6
Phone: (416) 546-0626

#427
New York Subway
Cuisines: Sandwiches, Ethnic Food
Average price: Under $10
Area: Alexandra Park, Queen Street West
Address: 520 Queen Street W
Toronto, ON M5V 2B3
Phone: (416) 703-4496

#428
Goods & Provisions
Cuisines: Bar, Gastropub
Average price: $31-$60
Area: Leslieville
Address: 1124 Queen Street E
Toronto, ON M4M
Phone: (647) 340-1738

#429
Cafe California Restaurant
Cuisines: Mediterranean, American
Average price: $11-$30
Area: Church-Wellesley Village, Downtown Core
Address: 538 Church St
Toronto, ON M4Y 2E1
Phone: (416) 960-6161

#430
Petit Four
Cuisines: Sandwiches, Bakery, Salad
Average price: Under $10
Area: Downtown Core
Address: 189 Bay Street
Toronto, ON M5L 1G7**>**
Phone: (416) 368-1221

#431
Korean Grill House
Cuisines: Korean
Average price: $11-$30
Area: Entertainment District, Queen Street West, Downtown Core
Address: 214 Queen St W
Toronto, ON M5V 1Z2
Phone: (416) 263-9850

#432
Gourmet Gringos
Cuisines: Mexican
Average price: $11-$30
Area: Casa Loma, Wychwood
Address: 1384 Bathurst St
Toronto, ON M5V 1V1
Phone: (416) 988-1900

#433
Paldo Gangsan
Cuisines: Korean
Average price: Under $10
Area: Koreatown, Palmerston, Bickford Park, Seaton Village
Address: 694 Bloor Street W
Toronto, ON M6G 1L4
Phone: (416) 536-7517

#434
Mexican Salsas
Cuisines: Mexican
Average price: Under $10
Area: Kensington Market
Address: 249 Augusta Avenue
Toronto, ON M5T 2L8
Phone: (416) 977-8226

#435
Rock Lobster Food Co
Cuisines: Seafood
Average price: $11-$30
Area: Ossington Strip, Trinity Bellwoods, Beaconsfield Village
Address: 110 Ossington Ave
Toronto, ON M6J 2Z2
Phone: (416) 312-7662

#436
Cafe Neon
Cuisines: Cafe
Average price: $11-$30
Area: Wallace Emerson
Address: 241 Wallace Avenue
Toronto, ON M6H 1V5
Phone: (647) 352-8366

#437
Kanga
Cuisines: Australian
Average price: Under $10
Area: Downtown Core
Address: 65 Duncan Street
Toronto, ON M5V 1Z4
Phone: (416) 324-9174

#438
Ravi Soups
Cuisines: Soup
Average price: $11-$30
Area: High Park
Address: 2535 Dundas Street W
Toronto, ON M6P
Phone: (416) 769-7284

#439
Sake Sushi Bar
Cuisines: Sushi Bar, Japanese
Average price: $11-$30
Area: Koreatown, Bickford Park, Seaton Village
Address: 699 Bloor St W
Toronto, ON M6G 1L5
Phone: (416) 916-0313

#440
Basil Thai Kitchen
Cuisines: Thai, Malaysian
Average price: $11-$30
Area: The Danforth
Address: 2326 Danforth Ave
Toronto, ON M4C 1K7
Phone: (416) 422-0617

#441
The Ceili Cottage
Cuisines: Irish, Pub
Average price: $11-$30
Area: Leslieville
Address: 1301 Queen Street East
Toronto, ON M4L 1C2
Phone: (416) 406-1301

#442
7 Numbers Danforth
Cuisines: Italian
Average price: $31-$60
Area: Riverdale
Address: 307 Danforth Avenue E
Toronto, ON M4K 1N7
Phone: (416) 469-5183

#443
Tokyo Grill
Cuisines: Japanese
Average price: Under $10
Area: Downtown Core
Address: 582 Yonge St
Toronto, ON M4Y 1Z3
Phone: (416) 968-7054

#444
Bloom Restaurant
Cuisines: Latin American
Average price: $31-$60
Area: Swansea
Address: 2315 Bloor Street W
Toronto, ON M6S 1P1
Phone: (416) 767-1315

#445
Eggspectation
Cuisines: Breakfast & Brunch, Juice Bar& Smoothies
Average price: Under $10
Area: Downtown Core
Address: 483 Bay Street
Toronto, ON M5G 2C9
Phone: (416) 979-3447

#446
Bus Terminal Diner
Cuisines: Diner, Breakfast & Brunch
Average price: $11-$30
Area: The Danforth
Address: 1606 Danforth Ave
Toronto, ON M4C
Phone: (416) 463-4680

#447
The Gem
Cuisines: Pub, American
Average price: $11-$30
Area: Wychwood
Address: 1159 Davenport Rd
Toronto, ON M6H 2G4
Phone: (416) 654-1182

#448
Smith
Cuisines: Breakfast & Brunch, Canadian
Average price: $11-$30
Area: Church-Wellesley Village, Downtown Core
Address: 553 Church Street
Toronto, ON M4Y 2E2
Phone: (416) 926-2501

#449
Le Kensington Bistro
Cuisines: French, Breakfast & Brunch
Average price: $11-$30
Area: Kensington Market
Address: 256 Augusta Avenue
Toronto, ON M5T 3A9
Phone: (416) 792-9440

#450
Fresh on Eglinton
Cuisines: Restaurants
Average price: $11-$30
Area: Mount Pleasant and Davisville, Yonge and Eglinton
Address: 90 Eglinton Avenue East
Toronto, ON M4P 2Y3
Phone: (416) 599-4442

#451
The Monarch Tavern
Cuisines: Pub, Gluten-Free, Sandwiches
Average price: $11-$30
Area: Little Italy
Address: 12 Clinton St
Toronto, ON M6J 2N8
Phone: (416) 531-5833

#452
Food Dudes Pantry
Cuisines: Cafe
Average price: Under $10
Area: Leslieville
Address: 24 Carlaw Avenue
Toronto, ON M4M 2R7
Phone: (647) 340-3833

#453
Ginger
Cuisines: Vietnamese
Average price: Under $10
Area: Church-Wellesley Village, Downtown Core
Address: 546 Church St
Toronto, ON M4Y 2E1
Phone: (416) 413-1053

#454
The Whippoorwill Restaurant & Tavern
Cuisines: Canadian, Cocktail Bar
Average price: $11-$30
Area: Brockton Village, Bloordale Village
Address: 1285 Bloor St W
Toronto, ON M6H 1N7
Phone: (416) 530-2999

#455
Rock 'n' Horse Saloon
Cuisines: Bar, Comfort Food
Average price: $11-$30
Area: Entertainment District, Downtown Core
Address: 250 Adelaide Street W
Toronto, ON M5H 1X6
Phone: (647) 344-1234

#456
E L Ruddy Co Cafe
Cuisines: Vegetarian, Vegan
Average price: $11-$30
Area: Little Portugal
Address: 1371 Dundas Street W
Toronto, ON M6J 1Y3
Phone: (647) 351-0423

#457
Rikishi Japanese Restaurant
Cuisines: Japanese
Average price: $11-$30
Area: Bickford Park
Address: 833 Bloor Street W
Toronto, ON M6G 1M1
Phone: (416) 538-0760

#458
Jacques' Bistro Du Parc
Cuisines: French
Average price: $31-$60
Area: Yorkville
Address: 126 Cumberland St
Toronto, ON M5R 1A6
Phone: (416) 961-1893

#459
Bamboo Buddha Chinese Resturant
Cuisines: Chinese
Average price: Under $10
Area: Niagara
Address: 752 King Street W
Toronto, ON M5V 1N3
Phone: (416) 504-9311

#460
Crème Brasserie
Cuisines: French, Cafe
Average price: $31-$60
Area: Yorkville
Address: 162 Cumberland Street
Toronto, ON M5R 3N5
Phone: (416) 962-7363

#461
Reliable Fish & Chips
Cuisines: Fish & Chips
Average price: Under $10
Area: Leslieville
Address: 954 Queen Street E
Toronto, ON M4M 1J7
Phone: (416) 465-4111

#462
Chew Chew's Diner
Cuisines: Diner, Breakfast & Brunch
Average price: $11-$30
Area: Cabbagetown
Address: 186 Carlton Street
Toronto, ON M5A 2K6
Phone: (416) 924-7583

#463
Kenzo Ramen
Cuisines: Japanese
Average price: $11-$30
Area: Downtown Core
Address: 522 Yonge Street
Toronto, ON M4Y 1X9
Phone: (647) 340-2112

#464
Fran's Restaurant
Cuisines: Diner, Breakfast & Brunch
Average price: $11-$30
Area: Downtown Core
Address: 20 College Street
Toronto, ON M5G 1K2
Phone: (416) 923-9867

#465
Ferro Bar & Cafe
Cuisines: Bar, Italian
Average price: $11-$30
Area: Wychwood
Address: 769 St Clair Avenue W
Toronto, ON M6C 1B4
Phone: (416) 654-9119

#466
Suki Japanese Restaurant
Cuisines: Japanese
Average price: $11-$30
Area: Yonge and St. Clair, Deer Park
Address: 48 Av Street Clair E
Toronto, ON M4T 1M9
Phone: (416) 929-8598

#467
Littlefish
Cuisines: Coffee & Tea, Breakfast & Brunch
Average price: $11-$30
Area: The Junction
Address: 3080 Dundas Street W
Toronto, ON M6P
Phone: (416) 604-3474

#468
Morning Glory Cafe
Cuisines: Breakfast & Brunch
Average price: $11-$30
Area: Corktown
Address: 457 King Street E
Toronto, ON M5A 1L6
Phone: (416) 703-4728

#469
Cafe Fiorentina
Cuisines: Breakfast & Brunch, Desserts, Coffee & Tea
Average price: $11-$30
Area: The Danforth
Address: 236 Danforth Avenue
Toronto, ON M4K 1N4
Phone: (416) 855-4240

#470
Roll Play Cafe
Cuisines: Cafe
Average price: $11-$30
Area: Downtown Core
Address: 10A Edward Street
Toronto, ON M5G 1C9
Phone: (416) 904-8483

#471
Betty's
Cuisines: Pub, Dive Bar, American
Average price: $11-$30
Area: Corktown
Address: 240 King Street E
Toronto, ON M5A 1K1
Phone: (416) 368-1300

#472
Queen Margherita Pizza
Cuisines: Pizza
Average price: $11-$30
Area: Leslieville
Address: 1402 Queen Street E
Toronto, ON M4L 1C9
Phone: (416) 466-6555

#473
Greenwood Smokehouse BBQ
Cuisines: Barbeque, Soul Food
Average price: $11-$30
Area: Greektown, Riverdale
Address: 673 Danforth Avenue
Toronto, ON M4J 1L2
Phone: (416) 469-2270

#474
Hot House Restaurant & Bar
Cuisines: Italian, Bar
Average price: $11-$30
Area: St. Lawrence, Downtown Core
Address: 35 Church Street
Toronto, ON M5E 1T3
Phone: (416) 366-7800

#475
Duck
Cuisines: Chinese
Average price: Under $10
Area: Downtown Core
Address: 444 Yonge St
Toronto, ON M5B 2H4
Phone: (416) 595-5188

#476
Pearl Harbourfront Chinese
Cuisines: Chinese
Average price: $31-$60
Area: Harbourfront
Address: 207 Queens Quay W, Ste 200
Toronto, ON M5J 1A7
Phone: (416) 203-1233

#477
Universal Grill
Cuisines: Canadian
Average price: $11-$30
Area: Christie Pits
Address: 1071 Shaw Street
Toronto, ON M6G 3N4
Phone: (416) 588-5928

#478
Little Anthony's
Cuisines: Bar, Italian
Average price: $11-$30
Area: Financial District, Downtown Core
Address: 121 Richmond Street W
Toronto, ON M5H 3K6
Phone: (416) 368-2223

#479
Celebrity Hotpot
Cuisines: Chinese
Average price: $11-$30
Area: Alexandra Park, Chinatown, Downtown Core
Address: 254 Spadina Avenue
Toronto, ON M5T 2C2
Phone: (647) 748-3588

#480
25 Liberty
Cuisines: Brasserie, Breakfast & Brunch, Comfort Food
Average price: $31-$60
Area: Liberty Village
Address: 25 Liberty Street
Toronto, ON M6K 3E7
Phone: (647) 748-8200

#481
25 Liberty
Cuisines: Brasserie, Breakfast & Brunch, Comfort Food
Average price: $31-$60
Area: Liberty Village
Address: 25 Liberty Street
Toronto, ON M6K 3E7
Phone: (647) 748-8200

#482
Poutini's House of Poutine
Cuisines: Fast Food, Poutineries
Average price: Under $10
Area: West Queen West, Beaconsfield Village
Address: 1112 Queen Street W
Toronto, ON M6J 1H9
Phone: (647) 342-3732

#483
Kenzo
Cuisines: Japanese
Average price: Under $10
Area: The Annex
Address: 372 Bloor Street W
Toronto, ON M5S 1X7
Phone: (416) 921-6787

#484
Papaya Restaurant
Cuisines: Thai
Average price: $11-$30
Area: Church-Wellesley Village, Downtown Core
Address: 545 Yonge St
Toronto, ON M4Y 1Y5
Phone: (416) 944-9731

#485
Ha Gow Dim Sum House
Cuisines: Food Delivery, Dim Sum
Average price: $11-$30
Area: The Danforth
Address: 988 Danforth Avenue
Toronto, ON M4J 1M1
Phone: (416) 461-8294

#486
College Falafel
Cuisines: Middle Eastern, Mediterranean, Vegetarian
Average price: Under $10
Area: Dufferin Grove, Bickford Park
Address: 450 Ossington Ave
Toronto, ON M6G 3T2
Phone: (416) 532-8698

#487
Belljar Cafe
Cuisines: Cafe
Average price: $11-$30
Area: Roncesvalles
Address: 2072 Dundas Street West
Toronto, ON M6R 1W9
Phone: (416) 535-0777

#488
Archeo
Cuisines: Italian
Average price: $11-$30
Area: Distillery District
Address: 31 Trinity Street
Toronto, ON M5A 3C4
Phone: (416) 815-9898

#489
Gallery Grill
Cuisines: Canadian
Average price: $31-$60
Area: University of Toronto, Downtown Core
Address: 7 Hart House Circle
Toronto, ON M5S 3H3
Phone: (416) 978-2445

#490
Oliver & Bonacini Café Grill
Cuisines: Canadian
Average price: $31-$60
Area: St. Lawrence, Downtown Core
Address: 33 Yonge Street
Toronto, ON M5E 1G4
Phone: (647) 260-2070

#491
Soho House Toronto
Cuisines: Lounge, Canadian
Average price: $31-$60
Area: Downtown Core
Address: 192 Adelaide St W
Toronto, ON M5H 4E7
Phone: (416) 599-7646

#492
Osgoode Hall Restaurant
Cuisines: French
Average price: $11-$30
Area: Downtown Core
Address: 130 Queen Street W
Toronto, ON M5H 2N6
Phone: (416) 947-3361

#493
Brickyard Grounds
Cuisines: Cafe, Coffee & Tea
Average price: Under $10
Area: Leslieville
Address: 1289 Gerrard Street E
Toronto, ON M4L 1Y5
Phone: (416) 465-4444

#494
Tre Mari Bakery
Cuisines: Bakery, Italian, Delicatessen
Average price: Under $10
Area: Corso Italia
Address: 1311 Saint Clair Avenue W
Toronto, ON M6E 1C2
Phone: (416) 654-8960

#495
Wanda's Belgian Waffles
Cuisines: Desserts, Breakfast & Brunch
Average price: Under $10
Area: Ryerson, Downtown Core
Address: 361 Yonge Street
Toronto, ON M5B
Phone: (416) 901-0766

#496
Canyon Creek
Cuisines: Steakhouse, Seafood
Average price: $11-$30
Area: Downtown Core
Address: 156 Front Street West
Toronto, ON M5J 2L6
Phone: (416) 596-2240

#497
Albion's Pizza Shawarma
Cuisines: Pizza
Average price: Under $10
Area: Dovercourt
Address: 1030 Bloor Street W
Toronto, ON M6H 1M4
Phone: (416) 792-5678

#498
Biff's Bistro
Cuisines: French
Average price: $31-$60
Area: St. Lawrence, Downtown Core
Address: 4 Front Street E
Toronto, ON M5E 1G4
Phone: (416) 860-0086

#499
Pero Restaurant & Lounge
Cuisines: African, Vegan, Vegetarian
Average price: $11-$30
Area: Christie Pits, Bickford Park
Address: 812 Bloor Street W
Toronto, ON M6G 1L9
Phone: (416) 915-7225

#500
Brownstone Bistro
Cuisines: Italian
Average price: $11-$30
Area: Church-Wellesley Village, Downtown Core
Address: 603 Yonge Street
Toronto, ON M4Y 1Z5
Phone: (416) 920-6288

TOP 500
ARTS & ENTERTAINMENT

The Most Recommended by Locals & Trevelers

(From #1 to #500)

#1
The Second City Mainstage Theatre
Category: Comedy Club, Performing Arts
Area: Entertainment District
Address: 51 Mercer Street
Toronto, ON M5V 9G9
Phone: (416) 343-0011

#2
CN Tower
Category: Landmark
Area: Entertainment District
Address: 301 Front St W
Toronto, ON M5V 2T6
Phone: (416) 868-6937

#3
Ripley's Aquarium of Canada
Category: Aquarium
Area: Entertainment District
Address: 288 Bremner Boulevard
Toronto, ON M5V 3L9
Phone: (647) 351-3474

#4
Allan Garden Conservatory
Category: Botanical Garden
Address: 19 Horticultural Ave
Toronto, ON M5A 2P2

#5
Art Gallery of Ontario
Category: Museum
Area: Downtown Core
Address: 317 Dundas St W
Toronto, ON M5T 1G4
Phone: (416) 977-0414

#6
Stuart Jackson Gallery
Category: Antiques, Art Gallery
Area: Niagara, West Queen West, Trinity Bellwoods
Address: 882 Queen St W
Toronto, ON M6J 1G3
Phone: (416) 967-9166

#7
Massey Hall
Category: Music Venues
Area: Downtown Core
Address: 178 Victoria St.
Toronto, ON M5B 1T7
Phone: (416) 872-4255

#8
Canadian National Exhibition
Category: Amusement Park
Address: 210 Princes' Boulevard
Toronto, ON M6K 3C3

#9
Goodhandy's
Category: Adult Entertainment, Gay Bar, Venues, Event Space
Area: Corktown, Downtown Core
Address: 120 Church Street
Toronto, ON M5C 2G8

#10
SPiN Toronto
Category: Social Club
Address: 461 King Street W
Toronto, ON M5V 1K4

#11
The Dakota Tavern
Category: Music Venues, Dive Bar
Area: Dufferin Grove, Little Italy, Little Portugal, Ossington Strip
Address: 249 Ossington Avenue
Toronto, ON M6J 3A1
Phone: (416) 850-4579

#12
Paul Petro Contemporary Art
Category: Art Gallery
Area: West Queen West, Trinity Bellwoods
Address: 980 Queen Street W
Toronto, ON M6J 1H1
Phone: (416) 979-7874

#13
Ontario Place
Category: Park, Amusement Park
Address: 955 Lake Shore Blvd W
Toronto, ON M6K 3B9

#14
Birch Libralato
Category: Art Gallery
Area: Niagara
Address: 129 Tecumseth Street
Toronto, ON M6J 2H2
Phone: (416) 365-3003

#15
TIFF Bell Lightbox
Category: Cinema
Area: Entertainment District, Downtown Core
Address: 350 King St W
Toronto, ON M5V 3X5
Phone: (416) 599-8433

#16
Bar + Karaoke Lounge
Category: Karaoke, Dance Club, Music Venues
Area: Ryerson, Downtown Core
Address: 360 Yonge Street
Toronto, ON M5B 1S5
Phone: (416) 340-7154

#17
Medieval Times Toronto
Category: Dinner & Tournament
Area: Downtown Core
Address: 10 Dufferin St
Toronto, ON M6K
Phone: (888) 935-6878

#18
Bellevue Square Park
Category: Park
Area: Kensington Market
Address: 5 Bellevue Ave
Toronto, ON M5T 2N4

#19
Magic Lantern Theatres
Category: Cinema
Area: Church-Wellesley Village, Downtown Core
Address: 20 Carlton Street
Toronto, ON M5B 2H5
Phone: (416) 494-9371

#20
High Park Zoo
Category: Zoo, Park
Area: High Park
Address: Deer Pen Road
Toronto, ON M6R

#21
Toronto Music Garden
Category: Botanical Garden, Park
Address: 475 Queen's Quay
Toronto, ON M5V 3G3

#22
Hockey Hall of Fame
Category: Museum
Area: Downtown Core
Address: 30 Yonge Street
Toronto, ON M5E 1X8
Phone: (416) 360-7765

#23
Rainbow Cinemas
Category: Cinema
Area: St. Lawrence, Downtown Core
Address: 80 Front St E
Toronto, ON M5E 1T4
Phone: (416) 494-9371

#24
Campbell House Museum
Category: Museum
Area: Queen Street West, Downtown Core
Address: 160 Queen St W
Toronto, ON M5H 3H3
Phone: (416) 597-0227

#25
The Danforth Music Hall
Category: Music Venues
Area: Riverdale
Address: 147 Danforth Avenue
Toronto, ON M4K 1N2
Phone: (416) 778-8163

#26
Harbourfront Centre
Category: Performing Arts, Venues, Event Space
Area: Harbourfront
Address: 235 Queens Quay W
Toronto, ON M5J 2G8
Phone: (416) 973-4000

#27
Bloor Hot Docs Cinema
Category: Cinema
Area: The Annex
Address: 506 Bloor St W
Toronto, ON M5S 1Y3
Phone: (416) 637-3123

#28
The Reservoir Lounge
Category: Jazz & Blues, Music Venues
Area: St. Lawrence, Downtown Core
Address: 52 Wellington St E
Toronto, ON M5E 1C8
Phone: (416) 955-0887

#29
Royal Ontario Museum
Category: Museum
Area: University of Toronto, Downtown Core
Address: 100 Queen's Park
Toronto, ON M5S 2C6
Phone: (416) 586-8000

#30
High Park
Category: Park, Zoo, Playground
Area: High Park
Address: 1873 Bloor St W
Toronto, ON M6P 3K7

#31
Cirque Du Soleil
Category: Performing Arts
Address: 51 Commissioners Street
Toronto, ON M5A 1A6

#33
Ed Mirvish Theatre
Category: Performing Arts
Area: Downtown Core
Address: 244 Victoria Street
Toronto, ON M5B 1V8
Phone: (416) 872-1212

#32
Hot Docs Canadian International Documentary Festival
Category: Cinema, Festival
Area: Entertainment District, Downtown Core
Address: 110 Spadina Avenue
Toronto, ON M5V 2K4
Phone: (416) 203-2155

#34
Polson Pier Entertainment
Category: Amusement Park, Swimming Pool
Address: 11 Polson St
Toronto, ON M5A 1A4

#35
Air Canada Centre
Category: Arena
Address: 50 Bay Street
Toronto, ON M5J 2L2

#36
Cameron House
Category: Music Venues, Bar
Area: Alexandra Park, Queen Street West
Address: 408 Queen St W
Toronto, ON M5V 2A7
Phone: (416) 703-0811

#37
Arnell Plaza
Category: Park
Area: Financial District, Downtown Core
Address: 333 Bay St
Toronto, ON M5H 2T4

#38
The Horseshoe Tavern
Category: Music Venues, Dive Bar
Area: Queen Street West, Downtown Core
Address: 370 Queen Street W
Toronto, ON M5V 2A2
Phone: (416) 598-4753

#39
Cherry Beach
Category: Beach, Dog Park
Address: 275 Unwin Ave
Toronto, ON M5H 2N2

#40
Cineplex Odeon Varsity and Varsity Cinemas
Category: Cinema
Area: Yorkville, Downtown Core
Address: 55 Bloor Street W
Toronto, ON M4W 1A5
Phone: (416) 961-6304

#41
Clint Roenisch Gallery
Category: Art Gallery
Area: West Queen West, Trinity Bellwoods
Address: 944 Queen Street W
Toronto, ON M6J 1G8
Phone: (416) 516-8593

#42
Arts On King
Category: Arts & Crafts, Art Gallery
Area: Corktown, Downtown Core
Address: 165 King Street East
Toronto, ON M5A 1J4
Phone: (416) 777-9701

#43
The Emmet Ray
Category: Jazz & Blues, Music Venues
Area: Dufferin Grove
Address: 924 College Street
Toronto, ON M6H 1A4
Phone: (416) 792-4497

#44
Queen Elizabeth Theatre
Category: Venues, Event Space
Address: 190 Princes Blvd
Toronto, ON M6K 3C3

#45
Casa Loma
Category: Museum
Area: Casa Loma
Address: 1 Austin Terrace
Toronto, ON M5R 1X8
Phone: (416) 923-1171

#46
The Boat
Category: Music Venues, Bar
Area: Kensington Market
Address: 158 Augusta Avenue
Toronto, ON M5T 2L5
Phone: (416) 593-9218

#47
Centennial Park Conservatory
Category: Park
Area: Etobicoke
Address: 151 Elmcrest Rd
Toronto, ON M9C 3S2
Phone: (416) 394-8543

#48
Orbit Room
Category: Music Venues
Area: Little Italy, Palmerston, Bickford Park
Address: 580A College St
Toronto, ON M6G 1B3
Phone: (416) 535-0613

#49
Museum of Contemporary Canadian Art
Category: Art Gallery
Area: West Queen West, Trinity Bellwoods
Address: 952 Queen St W
Toronto, ON M6J 1G8
Phone: (416) 395-0067

#50
Poetry Jazz Cafe
Category: Music Venues
Area: Kensington Market
Address: 224 Augusta Avenue
Toronto, ON M5T 1M5
Phone: (416) 599-5299

#51
Buddies In Bad Times Theatre
Category: Performing Arts, Gay Bar
Area: Church-Wellesley Village, Downtown Core
Address: 12 Alexander St
Toronto, ON M4Y 1B4
Phone: (416) 975-8555

#52
Little Norway park
Category: Playground, Park
Address: Queens Quay & Bathurst
Toronto, ON M5V

#53
The Rex Hotel Jazz & Blues Bar
Category: Pub, Jazz & Blues
Area: Entertainment District, Queen Street West, Downtown Core
Address: 194 Queen Street W
Toronto, ON M5V 1Z1
Phone: (416) 598-2475

#54
Dovercourt Park
Category: Park
Area: Dovercourt
Address: 160 Westmoreland Ave
Toronto, ON M6H

#55
El Mocambo
Category: Music Venues
Area: Chinatown, Kensington Market, Downtown Core
Address: 464 Spadina Ave
Toronto, ON M5T 2G8
Phone: (647) 748-6969

#56
Lower Ossington Theatre
Category: Performing Arts
Area: Ossington Strip, Beaconsfield Village
Address: 100A Ossington Ave
Toronto, ON M6J 2Z2
Phone: (416) 915-6747

#57
Toronto Mendelssohn Choir
Category: Performing Arts
Area: Entertainment District, Downtown Core
Address: 60 Simcoe Street
Toronto, ON M5J 2H5
Phone: (416) 598-0422

#58
The Elgin & Winter Garden Theatre Centre
Category: Performing Arts
Area: Downtown Core
Address: 189 Yonge St
Toronto, ON M5B 1M4
Phone: (416) 314-2901

#59
Kidnetix Edu-Play Centre
Category: Amusement Park, Playground
Address: 100 Bridgeland Ave
Toronto, ON M6A 2V1

#60
Tall Ship Cruises Toronto Tall Ship Kajama
Category: Tours
Area: Harbourfront
Address: 235 Queens Quay W
Toronto, ON M5J 2N5
Phone: (416) 203-2322

#61
Revue Cinema
Category: Cinema
Area: High Park, Roncesvalles
Address: 400 Roncesvalles Ave
Toronto, ON M6R 2M9
Phone: (416) 531-9959

#62
Mod Music Academy
Category: Performing Arts
Area: Mount Pleasant and Davisville, Yonge and Eglinton
Address: 120 Eglinton Ave E
Toronto, ON M4P 1E2
Phone: (416) 322-2911

#63
Royal Cinema
Category: Cinema
Area: Bickford Park
Address: 608 College Street
Toronto, ON M6G 1A1
Phone: (416) 466-4400

#64
Calgary Corn Maze & Fun Farm
Category: Zoo, Amusement Park
Area: Downtown Core
Address: 284022 Township Road 224, Toronto, ON
Phone: (403) 648-2719

#65
One Of A Kind Show And Sale
Category: Arts & Crafts, Festival
Area: Parkdale
Address: 100 Princes' Blvd
Toronto, ON M6K

#66
Mztv Museum of Television
Category: Museum
Area: Corktown
Address: 550 Queen Street E
Toronto, ON M5A 1V2
Phone: (416) 599-7339

#67
Vegetarian Food Festival
Category: Festival
Area: Harbourfront
Address: 235 Queens Quay W
Toronto, ON M5J 2G8

#68
Deleon White Gallerie
Category: Art Gallery
Area: Brockton Village
Address: 1139 College Street
Toronto, ON M6H 1B5
Phone: (416) 597-9466

#69
Simex
Category: Amusement Park
Address: 511 King Street W
Toronto, ON M5V 1K4

#70
The Gardiner Museum
Category: Museum
Area: Discovery District, Yorkville, Downtown Core
Address: 111 Queen's Park
Toronto, ON M5S 2C7
Phone: (416) 586-8080

#71
Great Escape
Category: Amusement Park, Party & Event Planning
Area: Willowdale
Address: 5291-A Yonge Street
Toronto, ON M2N 5R3
Phone: (647) 342-1627

#72
The Galleria Art & Frame
Category: Art Gallery
Area: Downtown Core
Address: 123 - 6464 Yonge St.
Toronto, ON M5H 1L6
Phone: (416) 223-4349

#73
Leslieville's Crazy Doll House
Category: Amusement Park
Area: Leslieville
Address: 37 Bertmount Avenue
Toronto, ON M4M 2X8

#74
Cineplex Odeon Yonge & Dundas Cinemas
Category: Cinema
Area: Ryerson, Downtown Core
Address: 10 Dundas Street E
Toronto, ON M5B 2G9
Phone: (416) 977-9262

#75
Toronto Underground Cinema
Category: Cinema
Area: Alexandra Park, Downtown Core
Address: 186 Spadina Avenue
Toronto, ON M5T
Phone: (647) 992-4335

#76
Phoenix Concert Theatre
Category: Music Venues
Area: Cabbagetown
Address: 410 Sherbourne St
Toronto, ON M4X 1K2
Phone: (416) 323-1251

#77
The Garrison
Category: Music Venues
Area: Little Portugal
Address: 1197 Dundas St W
Toronto, ON M6J
Phone: (416) 519-9439

#78
Toronto Island
Category: Park, Beach
Address: Toronto Island
Toronto, ON M5J 1A7

#79
Toronto's Festival of Beer
Category: Festival
Address: 200 Princes' Blvd
Toronto, ON M6K

#80
Velvet Underground
Category: Music Venues, Dance Club
Area: Alexandra Park, Queen Street West
Address: 510 Queen St W
Toronto, ON M5V 2B3
Phone: (416) 504-6688

#81
Holco Sales Reg'd
Category: Amusement Park
Area: Downtown Core
Address: 514 Yonge Street
Toronto, ON M4Y 1X9
Phone: (416) 922-5842

#82
Koerner Hall
Category: Music Venues
Area: University of Toronto, Downtown Core
Address: 273 Bloor St W
Toronto, ON M5S 1W2
Phone: (416) 408-0208

#83
Hollander Joseph & Sons
Category: Amusement Park
Area: Downtown Core
Address: 514 Yonge Street
Toronto, ON M4Y 1X9
Phone: (416) 922-5842

#84
Funnelz
Category: Amusement Park
Area: Scarborough
Address: 24 Lebovic Avenue
Toronto, ON M1L
Phone: (416) 759-9555

#85
Four Seasons Centre for the Performing Arts
Category: Performing Arts
Area: Queen Street West
Address: 145 Queen St W
Toronto, ON M5H 4G1
Phone: (416) 363-6671

#86
Spadina Historic House Museum
Category: Museum
Area: Casa Loma, South Hill
Address: 285 Spadina Road
Toronto, ON M5R 2V5
Phone: (416) 392-6910

#87
Hollander Amusements Limited
Category: Amusement Park
Area: Downtown Core
Address: 514 Yonge Street
Toronto, ON M4Y 1X9
Phone: (416) 922-5842

#88
Museum of Inuit Art
Category: Museum
Area: Harbourfront
Address: 207 Queens Quay W
Toronto, ON M5J 1A7
Phone: (416) 640-1571

#89
The Natrel Rink
Category: Skating Rinks
Area: Harbourfront
Address: 235 Queens Quay W
Toronto, ON M5J 2G8
Phone: (416) 973-4866

#90
Skeir Gallery
Category: Art Gallery
Area: Parkdale, Roncesvalles
Address: 1537 Queen Street W
Toronto, ON M6R 1A7
Phone: (416) 854-2862

#91
Latinada Tapas Restaurant
Category: Latin American, Music Venues
Area: High Park
Address: 1671 Bloor Street W
Toronto, ON M6P 1A6
Phone: (416) 913-9716

#92
The Opera House
Category: Music Venues
Area: Riverdale
Address: 735 Queen St. E.
Toronto, ON M4M 1H1
Phone: (416) 466-0313

#93
The Piston
Category: Music Venues, Lounge
Area: Dovercourt
Address: 937 Bloor St
Toronto, ON M6H 1L5
Phone: (416) 532-3989

#94
Milk Glass
Category: Art Gallery
Area: Little Portugal, Beaconsfield Village
Address: 1247 Dundas Street W
Toronto, ON M6J 1X5

#95
Scotiabank Buskerfest
Category: Festival
Area: St. Lawrence, Downtown Core
Address: St. Lawrence Market
Toronto, ON M5E 1C2

#96
Cartworld Toronto
Category: Amusement Park
Address: 11 Polson Street
Toronto, ON M5A 1A4

#97
Forest Hill Memorial Arena
Category: Arena, Skating Rinks
Address: 340 Chaplin Cres
Toronto, ON M5N 2N3 #98

#99
Isabel Bader Theatre
Category: Venues, Event Space
Area: Discovery District, University of Toronto, Downtown Core
Address: 93 Charles St W
Toronto, ON M5S
Phone: (416) 585-4498

#100
BMO Field
Category: Stadium
Address: 170 Princes' Blvd
Toronto, ON M6K 3C3

#101
The Princess of Wales Theatre
Category: Performing Arts
Area: Entertainment District, Downtown Core
Address: 300 King Street W
Toronto, ON M5V 1J2
Phone: (416) 872-1212

#102
Rustic Owl Café
Category: Art Gallery, Cafe
Area: Dovercourt, Dufferin Grove
Address: 993 Bloor St W
Toronto, ON M6H 1M1

#103
Graven Feather
Category: Art Gallery
Area: Niagara, West Queen West, Trinity Bellwoods
Address: 906 Queen St W
Toronto, ON M6J 1G9

#104
Textile Museum of Canada
Category: Museum
Area: Downtown Core
Address: 55 Centre Ave
Toronto, ON M5G 2H5
Phone: (416) 599-5321

#105
Oip Dance Centre
Category: Performing Arts, Dance School
Area: Corktown
Address: 190 Richmond Street E
Toronto, ON M5A 1P1
Phone: (647) 477-5225

#106
Toronto After Dark Film Festival
Category: Festival
Area: The Annex
Address: 506 Bloor St W
Toronto, ON M5S 1Y5

#107
Function 13
Category: Art Gallery, Books, Music & Video
Area: Kensington Market
Address: 156 Augusta Ave
Toronto, ON M5T 2L5
Phone: (416) 840-1010

#108
WestJet Stage
Category: Music Venues
Area: Harbourfront
Address: 235 Queens Quay W
Toronto, ON M5J 2G8

#109
Trinity Bellwoods Park
Category: Park
Area: Trinity Bellwoods
Address: 155 Crawford Street
Toronto, ON M6J 2Z0
Phone: (416) 392-0743

#110
The Guvernment
Category: Music Venues, Dance Club
Address: 132 Queen's Quay E
Toronto, ON M5A 3Y5

#111
Mackenzie House
Category: Museum
Area: Downtown Core
Address: 82 Bond Street
Toronto, ON M5B 1X2
Phone: (416) 392-6915

#112
Fort York: Garrison Common
Category: Museum
Address: 250 Fort York Blvd
Toronto, ON M5V 3K9

#113
Le Gallery
Category: Art Gallery
Area: Dufferin Grove, Little Portugal, Beaconsfield Village
Address: 1183 Dundas Street W
Toronto, ON M6J 1X3
Phone: (416) 532-8467

#114
Clinton's
Category: Pub, Music Venues
Area: Koreatown, Bickford Park
Address: 693 Bloor Street W
Toronto, ON M6G 1L5
Phone: (416) 535-9541

#115
Fantasy Fair
Category: Amusement Park
Area: Etobicoke
Address: 500 Rexdale Boulevard
Toronto, ON M9W 6K5
Phone: (416) 674-5200

#116
University of Toronto Athletic Centre
Category: Athletic Centre
Area: University of Toronto
Address: 55 Harbord Street
Toronto, ON M5S 2W6
Phone: (416) 978-3436

#117
The Wine Boutique
Category: Winery
Area: Palmerston
Address: 585 Markham Street
Toronto, ON M6G 2L7
Phone: (416) 516-9463

#118
FanExpo
Category: Festival
Area: Entertainment District, Downtown Core
Address: 255 Front St W
Toronto, ON M5V 2W6
Phone: (416) 241-7827

#119
Jazz Bistro
Category: Jazz & Blues
Area: Downtown Core
Address: 251 Victoria Street
Toronto, ON M5B 1T8
Phone: (416) 363-5299

#120
The Flying Beaver Pubaret
Category: Music Venues, Pub
Area: Cabbagetown
Address: 488 Parliament St
Toronto, ON M4X 1P3
Phone: (647) 347-6567

#121
Whippersnapper Gallery
Category: Music Venues, Art Gallery
Area: Chinatown, Kensington Market
Address: 594 Dundas St W
Toronto, ON M5T 1H5

#122
The Power Plant Contemporary Art Gallery
Category: Art Gallery
Area: Harbourfront
Address: 231 Queens Quay W
Toronto, ON M5J 2G8
Phone: (416) 973-4949

#123
Mysteriously Yours... Mystery Dinner Theatre
Category: Performing Arts
Area: Mount Pleasant and Davisville
Address: 2026 Yonge Street
Toronto, ON M4S 1Z9
Phone: (416) 486-7469

#124
Caribana
Category: Festival
Area: The Annex
Address: 263 Davenport Rd
Toronto, ON M5R 1J9
Phone: (416) 391-5608

#125
John M Kelly Library
Category: Library
Area: Discovery District, University of Toronto, Downtown Core
Address: 113 St. Joseph Street
Toronto, ON M5S

#126
Alliance Cinemas The Beach
Category: Cinema
Area: Upper Beach
Address: 1651 Queen Street E
Toronto, ON M4L 1G5
Phone: (416) 699-1327

#127
BanksyGuard With Balloon Dog
Category: Performing Arts
Area: Harbourfront
Address: 80 Harbour Street
Toronto, ON M5J

#128
Defcon Paintball
Category: Recreation Center, Paintball, Amusement Park
Address: 3550 Victoria Park Avenue
Toronto, ON M2H 2N5

#129
Factory Theatre
Category: Performing Arts
Address: 125 Bathurst Street
Toronto, ON M5V 2R2

#130
Toronto Sculpture Garden
Category: Art Gallery, Park
Area: Corktown, St. Lawrence, Downtown Core
Address: 115 King St E
Toronto, ON M5C
Phone: (416) 515-9658

#131
Downsview Park Allen Road
Category: Amusement Park, Venues, Event Space
Area: Downsview
Address: 35 Carl Hall Rd
Toronto, ON M3K 2B6
Phone: (416) 952-2222

#132
Toronto International Film Festival
Category: Festival
Area: Entertainment District, Downtown Core
Address: 350 King St W
Toronto, ON M5V 3X5
Phone: (416) 977-4560

#133
Royal Conservatory of Music
Category: Music Venues
Area: The Annex, University of Toronto
Address: 273 Bloor Street West
Toronto, ON M5S 1W2
Phone: (416) 408-1776

#134
Jessica Bradley Art & Projects
Category: Art Gallery
Area: Little Portugal
Address: 1450 Dundas Street W
Toronto, ON M6J 1Y6
Phone: (416) 537-3125

#135
Rouge Concept Gallery
Category: Art Gallery, Framing
Area: Riverdale
Address: 732 Queen Street E
Toronto, ON M4M 1H2
Phone: (416) 778-0555

#136
Omy
Category: Art Gallery
Area: West Queen West, Beaconsfield Village
Address: 1140 Queen St W
Toronto, ON M6J 1J3

#137
Bad Dog Theatre
Category: Performing Arts
Area: Dovercourt, Dufferin Grove
Address: 945 Bloor St W
Toronto, ON M6H 1L5
Phone: (416) 491-3115

#138
The Charlotte Room
Category: Pool Hall, Lounge,Venues
Area: Entertainment District, Downtown Core
Address: 19 Charlotte Street
Toronto, ON M5V 2H5
Phone: (416) 591-1738

#139
Habeeba's Dance Studio
Category: Performing Arts, Dance Studio
Area: Downtown Core
Address: 179 Dundas Street E
Toronto, ON M5A 1Z4
Phone: (416) 920-8580

#140
Centre Island
Category: Park, Boating, Amusement Park
Address: Toronto Island
Toronto Island, ON M5J 1A7

#141
Royal Alexandra Theatre
Category: Performing Arts
Area: Entertainment District
Address: 260 King St W
Toronto, ON M5V 1H9
Phone: (416) 872-1212

#142
The Ballroom Bowl Bar Bistro
Category: Bowling, Dance Club
Area: Entertainment District, Downtown Core
Address: 145 John Street
Toronto, ON M5V 2E4
Phone: (416) 597-2695

#143
Bathurst Bowlerama
Category: Amusement Park, Bowling, Venues, Event Space
Address: 2788 Bathurst Street North York, ON M6B 3A3

#144
Direct Energy Centre
Category: Convention Space
Address: 100 Princes Blvd
Toronto, ON M6K 3C3

#145
Trash Palace
Category: Cinema
Area: Niagara
Address: 89-B Niagara St
Toronto, ON M5V
Phone: (416) 203-2389

#146
TRANZAC Club
Category: Performing Arts, Music Venues, Community Service
Address: 292 Brunswick Ave
Toronto, ON M5S 2M7

#147
Scotiabank Theatre
Category: Cinema
Area: Entertainment District, Downtown Core
Address: 259 Richmond Street W
Toronto, ON M5V 3M6
Phone: (416) 368-5600

#148
Hart House Theatre
Category: Performing Arts
Area: University of Toronto, Downtown Core
Address: 7 Hart House Circle
Toronto, ON M5S 3H3
Phone: (416) 978-8849

#149
Telegramme Prints
Category: Art Gallery, Framing
Area: Leslieville
Address: 1103 Queen St E
Toronto, ON M4M 1K7
Phone: (416) 463-8998

#150
Frame It On Bloor
Category: Art Gallery, Framing
Area: High Park
Address: 1610 Bloor St W
Toronto, ON M6P 1A7
Phone: (416) 588-4226

#151
Rogers Centre
Category: Stadium, Landmark
Area: Entertainment District
Address: 1 Blue Jays Way
Toronto, ON M5V 1J3
Phone: (416) 341-3663

#152
Veld Music Festival
Category: Festival
Area: Downsview
Address: 35 Carl Hall Road
Toronto, ON M3K 2E2

#153
Gerstein Science Information Centre
Category: Library
Area: University of Toronto, Downtown Core
Address: 9 King's College Cir
Toronto, ON M5S 1A5
Phone: (416) 978-2280

#154
Toronto Botanical Garden
Category: Botanical Garden, Venues, Event Space
Address: 777 Lawrence Avenue E
Toronto, ON M3C 1P2

#155
Smiling Buddha
Category: Music Venues, Jazz & Blues, Comedy Club
Area: Dufferin Grove
Address: 961 College Street
Toronto, ON M6H 1A6
Phone: (416) 519-3332

#156
Roseland Antiques
Category: Antiques, Art Gallery
Area: Niagara, West Queen West, Trinity Bellwoods
Address: 702 Queen St W
Toronto, ON M6J 1E7
Phone: (416) 869-9229

#157
Capitol Event Theatre
Category: Venues, Event Space
Area: Mount Pleasant and Davisville, Yonge and Eglinton
Address: 2492 Yonge Street
Toronto, ON M4P 2H7
Phone: (647) 350-3313

#158
The Haunted Walk of Toronto
Category: Tours, Performing Arts
Area: Distillery District
Address: 30 Gristmill Lane
Toronto, ON M5A 4R2
Phone: (416) 238-1473

#159
Inabstracto
Category: Art Gallery, Furniture Store
Area: West Queen West
Address: 1160 Queen Street W
Toronto, ON M6J 1J5
Phone: (416) 533-6362

#160
Toronto Railway Heritage Centre
Category: Museum
Area: Entertainment District
Address: 255 Bremner Blvd
Toronto, ON M5V 3M9

#161
Molson Canadian Amphitheatre
Category: Music Venues, Amphitheatre
Address: 909 Lakeshore Boulevard W
Toronto, ON M6K 3L3

#162
The Silver Dollar Room
Category: Music Venues
Area: University of Toronto, Downtown Core
Address: 486 Spadina Avenue
Toronto, ON M5S 2H1
Phone: (416) 975-0909

#163
Panasonic Theatre
Category: Performing Arts
Area: Church-Wellesley Village, Downtown Core
Address: 651 Yonge Street
Toronto, ON M4Y 1Z9
Phone: (416) 928-5963

#164
Artscape Wychwood Barns
Category: Art Gallery, Community Service
Area: Wychwood
Address: 601 Christie Street
Toronto, ON M6G 4C7
Phone: (416) 653-3520

#165
CBC Museum
Category: Museum
Area: Entertainment District, Downtown Core
Address: 250 Front St W
Toronto, ON M5V 3G5
Phone: (416) 205-5574

#166
Pentimento Fine Art Gallery
Category: Art Gallery
Area: Leslieville
Address: 1164 Queen St E
Toronto, ON M4M 1L5
Phone: (416) 406-6772

#167
Humber Cinemas
Category: Cinema
Area: Swansea
Address: 2442 Bloor Street West
Toronto, ON M6S 1P8
Phone: (416) 769-2442

#168
SilverCity Yorkdale Cinemas
Category: Cinema
Address: 3401 Dufferin Street
Toronto, ON M6A 2T9

#169
Lula Lounge
Category: Latin American, Music Venues
Area: Brockton Village
Address: 1585 Dundas Street W
Toronto, ON M6K 1T9
Phone: (416) 588-0307

#170
Theatre Passe Muraille
Category: Performing Arts
Area: Alexandra Park
Address: 16 Ryerson Avenue
Toronto, ON M5T 2P3
Phone: (416) 504-7529

#171
The Green Iguana Glassworks
Category: Art Gallery
Area: Palmerston
Address: 589 Markham Street
Toronto, ON M6G 2L7
Phone: (416) 536-8655

#172
Bounce 123
Category: Amusement Park
Area: Etobicoke
Address: 83 Galaxy Boulevard
Toronto, ON M9W 5X6
Phone: (416) 871-1602

#173
Soulpepper Theatre Company
Category: Performing Arts, Music Venues
Area: Distillery District
Address: 50 Tank House Lane
Toronto, ON M5A 3C4
Phone: (416) 203-6264

#174
Grand Prix Kartways
Category: Amusement Park, Arcade, Social Club
Area: Downsview
Address: 75 Carl Hall Road
North York, ON M3K 2B9
Phone: (416) 638-5278

#175
Innis Town Hall
Category: Cinema
Area: University of Toronto, Downtown Core
Address: 2 Sussex Ave
Toronto, ON M5S 1J5

#176
Parts Gallery
Category: Art Gallery
Area: Leslieville
Address: 1150 Queen Street E
Toronto, ON M4M 1L2
Phone: (416) 465-8500

#177
Absolute Comedy
Category: Comedy Club
Area: Mount Pleasant and Davisville
Address: 2335 Yonge Street
Toronto, ON M4P 2C8
Phone: (416) 486-7700

#178
Atomic Toybot
Category: Comic Books, Hobby Shops, Art Gallery
Area: Leslieville
Address: 978 Queen Street E
Toronto, ON M4M 1K2
Phone: (416) 466-4506

#179
Foundery
Category: Art Gallery, Venues
Area: Little Italy
Address: 376 Bathurst Street
Toronto, ON M5T 2S6
Phone: (416) 938-1229

#180
Music Gallery
Category: Venues, Event Space
Area: Downtown Core
Address: 197 John Street
Toronto, ON M5T 1X6
Phone: (416) 204-1080

#181
Downsview Public Library
Category: Library
Area: Downsview
Address: 2793 Keele St
Toronto, ON M3M 2G3
Phone: (416) 395-5720

#182
Adelaide Hall
Category: Performing Arts
Area: Entertainment District
Address: 250 Adelaide Street W
Toronto, ON M5H 1X6
Phone: (416) 205-1234

#183
Georgia Scherman Projects
Category: Art Gallery
Area: Niagara
Address: 133 Tecumseth St
Toronto, ON M6J 2H2
Phone: (416) 554-4112

#184
Eglinton Park
Category: Park
Area: Yonge and Eglinton
Address: 160 Eglinton Avenue W
Toronto, ON M4P 3B5

#185
Origo Books
Category: Bookstore, Art Gallery
Area: St. Lawrence
Address: 49 Lower Jarvis Street
Toronto, ON M5E 1R8
Phone: (416) 703-3535

#186
NextRelic
Category: Amusement Park
Area: Scarborough
Address: 700 Progress Ave
Toronto, ON M1H 2Z7
Phone: (416) 792-0301

#187
High Park Outdoor Amphitheatre
Category: Performing Arts
Area: High Park
Address: 200 Parkide Dr
Toronto, ON M6R 2Z3

#188
Art Metropole
Category: Bookstore, Art Gallery
Area: Brockton Village
Address: 1490 Dundas Street W
Toronto, ON M6K 1T5
Phone: (416) 703-4400

#189
The Engine Gallery
Category: Art Gallery
Area: West Queen West, Beaconsfield Village
Address: 1112 Queen Street W
Toronto, ON M6J 1H9
Phone: (416) 531-9905

#190
Famous Players Canada Square Cinemas
Category: Cinema
Area: Mount Pleasant and Davisville, Yonge and Eglinton
Address: 2190 Yonge Street
Toronto, ON M4S 2C6
Phone: (416) 646-0444

#191
Banksy tiny tag
Category: Art Gallery
Area: St. Lawrence
Address: 3 Church Street
Toronto, ON M5E

#192
Cavalia Odysseo
Category: Performing Arts
Address: 429 Lakeshore Boulevard E
Toronto, ON M5A

#193
Ontario Science Centre
Category: Museum
Address: 770 Don Mills Rd North York, ON M3C 1T3

#194
Toronto Wine & Spirit Festival
Category: Festival
Address: 25 Dockside Dr
Toronto, ON M5A 0B5

#195
Goodfellas Gallery
Category: Art Gallery
Area: Parkdale
Address: 1266 Queen St W
Toronto, ON M6K 1J4
Phone: (647) 765-6627

#196
Gallery TPW
Category: Art Gallery
Area: Ossington Strip, Beaconsfield Village
Address: 1256 Dundas Street W
Toronto, ON M6J 1X5

#197
Tarragon Theatre
Category: Performing Arts
Area: Casa Loma
Address: 30 Bridgman Ave
Toronto, ON M5R 1X3
Phone: (416) 531-1827

#198
Bento Miso
Category: Arcade, Community Center
Area: Niagara
Address: 862 Richmond Street W
Toronto, ON M6J 1C9
Phone: (416) 848-3702

#199
Arta Gallery
Category: Art Gallery
Area: Distillery District
Address: 14 Distillery Lane
Toronto, ON M5A 3C4
Phone: (416) 364-2782

#200
Gilchrist Vending
Category: Amusement Park
Address: 30 Bertal Road
York, ON M6M 4M4

#201
Projection Booth Cinema
Category: Cinema, Performing Arts
Area: Leslieville
Address: 1035 Gerrard Street E
Toronto, ON M4M 1Z6
Phone: (416) 466-3636

#202
Extreme Fun
Category: Amusement Park
Address: 186 Bartley Drive
North York, ON M4A 1E1

#203
Metropolis Living
Category: Antiques, Furniture Store, Art Gallery
Area: The Junction
Address: 2989 Dundas St W
Toronto, ON M6P 1Z4
Phone: (647) 343-6900

#204
Jungle Cubs Indoor Playground
Category: Child Care & Day Care, Amusement Park
Area: Mount Pleasant and Davisville
Address: 1681 Av Bayview
East York, ON M4G 3C1
Phone: (416) 322-6005

#205
Young People's Theatre
Category: Performing Arts
Area: Corktown, St. Lawrence
Address: 165 Front Street E
Toronto, ON M5A 3Z4
Phone: (416) 862-2222

#206
Navillus Gallery
Category: Art Gallery
Area: Yorkville
Address: 110 Davenport Road
Toronto, ON M5R 3R3
Phone: (416) 921-6467

#207
Christopher Cutts Gallery
Category: Art Gallery
Area: Roncesvalles
Address: 21 Morrow Avenue
Toronto, ON M6R 2H9
Phone: (416) 532-5566

#208
Centennial Arena
Category: Arena
Area: Scarborough
Address: 1967 Ellesmere Road
Scarborough, ON M1H 2W5
Phone: (416) 438-8025

#209
Hugh's Room
Category: Music Venues
Area: High Park, Roncesvalles
Address: 2261 Dundas St W
Toronto, ON M6R 1X6
Phone: (416) 531-6604

#210
Comedy Bar
Category: Comedy Club
Area: Dovercourt, Dufferin Grove
Address: 945 Bloor St W
Toronto, ON M6H 1L5
Phone: (416) 551-6540

#211
Mary's Playland
Category: Amusement Park
Area: Etobicoke
Address: 2885 Bloor Street W
Etobicoke, ON M8X 1B3
Phone: (416) 236-5437

#212
City Dance Corps
Category: Performing Arts, Dance Studio
Address: 489 Queen St W
Toronto, ON M5V 2B4

#213
Halo Halo Village
Category: Art Gallery
Area: Christie Pits, Seaton Village
Address: 208 Christie Street
Toronto, ON M6G 1W8
Phone: (416) 910-9585

#214
Ultimate Improv
Category: Performing Arts
Area: The Annex
Address: 26 Bernard Ave
Toronto, ON M5R 1R2
Phone: (647) 898-8457

#215
Metro Theatre
Category: Cinema, Adult Entertainment
Area: Koreatown, Palmerston
Address: 677 Bloor St W
Toronto, ON M6G 1L3
Phone: (416) 534-0300

#216
Toronto Police Museum
Category: Museum
Area: Downtown Core
Address: 40 College St
Toronto, ON M5G 2J3
Phone: (416) 808-7020

#217
Japan Foundation Toronto
Category: Museum, Art Gallery
Area: Discovery District, Yorkville, Downtown Core
Address: 131 Bloor Street W
Toronto, ON M5S 1P7
Phone: (416) 966-1600

#218
Twin Pine Bowl
Category: Amusement Park, Bowling
Address: 1359 Av Lawrence O North York, ON M6L 1A4

#219
Arts & Letters Club
Category: Social Club
Area: Downtown Core
Address: 14 Elm St
Toronto, ON M5G 1G7
Phone: (416) 597-0223

#220
North Park Bowl
Category: Amusement Park, Bowling
Address: 1359 Av Lawrence O
North York, ON M6L 1A4

#221
Universal Shuffle Boards
Category: Amusement Park
Address: 30 Bertal Road
York, ON M6M 4M4

#222
Communication Art Gallery
Category: Art Gallery
Address: 209 Harbord St
Toronto, ON M5S 2R5

#223
Canvas Gallery
Category: Art Gallery
Area: Dovercourt
Address: 950 Dupont St
Toronto, ON M6H 1Z2
Phone: (416) 532-5275

#224
Monte Clark Gallery
Category: Art Gallery
Area: Distillery District
Address: 55 Mill Street
Toronto, ON M5A 3C4
Phone: (416) 703-1700

#225
Crozier Kenneth
Category: Amusement Park
Address: 250 Scarlett Road
York, ON M6N 4X5

#226
Centreville Amusement Park
Category: Amusement Park
Area: Etobicoke
Address: 84 Advance Road
Etobicoke, ON M8Z 2T7
Phone: (416) 234-2345

#227
T.O.TIX
Category: Performing Arts
Area: Ryerson, Downtown Core
Address: 1 Dundas Street E
Toronto, ON M5B 2R8

#228
Time Out Canada
Category: Amusement Park
Address: 85 Scarsdale Road
North York, ON M3B 2R2

#229
Randolph Theatre
Category: Music Venues
Area: Palmerston
Address: 736 Bathurst St.
Toronto, ON M5S 2R4
Phone: (855) 985-5000

#230
Partners For Kids
Category: Amusement Park
Address: 85 Scarsdale Road
North York, ON M3B 2R2

#231
Kidsway Indoor Playground
Category: Amusement Park
Area: Etobicoke
Address: 2885 Bloor Street W
Etobicoke, ON M8X 1B3
Phone: (416) 236-5437

#232
Elisabeth Legge Antique Prints
Category: Antiques, Home Decor, Art Gallery
Area: Yorkville
Address: 37b Hazelton Ave
Toronto, ON M5R 2E3
Phone: (416) 972-1378

#233
TD Jazz Festival Series
Category: Festival
Area: University of Toronto, Downtown Core
Address: 273 Bloor Street W
Toronto, ON M5S 1W2

#234
Flipside Studio
Category: Performing Arts, Event Planning & Services
Area: Yorkville
Address: 838 Yonge Street
Toronto, ON M4W 2H1
Phone: (647) 883-4343

#235
Sun Life Financial Museum + Arts Pass
Category: Museum, Library
Address: 789 Yonge Street
Toronto, ON M4W 2G8

#236
Starbust Coin Machines
Category: Amusement Park
Area: Etobicoke
Address: 717 Kipling Avenue
Etobicoke, ON M8Z 5G4
Phone: (416) 251-2122

#237
Fusion Artists
Category: Performing Arts
Area: Downtown Core
Address: 10 Saint Mary St
Toronto, ON M4Y 1P9
Phone: (416) 408-3304

#238
Tournamaxx Canada
Category: Amusement Park
Area: Etobicoke
Address: 717 Kipling Avenue
Etobicoke, ON M8Z 5G4
Phone: (416) 503-0845

#239
Kids Retreat Indoor Ground and Party Place
Category: Amusement Park
Area: Etobicoke
Address: 727 The Queensway
Etobicoke, ON M8Y 1L4
Phone: (416) 253-5437

#240
Puppetry of the Penis
Category: Performing Arts
Area: Downtown Core
Address: 189 Yonge St
Toronto, ON M5B 1M4
Phone: (416) 314-2901

#241
The Basement
Category: Music Venues
Area: Niagara, Queen Street West, West Queen West
Address: 178 Bathurst St
Toronto, ON M5V

#242
Studio 99
Category: Amusement Park
Address: 5926 Yonge Street
North York, ON M2M 3V9

#243
401 Mini-Indy Go-Karts
Category: Amusement Park
Area: Etobicoke
Address: 37 Stoffel Drive
Etobicoke, ON M9W 6A8
Phone: (416) 614-6789

#244
Comedy Lounge
Category: Performing Arts
Area: Bickford Park
Address: 875 Bloor W
Toronto, ON M5B 2K7
Phone: (647) 997-8775

#245
Esmeralda Enrique Spanish Dance Company
Category: Performing Arts, Dance Studio
Area: Entertainment District, Downtown Core
Address: 401 Richmond Street West
Toronto, ON M5V 3A8
Phone: (416) 595-5753

#246
I T S Canada
Category: Amusement Park
Area: Etobicoke
Address: 717 Kipling Avenue
Etobicoke, ON M8Z 5G4
Phone: (416) 252-5494

#247
Norman Felix Inc.
Category: Art Gallery, Cafe, Music Venues
Address: 445 Adelaide Street West
Toronto, ON M5V 1T1

#248
Snooker Club V I P
Category: Pool Hall, Casino, Amusement Park
Area: Scarborough
Address: 301 Ellesmere Road
Scarborough, ON M1R 4E4
Phone: (416) 391-1313

#249
Praxis Gallery
Category: Art Gallery
Area: Parkdale, Roncesvalles
Address: 1614 Queen Street W
Toronto, ON M6R 1A8
Phone: (416) 532-0250

#250
Agincourt District Library
Category: Library
Area: Scarborough
Address: 155 Bonis Avenue
Toronto, ON M1T 3W6
Phone: (416) 396-8943

#251
Diesel Playhouse
Category: Performing Arts
Area: Entertainment District, Downtown Core
Address: 56 Blue Jays Way
Toronto, ON M5V 2G3
Phone: (416) 971-5656

#252
Magic Mud Gallery
Category: Art Gallery
Address: 1408 Davenport Road
Toronto, ON M6H 2H7

#253
Loop Gallery
Category: Art Gallery
Area: Little Portugal, Beaconsfield Village
Address: 1273 Dundas St W
Toronto, ON M6J 1X8
Phone: (416) 516-2581

#254
Shao Design
Category: Art Gallery
Area: Distillery District, St. Lawrence
Address: 39 Parliament Street
Toronto, ON M5A 4R2
Phone: (416) 777-1313

#255
Mississauga Waterfront Festival
Category: Festival
Address: 20 Lakeshore Road East
Mississauga, ON L5H 2M9

#256
Comet Bowling Lanes
Category: Amusement Park, Bowling
Area: Scarborough
Address: 803 Brimley Road
Scarborough, ON M1J 1C9
Phone: (416) 267-1671

#257
PM Gallery
Category: Art Gallery, Arts & Crafts
Area: Brockton Village
Address: 1518 Dundas Street W
Toronto, ON M6K 1T6
Phone: (416) 937-3862

#258
Gate 403 Bar & Grill
Category: Jazz & Blues, American
Area: High Park, Roncesvalles
Address: 403 Roncesvalles Avenue
Toronto, ON M6R 2N1
Phone: (416) 588-2930

#259
SWEA Toronto Christmas Market
Category: Festival
Area: Harbourfront
Address: 235 Queens Quay W
Toronto, ON M5J 2G8
Phone: (416) 973-4000

#260
Proof Studio Gallery
Category: Art Gallery
Area: Distillery District
Address: 55 Mill Street
Toronto, ON M5A 3C4
Phone: (416) 504-6761

#261
Mario Racing Karts Manufacturing
Category: Amusement Park
Address: 96 Bowes Road
Concord, ON L4K 1J7

#262
Nightwood Theatre
Category: Cinema
Area: Distillery District
Address: 55 Mill Street
Toronto, ON M5A 3C4
Phone: (416) 944-1740

#263
National Ballet of Canada
Category: Performing Arts
Address: 470 Queens Quay W
Toronto, ON M5V 2Y3

#264
Woodie Wood Chuck's
Category: Amusement Park
Area: Scarborough
Address: 4466 Av Sheppard E
Scarborough, ON M1S 1V2
Phone: (416) 298-3555

#265
Art Collective CODA
Category: Arts & Crafts, Art Gallery
Address: 1643 Saint Clair Avenue W
Toronto, ON M6N 1H7

#266
The Bata Shoe Museum
Category: Museum
Area: The Annex, University of Toronto, Downtown Core
Address: 327 Bloor St W
Toronto, ON M5S 1W7
Phone: (416) 979-7799

#267
EcoCab Tours
Category: Bike Rentals, Tours
Area: Corktown, Downtown Core
Address: 6 Dalhousie Street
Toronto, ON M5C 1S1
Phone: (416) 467-9229

#268
Polson Pier Drive-In
Category: Cinema
Address: 11 Polson St
Toronto, ON M5A 1A4

#269
Walter's Antique Warehouse
Category: Antiques, Art Gallery
Address: 10 Canvarco Road
Toronto, ON M4G 3T4

#270
Distill
Category: Art Gallery
Area: Distillery District
Address: 24 Tank House Lane
Toronto, ON M5A 3C4
Phone: (416) 304-0033

#271
Marbello
Category: Amusement Park
Address: 96 Bowes Road
Concord, ON L4K 1J7

#272
ReelHeART International Film Festival
Category: Festival
Area: Leslieville
Address: 1035 Gerrard Street
Toronto, ON M4M 1Z4

#273
Space II Metal Products
Category: Amusement Park
Address: 96 Bowes Road
Concord, ON L4K 1J7

#274
Big Picture Cinema
Category: Cinema
Area: Leslieville
Address: 1035 Gerrard Street E
Toronto, ON M4M 1Z6
Phone: (416) 466-3636

#275
Jiggles & Giggles
Category: Amusement Park
Address: 120 Carlauren Road
Woodbridge, ON L4L 8E5

#276
The Design Exchange
Category: Museum
Area: Downtown Core
Address: 234 Bay Street
Toronto, ON M5K 1B2
Phone: (416) 363-6121

#277
Echo Beach
Category: Music Venues
Address: 909 Lakeshore Boulevard
Toronto, ON M6K

#278
M S R Electronic
Category: Amusement Park
Address: 207 Edgeley Boulevard
Concord, ON L4K 4B5

#279
Bounce 'n Play
Category: Amusement Park
Address: 71 Marycroft Avenue
Woodbridge, ON L4L 5Y6

#280
Hip Kik
Category: Performing Arts
Area: The Junction
Address: 3070 Dundas St W
Toronto, ON M6P 1Z7
Phone: (647) 892-5171

#281
Church Street Fetish Fair
Category: Festival
Area: Church-Wellesley Village, Downtown Core
Address: Church Street & Wellesley Street, Toronto, ON M4Y

#282
The Parke Gallery
Category: Art Gallery
Area: Greektown, Riverdale
Address: 707 Pape Avenue
Toronto, ON M4K 3S6
Phone: (416) 346-6826

#283
CAMERA
Category: Cinema, Art Gallery, Bar
Area: West Queen West, Beaconsfield Village
Address: 1026 Queen Street W
Toronto, ON M6J 1H6
Phone: (416) 530-0011

#284
Village Playhouse
Category: Cinema
Area: Bloor-West Village, Swansea
Address: 2190 Bloor Street W
Toronto, ON M6S 1N3
Phone: (416) 767-7702

#285
Redpath Sugar Museum
Category: Museum
Address: 95 Queens Quay E
Toronto, ON M5E 1L7

#286
The Canadian Stage Company
Category: Performing Arts
Area: St. Lawrence
Address: 26 Berkeley Street
Toronto, ON M5A 2W3
Phone: (416) 368-3110

#287
Delta Bingo
Category: Casino
Area: The Junction
Address: 1799 Street Clair Avenue W
Toronto, ON M6N 1J9
Phone: (416) 656-8888

#288
Food Truck Festival
Category: Festival
Area: Distillery District
Address: 55 Mill St
Toronto, ON M5A 3C4
Phone: (416) 922-9760

#289
The Culinary Adventure
Category: Tours
Area: Entertainment District, Downtown Core
Address: 26 Dalhousie St
Toronto, ON M5V 3P7
Phone: (416) 565-1730

#290
2 Pianos 4 Hands
Category: Performing Arts
Area: Church-Wellesley Village, Downtown Core
Address: 651 Yonge St
Toronto, ON M4Y 1Z9

#291
Videofag
Category: Cinema, Art Gallery
Area: Kensington Market
Address: 187 Augusta Ave
Toronto, ON M5T
Phone: (647) 238-3048

#292
Black Swan Tavern
Category: Pub, Music Venues
Area: The Danforth
Address: 154 Danforth Avenue
Toronto, ON M4K 1N1
Phone: (416) 469-0537

#293
Beach Streetfest
Category: Performing Arts
Area: The Beach
Address: 1798 Queen Street E
Toronto, ON M4L 1G8
Phone: (416) 698-2152

#294
Cineplex Odeon Yorkdale
Category: Cinema
Address: 3401 Dufferin Street
Toronto, ON M6A 2T9

#295
Enoch Turner Schoolhouse
Category: Venues, Museum
Area: Corktown
Address: 106 Trinity St
Toronto, ON M5A 3C6
Phone: (416) 327-6997

#296
Tibetan Arts
Category: Art Gallery
Area: Mount Pleasant and Davisville
Address: 2487-A Yonge Street
Toronto, ON M4P 2H5
Phone: (416) 932-8684

#297
Petroff Gallery
Category: Art Gallery
Address: 1016 Eglinton Avenue W
Toronto, ON M6C 2C5

#298
The Cage 292
Category: Music Venues
Address: 292 College Street
Toronto, ON M5T 1S2

#299
The Sixth
Category: Art Gallery
Area: Parkdale, Roncesvalles
Address: 1642 Queen Street W
Toronto, ON M6R 1B2
Phone: (416) 535-7541

#300
ShopDineTour Toronto
Category: Tours
Area: Downtown Core
Address: Yonge-Dundas Sq
Toronto, ON M5B 2R8
Phone: (416) 463-7467

#301
Monarch Park Stadium
Category: Stadium
Area: The Danforth
Address: 1 Hanson Street
Toronto, ON M4J 4V3
Phone: (416) 466-2255

#302
May
Category: Music Venues, Lounge
Area: Little Italy, Trinity Bellwoods
Address: 876 Dundas Street W
Toronto, ON M6J 1V7
Phone: (416) 568-5510

#303
Sound Academy
Category: Music Venues
Address: 11 Polson St.
Toronto, ON M5A 1A4

#304
Thompson Landry Gallery
Category: Art Gallery
Area: Distillery District
Address: 55 Mill Street
Toronto, ON M5A 3C4
Phone: (416) 364-4955

#305
Gelico Gallery
Category: Art Gallery
Area: Christie Pits
Address: 264A Christie Street
Toronto, ON M6G 3B9
Phone: (647) 774-6262

#306
Cinematheque Ontario
Category: Cinema
Area: Downtown Core
Address: 317 Dundas St W
Toronto, ON M5T 1G4
Phone: (416) 968-3456

#307
The Kathedral
Category: Music Venues
Area: Alexandra Park, Niagara, Queen Street West, West Queen West
Address: 651 Queen Street W
Toronto, ON M5V 2B7
Phone: (416) 504-6699

#308
Festival On Bloor
Category: Festival
Area: The Annex, Downtown Core
Address: Bloor St W
Toronto, ON M6S 3E7

#309
The Antler Room
Category: Music Venues, Sports Bar
Area: Downtown Core
Address: 146 Front Street West
Toronto, ON M5J 1G2
Phone: (416) 977-8840

#310
Scotiabank Caribana Parade
Category: Festival
Address: Exhibition Place & Lakeshore Blvd, Toronto, ON M6K

#311
Greenwood Off-Track Wagering
Category: Casino
Area: Upper Beach
Address: 1661 Queen St E
Toronto, ON M4L 1G5
Phone: (416) 698-3136

#312
Allan Lamport Stadium
Category: Stadium
Area: Liberty Village
Address: 1151 King Street W
Toronto, ON M6K 3N3
Phone: (416) 392-1366

#313
Fringe Festival
Category: Performing Arts, Festival
Area: Palmerston
Address: 720 Bathurst Street
Toronto, ON M5S 2R4
Phone: (416) 966-1062

#314
University of Toronto Art Centre
Category: Art Gallery
Area: University of Toronto, Downtown Core
Address: 15 King's College Cir
Toronto, ON M5S 3H7
Phone: (416) 978-1838

#315
White House Studio Project
Category: Music Venues
Area: Kensington Market
Address: 277.5 Augusta Avenue
Toronto, ON M5T 2L7

#316
Orbital Arts
Category: Art Gallery
Area: Kensington Market
Address: 275 Augusta Avenue
Toronto, ON M5T 2M1
Phone: (416) 598-5623

#317
Granite Club
Category: Venues, Event Space
Address: 2350 Bayview Ave
Toronto, ON M2L 1E4

#318
Bau-Xi Photo
Category: Art Gallery
Area: Downtown Core
Address: 324 Dundas St. W
Toronto, ON M5T 1G5
Phone: (416) 977-0400

#319
Family Sundays
Category: Art Gallery
Area: Downtown Core
Address: 317 Dundas St W
Toronto, ON M5T 1G4
Phone: (416) 979-6648

#320
Method Lab
Category: Art Gallery
Area: Kensington Market
Address: 148 Augusta Ave
Toronto, ON M5T 1J2

#321
Posterity Graphics
Category: Art Gallery
Area: Cabbagetown
Address: 523 Parliament St
Toronto, ON M4X 1P3
Phone: (416) 323-0196

#322
The Angell Gallery
Category: Art Gallery
Area: Ossington Strip, West Queen West, Beaconsfield Village
Address: 12 Ossington Ave
Toronto, ON M6J 2Y7
Phone: (416) 530-0444

#323
Canadian Contemporary Dance Theatre
Category: Performing Arts
Area: Cabbagetown
Address: 509 Parliament Street
Toronto, ON M4X 1P3
Phone: (416) 924-5657

#324
Beaver Hall Artists Gallery
Category: Art Gallery
Area: Downtown Core
Address: 29 McCaul Street
Toronto, ON M5T 1V7
Phone: (416) 340-7168

#325
Sleeping Giant Gallery
Category: Venues, Art Gallery
Area: Little Italy, Trinity Bellwoods
Address: 789 Dundas Street West
Toronto, ON M6J
Phone: (647) 345-4425

#326
Galleria 814
Category: Art Gallery
Area: Wychwood
Address: 814 St. Clair Ave. West
Toronto, ON M6C 1B6
Phone: (416) 658-8814

#327
The Storefront Theatre
Category: Performing Arts
Area: Dovercourt
Address: 955 Bloor Street W
Toronto, ON M6H 1L6

#328
Moss Park Arena
Category: Arena
Area: Corktown
Address: 140 Sherbourne Street
Toronto, ON M5A 2R6
Phone: (416) 392-1060

#329
The Luminous Landscape
Category: Art Gallery
Area: Leslieville
Address: 270 Carlaw Avenue
Toronto, ON M4M 3L1
Phone: (416) 462-1170

#330
Waterfall Stage
Category: Music Venues
Area: Financial District, Downtown Core
Address: 100 King St W
Toronto, ON M5X 1B8

#331
Toronto Zombie Walk
Category: Festival
Area: Little Italy, Trinity Bellwoods
Address: 1053 Dundas St W
Toronto, ON M6J 1X1

#332
Todmorden Mills Heritage Site
Category: Venues, Museum
Area: East York
Address: 67 Pottery Rd
Toronto, ON M4K 2B9
Phone: (416) 396-2819

#333
COBA Collective Of Black Artists
Category: Performing Arts, Dance School, Dance Studio
Address: 585 Dundas Street E
Toronto, ON M5A 2B7

#334
Niagara Falls Museum Collection
Category: Art Gallery
Address: 468 Wellington Street W
Toronto, ON M5V 1E3

#335
Jane Mallett Theatre
Category: Performing Arts
Area: St. Lawrence, Downtown Core
Address: 27 Front St E
Toronto, ON M5E 1B4
Phone: (416) 366-7723

#336
Luminato
Category: Festival
Address: 55 John Street
Toronto, ON M5V 0C4

#337
Mount Pleasant Cinema
Category: Cinema
Area: Mount Pleasant and Davisville
Address: 675 Mt Pleasant Rd
Toronto, ON M4S 2N2
Phone: (416) 489-8484

#338
Elaine Fleck Gallery
Category: Art Gallery
Area: Niagara, West Queen West, Trinity Bellwoods
Address: 888 Queen St W
Toronto, ON M6J 1G3
Phone: (416) 469-8005

#339
Awol Gallery Studio
Category: Art Gallery
Area: Ossington Strip, Trinity Bellwoods, Beaconsfield Village
Address: 78 Ossington Avenue
Toronto, ON M6J 2Y7
Phone: (416) 535-5637

#340
Edward Day Gallery
Category: Art Gallery
Area: West Queen West, Trinity Bellwoods
Address: 952 Queen Street W
Toronto, ON M6J 1G8
Phone: (416) 921-6540

#341
Parliament Interpretive Centre
Category: Museum
Area: Corktown, St. Lawrence
Address: 265 Front Street E
Toronto, ON M5A 1G1
Phone: (416) 212-8897

#342
The Department
Category: Art Gallery
Area: Little Portugal, Beaconsfield Village
Address: 1389 Dundas St W
Toronto, ON M6J 3L5
Phone: (416) 716-8273

#343
Field Trip
Category: Festival
Address: 250 Fort York Boulevard
Toronto, ON M5V 3K9

#344
Pitter Patter Festival
Category: Festival
Area: Bloordale Village, Wallace Emerson
Address: 1238 Bloor St W
Toronto, ON M6H

#345
Funktion Gallery
Category: Art Gallery, Music Venues
Area: Brockton Village, Bloordale Village, Wallace Emerson
Address: 1244 Bloor St. W.
Toronto, ON M6H 1N5

#346
Toronto Roundhouse Park
Category: Museum
Area: Entertainment District
Address: 255 Bremner Boulevard
Toronto, ON M5V 3M9

#347
Katharine Mulherin Gallery
Category: Art Gallery
Area: West Queen West, Beaconsfield Village
Address: 1086 Queen Street W
Toronto, ON M6J 1H8
Phone: (416) 993-6510

#348
The Theatre Centre
Category: Performing Arts
Area: West Queen West, Beaconsfield Village
Address: 1087 Queen St W
Toronto, ON M6J 1H3
Phone: (416) 538-0988

#349
The Wine Shop
Category: Winery
Area: Harbourfront
Address: 228 Queens Quay W
Toronto, ON M5J 2Y7
Phone: (416) 598-8880

#350
Twist Gallery
Category: Art Gallery
Area: West Queen West, Beaconsfield Village
Address: 1100 Queen St W
Toronto, ON M6J 1H9
Phone: (416) 588-2222

#351
Omy
Category: Art Gallery
Area: West Queen West, Beaconsfield Village
Address: 1140 Queen St W
Toronto, ON M6J 1J3

#352
The Varsity Centre
Category: Stadiums & Arenas
Area: University of Toronto, Downtown Core
Address: 299 Bloor St. West
Toronto, ON M5S
Phone: (416) 978-4847

#353
Victoria Memorial Square
Category: Museum, Dog Park
Address: Wellington W and Portland
Toronto, ON M5V

#354
Dubon Chicken
Category: Festival
Area: Downtown Core
Address: 35 Baldwin Street
Toronto, ON M5T 1L3

#355
Lorraine Kimsa Theatre For Young People
Category: Performing Arts
Area: Corktown, St. Lawrence
Address: 165 Front Street E
Toronto, ON M5A 3Z4
Phone: (416) 363-5131

#356
Joy of Dance Studio & Teachers College
Category: Performing Arts
Area: Riverdale
Address: 95 Danforth Ave
Toronto, ON M4K 1N2
Phone: (416) 406-3262

#357
Sensation Canada
Category: Festival
Area: Entertainment District
Address: 1 Blue Jays Way
Toronto, ON M5V 1J3

#358
Paradise Sports Bar & Billiards
Category: Pool Hall, Casino
Area: The Danforth
Address: 940 Danforth Avenue
Toronto, ON M4J 1L9
Phone: (416) 466-7981

#359
Creative Childrens Dance Centre
Category: Performing Arts, Dance School
Area: The Junction
Address: 2968 Dundas Street W
Toronto, ON M6P 1Y8
Phone: (416) 762-9200

#360
The Blue Dot Gallery
Category: Art Gallery
Area: Distillery District
Address: 55 Mill Street
Toronto, ON M5A 3C4
Phone: (416) 487-1500

#361
Festival of South Asia
Category: Festival
Address: 1426 Gerrard St E
Toronto, ON M4L 1Z6

#362
Colborne Lodge
Category: Museum
Area: High Park
Address: 11 Colborne Lodge Drive
Toronto, ON M6R
Phone: (416) 392-6916

#363
Tattoo Rock Parlour
Category: Music Venues, Bar
Area: Alexandra Park, Queen Street West
Address: 567 Queen St W
Toronto, ON M5V 2B6

#364
Brayham Contemporary Art
Category: Art Gallery
Area: Leslieville
Address: 1318 Queen Street E
Toronto, ON M4L 1C5
Phone: (647) 435-7367

#365
Ryerson Theatre
Category: Performing Arts, Specialty School
Area: Ryerson, Downtown Core
Address: 43 Gerrard St E
Toronto, ON M5G 2A7
Phone: (416) 979-5118

#366
Lee's Palace
Category: Music Venues
Address: 529 Bloor Street W
Toronto, ON M5S 1Y5

#367
The Artic Bear
Category: Art Gallery
Area: Yorkville
Address: 125 Yorkville Ave
Toronto, ON M4W 1A7
Phone: (416) 967-7885

#368
Hot and Spicy Festival
Category: Festival
Area: Harbourfront
Address: 235 Queen Quay W
Toronto, ON M5J 2G8
Phone: (416) 973-4600

#369
GlobalAware
Category: Art Gallery
Area: Kensington Market
Address: 19 Kensington Avenue
Toronto, ON M5T 2J8
Phone: (416) 204-1984

#370
Bau-Xi Gallery
Category: Art Gallery
Area: Downtown Core
Address: 340 Dundas Street W
Toronto, ON M5T 1G5
Phone: (416) 977-0600

#371
Kube
Category: Art Gallery, Furniture Store
Area: Niagara, West Queen West, Trinity Bellwoods
Address: 677 Queen Street West
Toronto, ON M6J

#372
NARWHAL
Category: Art Gallery
Area: Roncesvalles
Address: 2104 Dundas Street West
Toronto, ON M6P 1X6
Phone: (647) 346-5317

#373
The ROM Theatre
Category: Cinema
Area: University of Toronto, Downtown Core
Address: 100 Queen's Park
Toronto, ON M5S 2C6
Phone: (416) 586-8000

#374
George Ignatieff Theatre
Category: Performing Arts
Area: University of Toronto, Downtown Core
Address: 15 Devonshire Pl
Toronto, ON M5S
Phone: (416) 978-4166

#375
Cineforum
Category: Cinema
Area: Kensington Market, Little Italy
Address: 463 Bathurst St
Toronto, ON M5T 2S9
Phone: (416) 603-6643

#376
Cinecycle
Category: Cinema
Area: Entertainment District, Downtown Core
Address: 129 Spadina Avenue
Toronto, ON M5V 2L7
Phone: (416) 971-4273

#377
Regent Theatre
Category: Cinema
Area: Mount Pleasant and Davisville
Address: 551 Mount Pleasant Road
Toronto, ON M4S 2M5
Phone: (416) 480-9884

#378
Taste of Toronto
Category: Festival
Area: City Place
Address: 250 Fort York Boulevard
Toronto, ON M5V

#379
Thrush Holmes Empire
Category: Art Gallery
Area: West Queen West, Beaconsfield Village
Address: 1093 Queen Street W
Toronto, ON M6J 1J1
Phone: (416) 530-4747

#380
Deaf Culture Centre
Category: Museum
Area: Distillery District
Address: 55 Mill Street, Suite 101
Toronto, ON M5A 3C4
Phone: (416) 203-9168

#381
The Hangman Artist Gallery
Category: Art Gallery
Area: Riverdale
Address: 756 Queen Street East
Toronto, ON M4M 1H4
Phone: (416) 465-0302

#382
Gallery 888
Category: Art Gallery
Area: Leslieville
Address: 888 Queen St E
Toronto, ON M4M 1J3
Phone: (416) 462-9930

#383
The Rose & Crown
Category: Music Venues, Pub
Area: Mount Pleasant and Davisville, Yonge and Eglinton
Address: 2335 Yonge St
Toronto, ON M4P 2C8
Phone: (416) 487-7673

#384
Pointing Baby Gallery
Category: Art Gallery
Area: Bloor-West Village
Address: 355 Jane Street
Toronto, ON M6S 3Z3

#385
Gallery Singidunum
Category: Art Gallery
Area: The Junction
Address: 3101 Dundas St W
Toronto, ON M6P 1Z9
Phone: (416) 766-0300

#386
Portico Art
Category: Art Gallery
Area: Lawrence Park
Address: 65 Lawrence Ave East
Toronto, ON M4N 1S5
Phone: (416) 485-0365

#387
The Guild Shop
Category: Art Gallery
Area: Yorkville
Address: 118 Cumberland Street
Toronto, ON M5R 1A6
Phone: (416) 921-1721

#388
Creative Children's Dance Centre
Category: Performing Arts
Area: The Junction
Address: 2968 Dundas Street West
Toronto, ON M6P 1Y8
Phone: (416) 762-9200

#389
Sevan Art Gallery
Category: Art Gallery, Interior Design
Area: Church-Wellesley Village
Address: 619A Yonge Street
Toronto, ON M4Y 1Z5
Phone: (416) 920-8809

#390
Billiards Academy
Category: Pool Hall, Casino
Area: Greektown, Riverdale
Address: 485 Danforth Avenue
Toronto, ON M4K 1P5
Phone: (416) 466-9696

#391
Mascotts
Category: Performing Arts
Area: Leslieville
Address: 1555 Queen St E
Toronto, ON M4L 1E6
Phone: (415) 469-0999

#392
Opera Atelier
Category: Performing Arts
Area: St. Lawrence, Downtown Core
Address: 157 King Street E
Toronto, ON M5C 1G9
Phone: (416) 703-3767

#393
Tibet Gallery
Category: Art Gallery
Area: Yorkville
Address: 4-24 Bellair Street
Toronto, ON M5R 2C7
Phone: (647) 345-4422

#394
The Baitshop
Category: Art Gallery, Sports Wear, Men's Clothing
Area: Parkdale
Address: 358 Dufferin St
Toronto, ON M6K 1Z8
Phone: (416) 536-6000

#395
YU Rock Cafe
Category: Music Venues, Cafe
Area: East York
Address: 978 Pape Ave
Toronto, ON M4K 3V7
Phone: (647) 342-3539

#396
Hurricane Simulator
Category: Arcade
Area: Upper Beach
Address: 1651 Queen St E
Toronto, ON M4L 1G5
Phone: (416) 699-1327

#397
Ellington's Music & Cafe
Category: Jazz & Blues, Coffee & Tea
Area: Wychwood
Address: 805 St Clair Avenue W
Toronto, ON M6C 1B9
Phone: (416) 652-9111

#398
Banksy - Spadina Rat
Category: Art Gallery
Area: Alexandra Park, Downtown Core
Address: 185 Spadina Avenue
Toronto, ON M5T 2C3

#399
JaZie's Magic Bar
Category: Performing Arts
Area: Roncesvalles
Address: 149 Sorauren Ave
Toronto, ON M6R 2E6
Phone: (647) 267-1214

#400
Banksy
Category: Art Gallery
Address: 391 Adelaide Street W
Toronto, ON M5V 3C1

#401
Meta Gallery
Category: Art Gallery
Area: Ossington Strip, Trinity Bellwoods, Beaconsfield Village
Address: 124 Ossington Avenue
Toronto, ON M6J 2Z5
Phone: (416) 955-0500

#402
Trinity-St Paul's United Church
Category: Church, Music Venues
Address: 427 Bloor Street W
Toronto, ON M5S 1X7

#403
Median Contemporary
Category: Art Gallery
Area: West Queen West, Beaconsfield Village
Address: 1142 Queen Street W
Toronto, ON M6J

#404
Woofstock
Category: Pets, Festival
Area: St. Lawrence, Downtown Core
Address: 92 Front St E
Toronto, ON M5E 1C4

#405
Ingram Gallery
Category: Art Gallery
Area: The Annex
Address: 49 Avenue Road
Toronto, ON M5R 2G3
Phone: (416) 929-2220

#406
Klim Art Gallery
Category: Art Gallery
Area: Mount Pleasant and Davisville, Yonge and Eglinton
Address: 2473 Yonge Street
Toronto, ON M4P 2H6
Phone: (416) 932-9221

#407
Gallery Arcturus
Category: Art Gallery
Area: Downtown Core
Address: 80 Gerrard St E
Toronto, ON M5B 1G6
Phone: (416) 977-1077

#408
Round Venue
Category: Music Venues
Area: Kensington Market
Address: 152 Augusta Avenue
Toronto, ON M5T 2L5
Phone: (416) 451-6346

#409
The Box
Category: Performing Arts
Area: Niagara
Address: 89 Niagara Street
Toronto, ON M5V 1C3
Phone: (416) 949-9252

#410
Kinsman Robinson Gallery
Category: Art Gallery
Area: Yorkville
Address: 108 Cumberland St
Toronto, ON M5R 1A6
Phone: (416) 964-2374

#411
Banksy - Rat Sign
Category: Art Gallery
Address: 54 Polson Street
Toronto, ON M5A 3L2

#412
Gallery 44
Category: Art Gallery
Area: Entertainment District, Downtown Core
Address: 401 Richmond Street W
Toronto, ON M5V 3A8
Phone: (416) 979-3941

#413
Mindzai
Category: Arts & Crafts, Art Gallery, Hobby Shops
Address: 11 Camden Street
Toronto, ON M5V 1V2

#414
ATTI Gallery
Category: Art Gallery
Area: Mount Pleasant and Davisville, Yonge and Eglinton
Address: 2152 Yonge Street
Toronto, ON M4S 2A8
Phone: (416) 484-6266

#415
Artscape Youngplace
Category: Art Gallery
Area: Trinity Bellwoods
Address: 180 Shaw Street
Toronto, ON M6J 2W5
Phone: (416) 530-2787

#416
Studio 561
Category: Art Gallery, Venues
Address: 561 Bloor St W
Toronto, ON M5Y 1S6

#417
52 McCaul
Category: Venues, Art Gallery
Area: Downtown Core
Address: 52 McCaul Street
Toronto, ON M5T 1V9
Phone: (416) 722-7074

#418
Best of China- Gift & Art Gallery
Category: Art Gallery
Area: Chinatown, Downtown Core
Address: 419 Dundas Street W
Toronto, ON M5T 1G6
Phone: (416) 847-0333

#419
Winter Garden Theatre
Category: Music Venues
Area: Downtown Core
Address: 189 Yonge St.
Toronto, ON M5B 1M4
Phone: (855) 985-5000

#420
Graffiti Alley
Category: Art Gallery
Area: Queen Street West
Address: 513 Queen Street W
Toronto, ON M5V

#421
Amber Group Fine Art Gallery
Category: Art Gallery
Address: 966 Saint Clair Avenue W
Toronto, ON M6E 1A1

#422
The Great Escape Canada
Category: Arcade
Address: 165 Geary Avenue
Toronto, ON M6H 2B8

#423
Ben Navaee Gallery
Category: Art Gallery
Area: Leslieville
Address: 1107 Queen Street E
Toronto, ON M4M 1K7
Phone: (416) 466-3996

#424
Roberts Gallery
Category: Art Gallery
Area: Church-Wellesley Village, Downtown Core
Address: 641 Yonge Street
Toronto, ON M4Y 1Z9
Phone: (416) 924-8731

#425
Improv Your Acting
Category: Performing Arts
Area: Riverdale
Address: 184 Munro Street
Toronto, ON M4K 1K8
Phone: (647) 688-9668

#426
Noon River Gallery
Category: Art Gallery, Jewelry
Area: City Place
Address: 20 Capreol Court
Toronto, ON M5V 4A3
Phone: (647) 261-1586

#427
The Bulger Stephen Gallery
Category: Art Gallery
Area: West Queen West, Beaconsfield Village
Address: 1026 Queen Street W
Toronto, ON M6J 1H6
Phone: (416) 504-0575

#428
Arraymusic
Category: Performing Arts
Area: Liberty Village
Address: 60 Atlantic Avenue
Toronto, ON M6K 1X9
Phone: (416) 532-3019

#429
IX Gallery & Event Place
Category: Art Gallery
Area: Riverdale
Address: 11 Davies Ave
Toronto, ON M4M 2A9
Phone: (416) 461-3233

#430
Artwork by Collins & Chandler Gallery
Category: Antiques, Jewelry, Art Gallery
Area: Summer Hill
Address: 181 Avenue Rd
Toronto, ON M5R 2J2
Phone: (416) 922-8784

#431
Odon Wagner Gallery & Odon Wagner Contemporary
Category: Art Gallery
Area: Yorkville
Address: 196 & 198 Davenport Road
Toronto, ON M5R 1J2
Phone: (416) 962-0438

#432
Gallery Hittite
Category: Art Gallery
Area: Yorkville
Address: 107 Scollard Street
Toronto, ON M5R 1G4
Phone: (416) 924-4450

#433
Eskimo Art Gallery
Category: Art Gallery
Area: Distillery District
Address: 8 Casegoods Lane
Toronto, ON M5A 3C4
Phone: (416) 366-3000

#434
Corkin Gallery
Category: Art Gallery
Area: Distillery District
Address: 55 Mill Street
Toronto, ON M5A 3C4
Phone: (416) 979-1980

#435
Parkside Drive
Category: Performing Arts, DJs
Area: High Park, Roncesvalles
Address: 2252 Dundas Street W
Toronto, ON M6R 1X3
Phone: (647) 226-7477

#436
Canadian Opera Company
Category: Performing Arts
Area: Corktown, St. Lawrence
Address: 227 Front Street E
Toronto, ON M5A 1E8
Phone: (416) 363-6671

#437
Geo Bell Hockey Association
Category: Arena
Area: The Junction
Address: 215 Ryding Avenue
Toronto, ON M6N 1H6
Phone: (416) 762-6715

#438
Theatre francais de Toronto
Category: Performing Arts
Area: Downtown Core
Address: 21 College Street
Toronto, ON M5G 2B3
Phone: (416) 534-6604

#439
Mattamy Athletic Centre at TheGarden
Category: Music Venues
Area: Church-Wellesley Village
Address: 50 Carlton Street
Toronto, ON M5B 1J2
Phone: (855) 985-5000

#440
Sharin Barber
Category: Art Gallery
Area: Yonge and St. Clair, Deer Park
Address: 42 Glen Elm Avenue
Toronto, ON M4T 1T7
Phone: (647) 348-0580

#441
Lausberg Contemporary
Category: Art Gallery
Area: Downtown Core
Address: 326 Dundas Street West
Toronto, ON M5T 1G5
Phone: (416) 516-4440

#442
Art Frame N Copy Co.
Category: Art Gallery, Framing
Area: Discovery District, Downtown Core
Address: 189 Dundas St W
Toronto, ON M5G 1C7
Phone: (416) 599-3334

#443
The Number9 Recording Studio
Category: Music Venues
Address: 222 Gerrard Street East
Toronto, ON M5A 2E8

#444
Broadway Arts Centre
Category: Performing Arts
Area: Roncesvalles
Address: 35 Golden Avenue
Toronto, ON M6R 2J5
Phone: (647) 294-3211

#445
Gallery Creatures Creating
Category: Art Gallery, Music Venues
Area: Little Italy, Trinity Bellwoods
Address: 822 Dundas Street W
Toronto, ON M6J 1V3
Phone: (647) 709-8337

#446
The Acacia Centre
Category: Performing Arts, Cinema
Area: Alexandra Park, Downtown Core
Address: 186 Spadina Ave
Toronto, ON M5R 1A1
Phone: (647) 348-3420

#447
Elgin Theatre
Category: Music Venues
Area: Downtown Core
Address: 189 Yonge St.
Toronto, ON M5B 1M4
Phone: (855) 985-5000

#448
Wynick-Tuck Gallery
Category: Art Gallery
Area: Entertainment District,
Downtown Core
Address: 401 Richmond Street W
Toronto, ON M5V 3A8
Phone: (416) 504-8716

#449
Gallery 44 Centre For Contemporary Photography
Category: Art Gallery
Area: Entertainment District
Address: 401 Richmond Street W
Toronto, ON M5V 3A8
Phone: (416) 979-3941

#450
Dance Collection Danse
Category: Museum
Area: Corktown
Address: 145 George Street
Toronto, ON M5A 2M6
Phone: (416) 365-3233

#451
STUDIO Event Theatre
Category: Music Venues, Art Gallery
Area: Entertainment District
Address: 333 King Street W
Toronto, ON M5V 1J5
Phone: (416) 226-4636

#452
Feheley Fine Arts
Category: Art Gallery
Area: Corktown
Address: 65 George Street
Toronto, ON M5A 4L8
Phone: (416) 323-1373

#453
Project Gallery
Category: Art Gallery
Area: Leslieville
Address: 1109 Queen Street E
Toronto, ON M4M 1K7
Phone: (416) 315-1192

#454
Canadian Exhibition Centre
Category: Art Gallery
Area: Entertainment District
Address: 255 Front Street W
Toronto, ON M5V 2W6
Phone: (416) 585-8120

#455
Talent, Inc.
Category: Performing Arts
Area: Corktown
Address: 550 Queen Street E
Toronto, ON M5A 1V2
Phone: (647) 748-7200

#456
Dual Audio Services Corp.
Category: Performing Arts, Party Supplies
Address: 7 Labatt Avenue
Toronto, ON M5A 1Z1

#457
Bernardi's Antiques
Category: Antiques, Art Gallery
Area: Mount Pleasant and Davisville, Yonge and Eglinton
Address: 699 Mount Pleasant Road
Toronto, ON M4S 2N4
Phone: (416) 483-6471

#458
The Box Toronto Studio and Theatre
Category: Performing Arts
Area: Niagara
Address: 89 Niagara Street
Toronto, ON M5V 1C3
Phone: (416) 949-9252

#459
Toronto Film Society
Category: Cinema
Area: Corktown, St. Lawrence
Address: 2 Sussex Ave
Toronto, ON M5A 3Z4
Phone: (416) 363-7222

#460
Diaz Contemporary
Category: Art Gallery
Area: Niagara
Address: 100 Niagara Street
Toronto, ON M5V 1C5
Phone: (416) 361-2972

#461
GTA Strings
Category: Performing Arts, Wedding Planning, Professional Services
Area: Swansea
Address: 2555 Bloor Street W
Toronto, ON M6S 1S1
Phone: (647) 707-0348

#462
De Luca Fine Art Gallery
Category: Art Gallery
Area: The Annex, Summer Hill
Address: 217 Avenue Road
Toronto, ON M5R 2J3
Phone: (416) 537-4699

#463
Mayberry Fine Art
Category: Art Gallery
Area: Yorkville
Address: 110 Yorkville Avenue
Toronto, ON M5R

#464
Cineplex Odeon Corporation
Category: Cinema
Area: Summer Hill
Address: 1303 Yonge Street
Toronto, ON M4T 2Y9
Phone: (416) 323-6600

#465
Art Yard
Category: Art Gallery
Area: West Queen West
Address: 30 Abell Street
Toronto, ON M6J 0A9
Phone: (416) 659-3077

#466
Medina & Grinkov Music
Category: Performing Arts
Area: Casa Loma
Address: 612 Davenport Road
Toronto, ON M5R 1K9
Phone: (416) 895-7453

#467
Wallace Film Studio
Category: Performing Arts
Area: Wallace Emerson
Address: 258 Wallace Ave
Toronto, ON M6P 3M9
Phone: (416) 538-3535

#468
Rancho Relaxo Lounge aka Upstairs Rancho Relaxo
Category: Festival, Music Venues
Address: 300 College Street
Toronto, ON M5S 2K2

#469
TFNS Toronto Fight Night Series
Category: Arcade
Area: The Junction
Address: 1444 Dupont St
Toronto, ON M6P 4H3

#470
The Design Exchange
Category: Museum
Area: Downtown Core
Address: 234 Bay Street
Toronto, ON M5K 1B2
Phone: (416) 363-6121

#471
Scollard Street Gallery
Category: Art Gallery
Address: 112 Scollard Street
Toronto, ON M5R 1G2

#472
Art Interiors
Category: Art Gallery
Address: 446 Spadina Rd
Toronto, ON M5P 3M2

#473
Gallery Louise Smith
Category: Art Gallery
Area: The Annex
Address: 238 Davenport Road
Toronto, ON M5R 1J6
Phone: (416) 485-3487

#474
Royal Hermitage
Category: Art Gallery
Area: The Annex
Address: 131 Avenue Road
Toronto, ON M5R 2H7
Phone: (416) 966-2771

#475
Red Pepper Spectacle Arts
Category: Performing Arts
Area: Kensington Market
Address: 160 Baldwin St
Toronto, ON M5T 3K7
Phone: (416) 598-3729

#476
Theatre Direct Canada
Category: Performing Arts
Area: Wychwood
Address: 601 Christie Street
Toronto, ON M6G 4C7
Phone: (416) 537-4191

#477
Salvador Sculptures & Collectables
Category: Art Gallery
Area: The Annex
Address: 160 Pears Avenue
Toronto, ON M5R 3P8
Phone: (416) 929-2320

#478
Hotshot
Category: Art Gallery
Area: Kensington Market
Address: 181 Augusta Ave
Toronto, ON M5T
Phone: (416) 979-7574

#479
CB Gallery
Category: Art Gallery
Area: Little Italy
Address: 376 Bathurst Street
Toronto, ON M5T 2S6

#480
Gilchrist Games
Category: Arcade, Antiques
Address: 30 Bertal Road
Toronto, ON M6M 4M4

#481
Toronto Dance Theatre
Category: Performing Arts
Area: Cabbagetown
Address: 80 Winchester Street
Toronto, ON M4X 1B2
Phone: (416) 967-1365

#482
Spruce
Category: Art Gallery, Home Decor
Area: Cabbagetown
Address: 455 Parliament Street
Toronto, ON M5A 3A3
Phone: (647) 748-4060

#483
Rebellion Gallery & Art Academy
Category: Art Gallery, Art Classes
Area: Leslieville
Address: 914 Eastern Avenue
Toronto, ON M4L 1A4
Phone: (416) 469-1777

#484
Westwood Concerts
Category: Performing Arts
Area: Yorkville
Address: 35 Hazelton Avenue
Toronto, ON M5R 1M6
Phone: (647) 403-4877

#485
Jazz In Toronto
Category: Jazz & Blues
Area: Entertainment District
Address: 194 Queen Street W
Toronto, ON M5V 1Z1
Phone: (416) 599-5486

#486
Canadian Opera House Corporation
Category: Cinema
Area: Downtown Core
Address: 145 Queen Street W
Toronto, ON M5H 4G1
Phone: (416) 368-4227

#487
Cahoots Theatre Projects
Category: Cinema
Area: Alexandra Park
Address: 174 Av Spadina
Toronto, ON M5T 2C2
Phone: (416) 203-9000

#488
Mainstage Marquee at Nathan Phillips Square
Category: Music Venues
Area: Downtown Core
Address: Queen Street West
Toronto, ON M5H 2N2
Phone: (855) 985-5000

#489
Speakeasy at Revival
Category: Performing Arts
Area: Little Italy, Bickford Park
Address: 783 College St
Toronto, ON M6G 1C5
Phone: (877) 821-7803

#490
Northern Lights
Category: Musicians, Performing Arts
Area: Downtown Core
Address: 56 Queen Street E
Toronto, ON M5C 1R8
Phone: (866) 744-7464

#491
Fourth Eye Gallery
Category: Art Gallery
Area: Cabbagetown
Address: 438 Parliament Street
Toronto, ON M5A 3A1
Phone: (416) 519-6456

#492
Red Sky Performance
Category: Cinema, Performing Arts
Area: Entertainment District, Downtown Core
Address: 401 Richmond St W
Toronto, ON M5V 3A8
Phone: (416) 585-9969

#493
Open Studio
Category: Art Gallery
Area: Entertainment District, Downtown Core
Address: 401 Richmond Street W
Toronto, ON M5V 3A8
Phone: (416) 504-8238

#494
A Space
Category: Art Gallery
Area: Entertainment District, Downtown Core
Address: 401 Richmond Street W
Toronto, ON M5V 3A8
Phone: (416) 979-9633

#495
The Red Head Gallery
Category: Art Gallery
Area: Entertainment District, Downtown Core
Address: 401 Richmond Street W
Toronto, ON M5V 3A8
Phone: (416) 504-5654

#496
Women's Art Resource
Category: Art Gallery
Area: Entertainment District, Downtown Core
Address: 401 Richmond Street W
Toronto, ON M5V 3A8
Phone: (416) 977-0097

#497
Toronto Outdoor Art
Category: Art Gallery
Area: Entertainment District, Downtown Core
Address: 401 Richmond Street W
Toronto, ON M5V 3A8
Phone: (416) 408-2754

#498
ArtSocket
Category: Art Gallery
Area: East York
Address: 15 Lesmount Avenue
Toronto, ON M4J 3V5
Phone: (718) 404-9278

#499
The Fifth Wall
Category: Art Gallery, Interior Design
Area: Corktown, Downtown Core
Address: 101 Richmond St E
Toronto, ON M5C 1N9
Phone: (416) 850-4222

#500
IMA Gallery
Category: Art Gallery
Area: Downtown Core
Address: 80 Avenue Spadina
Toronto, ON M5V 2J4
Phone: (416) 703-2235

TOP 500 NIGHTLIFE

The Most Recommended by Locals & Trevelers

(From #1 to #500)

#1
Black Hoof
Category: Gastropub, Cocktail Bar
Average price: Expensive
Area: Little Italy
Address: 928 Dundas Street W
Toronto, ON M6J 1W3
Phone: (416) 551-8854

#2
Communist's Daughter
Category: Bar
Average price: Inexpensive
Area: Dufferin Grove, Little Portugal, Ossington Strip, Beaconsfield Village
Address: 1149 Dundas Street W
Toronto, ON M6J 1X3
Phone: (647) 435-0103

#3
Barhop
Category: Bar
Average price: Modest
Area: Entertainment District, Downtown Core
Address: 391 King Street W
Toronto, ON M5V 1K1
Phone: (647) 352-7476

#4
Bovine Sex Club
Category: Bar
Average price: Inexpensive
Area: Alexandra Park, Queen Street West
Address: 542 Queen St W
Toronto, ON M5V 2B5
Phone: (416) 504-4239

#5
Bar + Karaoke Lounge
Category: Karaoke, Dance Club, Music Venues
Average price: Modest
Area: Ryerson, Downtown Core
Address: 360 Yonge Street
Toronto, ON M5B 1S5
Phone: (416) 340-7154

#6
The Hole In the Wall
Category: Pub, Canadian
Average price: Modest
Area: The Junction
Address: 2867 Dundas Street W
Toronto, ON M6P 1Y9
Phone: (647) 350-3564

#7
The Caledonian
Category: Pub, Scottish
Average price: Modest
Area: Dufferin Grove
Address: 856 College Street
Toronto, ON M6H 1A1
Phone: (647) 547-9827

#8
Beerbistro
Category: Canadian, Pub
Average price: Modest
Area: Downtown Core
Address: 18 King Street E
Toronto, ON M5C 1C4
Phone: (416) 861-9872

#9
BarChef
Category: Lounge, Cocktail Bar
Average price: Expensive
Area: Alexandra Park, Queen Street West
Address: 472 Queen Street W
Toronto, ON M5V 2B2
Phone: (416) 868-4800

#10
Reposado Bar & Lounge
Category: Lounge, Tapas, Mexican
Average price: Expensive
Area: Ossington Strip, Trinity Bellwoods, Beaconsfield Village
Address: 136 Ossington Avenue
Toronto, ON M6J 2Z5
Phone: (416) 532-6474

#11
The Done Right Inn
Category: Dive Bar
Average price: Inexpensive
Area: Niagara, West Queen West, Trinity Bellwoods
Address: 861 Queen St W
Toronto, ON M6J 1G4
Phone: (416) 364-9102

#12
Hair Of The Dog
Category: Pub, Comfort Food, Breakfast & Brunch
Average price: Modest
Area: Church-Wellesley Village, Downtown Core
Address: 425 Church Street
Toronto, ON M4Y 2C3
Phone: (416) 964-2708

#13
The Queen & Beaver Pub
Category: Pub, British, Sports Bar
Average price: Modest
Area: Downtown Core
Address: 35 Elm St
Toronto, ON M5G 1H1
Phone: (647) 347-2712

#14
The Reservoir Lounge
Category: Jazz & Blues, Music Venues
Average price: Modest
Area: St. Lawrence, Downtown Core
Address: 52 Wellington St E
Toronto, ON M5E 1C8
Phone: (416) 955-0887

#15
Handlebar
Category: Bar, Dance Club, Music Venues
Average price: Inexpensive
Area: Kensington Market
Address: 159 Augusta Avenue
Toronto, ON M5T 2L4
Phone: (647) 748-7433

#16
BarVolo
Category: Bar, Brasserie, Canadian
Average price: Modest
Area: Church-Wellesley Village, Downtown Core
Address: 587 Yonge St
Toronto, ON M4Y 1Z4
Phone: (416) 928-0008

#17
Union
Category: French, Wine Bar
Average price: Expensive
Area: Ossington Strip, Trinity Bellwoods, Beaconsfield Village
Address: 72A Ossington Avenue
Toronto, ON M6J 2Y7
Phone: (416) 850-0093

#18
Grand Electric
Category: Bar, Mexican
Average price: Modest
Area: Parkdale
Address: 1330 Queen Street W
Toronto, ON M6K 1L4
Phone: (416) 627-3459

#19
The Dakota Tavern
Category: Music Venues, Dive Bar
Average price: Modest
Area: Dufferin Grove, Little Italy, Little Portugal, Ossington Strip
Address: 249 Ossington Avenue
Toronto, ON M6J 3A1
Phone: (416) 850-4579

#20
Sweaty Betty's
Category: Dive Bar
Average price: Modest
Area: Ossington Strip, West Queen West, Trinity Bellwoods, Beaconsfield Village
Address: 13 Ossington Avenue
Toronto, ON M6J 2Y8
Phone: (416) 535-6861

#21
Drift
Category: Lounge
Average price: Modest
Area: Dovercourt, Dufferin Grove
Address: 1063 Bloor St W
Toronto, ON M6H 1M3
Phone: (647) 352-5335

#22
C'est What?
Category: Brewery, Music Venues
Average price: Modest
Area: St. Lawrence, Downtown Core
Address: 67 Front Street E
Toronto, ON M5E 1B5
Phone: (416) 867-9499

#23
The Comrade
Category: Lounge, Canadian
Average price: Modest
Area: Riverdale
Address: 758 Queen Street E
Toronto, ON M4M 1H4
Phone: (416) 778-9449

#24
The Boat
Category: Music Venues, Bar
Average price: Inexpensive
Area: Kensington Market
Address: 158 Augusta Avenue
Toronto, ON M5T 2L5
Phone: (416) 593-9218

#25
Cocktail Bar
Category: Bar
Average price: Expensive
Area: Little Italy, Trinity Bellwoods
Address: 923 Dundas St W
Toronto, ON M6J 1W3
Phone: (416) 792-7511

#26
Aft Kitchen & Bar
Category: Bar, American, Barbeque
Average price: Modest
Area: Riverdale
Address: 686 Queen Street E
Toronto, ON M4M 1H1
Phone: (647) 346-1541

#27
Cold Tea
Category: Bar
Average price: Modest
Area: Kensington Market
Address: 60 Kensington Ave
Toronto, ON M5T 2K2
Phone: (416) 546-4536

#28
The Monk's Table
Category: Pub, British
Average price: Modest
Area: Summer Hill
Address: 1276 Yonge Street
Toronto, ON M4T 1W5
Phone: (416) 920-9074

#29
The Second City Mainstage Theatre
Category: Comedy Club, Performing Arts
Average price: Modest
Area: Entertainment District
Address: 51 Mercer Street
Toronto, ON M5V 9G9
Phone: (416) 343-0011

#30
The Red Light
Category: Bar
Average price: Modest
Area: Little Portugal
Address: 1185 Dundas St W
Toronto, ON M6J 1X3
Phone: (416) 533-6667

#31
Prohibition Gastrohouse
Category: Pub, Gastropub, Sports Bar
Average price: Modest
Area: Riverdale
Address: 696 Queen Street E
Toronto, ON M4M 1G9
Phone: (416) 406-2669

#33
Town Crier Pub
Category: Pub
Average price: Modest
Area: Entertainment District, Downtown Core
Address: 115 John St
Toronto, ON M5V 3Y8
Phone: (416) 204-9588

#32
Pravda Vodka Bar
Category: Lounge
Average price: Expensive
Area: St. Lawrence, Downtown Core
Address: 44 Wellington St E
Toronto, ON M5E 1C7
Phone: (416) 366-0303

#34
No One Writes To The Colonel
Category: Bar, Italian
Average price: Modest
Area: Little Italy, Palmerston
Address: 460 College Street
Toronto, ON M6G 1A4
Phone: (416) 551-7647

#35
Souz Dal
Category: Lounge
Average price: Modest
Area: Little Italy, Bickford Park
Address: 612 College Street
Toronto, ON M6G 1B4
Phone: (416) 537-8755

#36
Sauce
Category: Champagne Bar, Lounge
Average price: Modest
Area: The Danforth
Address: 1376 Danforth Avenue
Toronto, ON M4J 1M9
Phone: (647) 748-1376

#37
The Emmet Ray
Category: Jazz & Blues, Music Venues
Average price: Modest
Area: Dufferin Grove
Address: 924 College Street
Toronto, ON M6H 1A4
Phone: (416) 792-4497

#38
7 West Cafe
Category: Italian, Breakfast & Brunch
Average price: Modest
Area: Downtown Core
Address: 7 Charles St W
Toronto, ON M4Y 1R4
Phone: (416) 928-9041

#39
The Horseshoe Tavern
Category: Music Venues, Dive Bar
Average price: Inexpensive
Area: Queen Street West,
Downtown Core
Address: 370 Queen Street W
Toronto, ON M5V 2A2
Phone: (416) 598-4753

#40
Earl's Kitchen & Bar
Category: American, Bar
Average price: Modest
Area: Financial District, Downtown Core
Address: 150 King Street W
Toronto, ON M5H 2B6
Phone: (416) 916-0227

#41
The Blake House
Category: Pub
Average price: Modest
Area: Downtown Core
Address: 449 Jarvis Street
Toronto, ON M4Y 2G6
Phone: (416) 975-1867

#42
The Wren
Category: Bar, American
Average price: Modest
Area: The Danforth
Address: 1382 Danforth Avenue
Toronto, ON M4J 1M9
Phone: (647) 748-1382

#43
Cameron House
Category: Music Venues, Bar
Average price: Inexpensive
Area: Alexandra Park,
Queen Street West
Address: 408 Queen St W
Toronto, ON M5V 2A7
Phone: (416) 703-0811

#44
Koerner Hall
Category: Music Venues
Average price: Expensive
Area: University of Toronto,
Downtown Core
Address: 273 Bloor St W
Toronto, ON M5S 1W2
Phone: (416) 408-0208

#45
Fifth Social Club
Category: Dance Club, Lounge
Average price: Expensive
Area: Entertainment District,
Downtown Core
Address: 225 Richmond Street W
Toronto, ON M5V 1W2
Phone: (416) 979-3000

#46
Drake Hotel
Category: Hotel, Lounge, Canadian
Average price: Expensive
Area: West Queen West,
Beaconsfield Village
Address: 1150 Queen Street W
Toronto, ON M6J 1J3
Phone: (416) 531-5042

#47
Mill Street Brew Pub
Category: Bar, Brasserie
Average price: Modest
Area: Distillery District
Address: 55 Mill St
Toronto, ON M5A 3C4
Phone: (416) 681-0338

#48
Bryden's
Category: Pub, Sandwiches
Average price: Modest
Area: Swansea
Address: 2455 Bloor Street W
Toronto, ON M6S 1P7
Phone: (416) 760-8069

#49
Crooked Star
Category: Dive Bar
Average price: Inexpensive
Area: Little Portugal, Ossington Strip, Beaconsfield Village
Address: 202 Ossington Avenue
Toronto, ON M6J 2Z7
Phone: (416) 536-7271

#50
The Rebel House
Category: Pub, Gastropub
Average price: Modest
Area: Summer Hill
Address: 1068 Yonge Street
Toronto, ON M4W 2L4
Phone: (416) 927-0704

#51
The Embassy Bar
Category: Bar
Average price: Inexpensive
Area: Kensington Market
Address: 223 Augusta Ave
Toronto, ON M5T 2L4
Phone: (416) 591-1132

#52
The Gem
Category: Pub, American
Average price: Modest
Area: Wychwood
Address: 1159 Davenport Rd
Toronto, ON M6H 2G4
Phone: (416) 654-1182

#53
WAYLA Lounge
Category: Lounge, Venues
Average price: Modest
Area: Leslieville
Address: 996 Queen St E
Toronto, ON M4M
Phone: (416) 901-5570

#54
Victory Café
Category: Pub, Canadian
Average price: Modest
Area: Palmerston
Address: 581 Markham St
Toronto, ON M6G 2L7
Phone: (416) 516-5787

#55
Thirsty & Miserable
Category: Dive Bar
Average price: Modest
Area: Kensington Market
Address: 197 Baldwin Street
Toronto, ON M5T 1M1
Phone: (647) 607-0134

#56
DEQ Terrace & Lounge
Category: Lounge
Average price: Exclusive
Area: Entertainment District, Downtown Core
Address: 181 Wellington Street West
Toronto, ON M5V 3G7
Phone: (416) 585-2500

#57
The Beaconsfield
Category: Pub, Canadian
Average price: Modest
Area: West Queen West, Beaconsfield Village
Address: 1154 Queen St W
Toronto, ON M6J 1J5
Phone: (416) 516-2550

#58
P.J. O'Brien's
Category: Pub
Average price: Modest
Area: St. Lawrence, Downtown Core
Address: 39 Colborne St
Toronto, ON M5E 1E3
Phone: (416) 815-7562

#59
The Roof Lounge
Category: Lounge
Average price: Expensive
Area: The Annex, Discovery District, University of Toronto, Downtown Core
Address: 4 Avenue Rd
Toronto, ON M5S 1T9
Phone: (416) 925-1234

#60
The Hideout On Queen
Category: Dance Club, Music Venues
Average price: Modest
Area: Alexandra Park, Queen Street West
Address: 484 Queen St W
Toronto, ON M5V 2B2
Phone: (647) 438-7664

#61
Ellington's Music & Cafe
Category: Jazz & Blues, Coffee & Tea
Average price: Inexpensive
Area: Wychwood
Address: 805 St Clair Avenue W
Toronto, ON M6C 1B9
Phone: (416) 652-9111

#62
Massey Hall
Category: Music Venues
Average price: Modest
Area: Downtown Core
Address: 178 Victoria St.
Toronto, ON M5B 1T7
Phone: (416) 872-4255

#63
The Saint Tavern
Category: Bar, Gastropub
Average price: Expensive
Area: Little Portugal, Ossington Strip, Trinity Bellwoods, Beaconsfield Village
Address: 227 Ossington Ave
Toronto, ON M6J 3A1
Phone: (647) 350-2100

#64
Betty's
Category: Pub, Dive Bar, American
Average price: Modest
Area: Corktown
Address: 240 King Street E
Toronto, ON M5A 1K1
Phone: (416) 368-1300

#65
Soho House Toronto
Category: Social Club, Lounge
Average price: Expensive
Area: Downtown Core
Address: 192 Adelaide St W
Toronto, ON M5H 4E7
Phone: (416) 599-7646

#66
Sin & Redemption
Category: Pub
Average price: Modest
Area: Downtown Core
Address: 126 McCaul St
Toronto, ON M5T 1W2
Phone: (416) 640-9197

#67
The Opera House
Category: Music Venues
Average price: Modest
Area: Riverdale
Address: 735 Queen St. E.
Toronto, ON M4M 1H1
Phone: (416) 466-0313

#68
The Brass Rail
Category: Adult Entertainment, Bar
Average price: Expensive
Area: Church-Wellesley Village, Downtown Core
Address: 701 Yonge St
Toronto, ON M4Y 2B2
Phone: (416) 924-1241

#69
The Mugshot Tavern
Category: Bar
Average price: Modest
Area: High Park
Address: 1729 Bloor Street W
Toronto, ON M6P 1B2
Phone: (416) 901-7468

#70
Montauk Bar
Category: Bar
Average price: Modest
Area: Little Italy, Trinity Bellwoods
Address: 765 Dundas St W
Toronto, ON M6J 1T9
Phone: (647) 281-9897

#71
Orbit Room
Category: Music Venues
Average price: Modest
Area: Little Italy, Palmerston, Bickford Park
Address: 580A College St
Toronto, ON M6G 1B3
Phone: (416) 535-0613

#72
The Library Bar
Category: Lounge, Canadian, Diner
Average price: Expensive
Area: Financial District, Downtown Core
Address: 100 Front Street W
Toronto, ON M5J 1E3
Phone: (416) 368-2511

#73
AAA Bar
Category: Barbeque, Pub
Average price: Modest
Area: Corktown, Downtown Core
Address: 138 Adelaide Street E
Toronto, ON M5C 1K9
Phone: (416) 850-2726

#74
416 Snack Bar
Category: Tapas, Bar
Average price: Modest
Area: Alexandra Park, Queen Street West, West Queen West, Trinity Bellwoods
Address: 181 Bathurst St
Toronto, ON M5T
Phone: (416) 364-9320

#75
Allen's
Category: Irish, Pub
Average price: Modest
Area: Riverdale
Address: 143 Danforth Avenue
Toronto, ON M4K 1N2
Phone: (416) 463-3086

#76
The County General
Category: Bar, Canadian
Average price: Modest
Area: Niagara, West Queen West, Trinity Bellwoods
Address: 936 Queen St W
Toronto, ON M6J 1G9
Phone: (416) 531-4447

#77
Bedford Academy
Category: Pub
Average price: Modest
Area: The Annex
Address: 36 Prince Arthur Avenue
Toronto, ON M5R 1A9
Phone: (416) 921-4600

#78
Fly Nightclub
Category: Dance Club, Gay Bar
Average price: Expensive
Area: Church-Wellesley Village, Downtown Core
Address: 8 Gloucester Street
Toronto, ON M4Y
Phone: (416) 410-5426

#79
Rasputin Vodka Bar
Category: Lounge
Average price: Modest
Area: Riverdale
Address: 780 Queen St E
Toronto, ON M4M 1H4
Phone: (416) 469-3737

#80
The Rex Hotel Jazz & Blues Bar
Category: Pub, Jazz & Blues
Average price: Modest
Area: Entertainment District, Queen Street West, Downtown Core
Address: 194 Queen Street W
Toronto, ON M5V 1Z1
Phone: (416) 598-2475

#81
Cadillac Lounge
Category: Dive Bar, Music Venues
Average price: Modest
Area: Parkdale
Address: 1296 Queen St W
Toronto, ON M6K 1L4
Phone: (416) 536-7717

#82
Buddies In Bad Times Theatre
Category: Performing Arts, Gay Bar
Average price: Inexpensive
Area: Church-Wellesley Village, Downtown Core
Address: 12 Alexander St
Toronto, ON M4Y 1B4
Phone: (416) 975-8555

#83
DBar
Category: Lounge
Average price: Expensive
Area: Yorkville
Address: 60 Yorkville Ave
Toronto, ON M5R 3V6
Phone: (416) 964-0441

#84
Castro's Lounge
Category: Pub
Average price: Modest
Area: The Beach
Address: 2116 Queen St E
Toronto, ON M4E 1E2
Phone: (416) 699-8272

#85
Northwood
Category: Bar, Cafe
Average price: Modest
Area: Bickford Park
Address: 815 W Bloor Street
Toronto, ON M6G 1M1
Phone: (416) 846-8324

#86
Get Well
Category: Dive Bar
Average price: Modest
Area: Little Portugal, Beaconsfield Village
Address: 1181 Dundas Street W
Toronto, ON M6J 1X4
Phone: (647) 351-2337

#87
Proof The Vodka Bar
Category: Lounge, Pub
Average price: Modest
Area: The Annex, Downtown Core
Address: 220 Bloor Street West
Toronto, ON M5S 1T8
Phone: (416) 800-3152

#88
Panorama Lounge & Restaurant
Category: Lounge, Dance Club
Average price: Expensive
Area: Yorkville, Downtown Core
Address: 55 Bloor Street W
Toronto, ON M4W 1A5
Phone: (416) 967-0000

#89
Labyrinth Lounge
Category: Dive Bar, Lounge
Average price: Inexpensive
Area: The Annex
Address: 298 Brunswick Avenue
Toronto, ON M5S 2M7
Phone: (416) 925-7775

#90
Goods & Provisions
Category: Bar, Gastropub
Average price: Expensive
Area: Leslieville
Address: 1124 Queen Street E
Toronto, ON M4M
Phone: (647) 340-1738

#91
Brooklynn
Category: Bar, Comedy Club, Music Venues
Average price: Modest
Area: West Queen West, Beaconsfield Village
Address: 1186 Queen Street W
Toronto, ON M6J 1J6
Phone: (416) 536-7700

#92
Bar Vespa
Category: Italian, Bar
Average price: Modest
Area: Liberty Village
Address: 167 E Liberty Street
Toronto, ON M6K 3K4
Phone: (416) 533-8377

#93
The Keg Steakhouse + Bar
Category: Steakhouse, Bar, Seafood
Average price: Expensive
Area: Financial District, Downtown Core
Address: 165 York Street
Toronto, ON M5H 3R8
Phone: (416) 703-1773

#94
Unicorn Pub
Category: Pub
Average price: Modest
Area: Mount Pleasant and Davisville, Yonge and Eglinton
Address: 175 Eglinton Ave E
Toronto, ON M4P 1J4
Phone: (416) 482-0115

#95
The Drake Underground
Category: Lounge
Average price: Modest
Area: West Queen West, Beaconsfield Village
Address: 1150 Queen St W
Toronto, ON M6J 1J3
Phone: (416) 531-5042

#96
Disgraceland
Category: Pub, Breakfast & Brunch
Average price: Modest
Area: Dovercourt
Address: 965 Bloor Street West
Toronto, ON M6H 1L7
Phone: (647) 347-5263

#97
Club V
Category: Dance Club, Lounge
Average price: Modest
Area: Yorkville
Address: 88 Yorkville Avenue
Toronto, ON M5R 1B9
Phone: (416) 975-4397

#98
Bar 244
Category: Bar, Dance Club
Average price: Inexpensive
Area: Entertainment District, Downtown Core
Address: 244 Adelaide St W
Toronto, ON M5H
Phone: (416) 599-2442

#99
3030
Category: Bar, Music Venues
Average price: Modest
Area: The Junction
Address: 3030 Dundas W
Toronto, ON M6P 1Z3
Phone: (416) 769-5736

#100
The Roy Public House
Category: Pub
Average price: Modest
Area: Leslieville
Address: 894 Queen Street E
Toronto, ON M4M 1J3
Phone: (416) 465-3331

#101
Village Idiot Pub & Grill
Category: Pub
Average price: Modest
Area: Downtown Core
Address: 126 McCaul St
Toronto, ON M5T 1W2
Phone: (416) 597-1175

#102
Tappo Wine Bar & Restaurant
Category: Wine Bar, Canadian
Average price: Expensive
Area: Distillery District
Address: 55 Mill Street
Toronto, ON M5A 3C4
Phone: (647) 430-1111

#103
Hawker Bar
Category: Bar, Asian Fusion
Average price: Modest
Area: Ossington Strip, Trinity Bellwoods, Beaconsfield Village
Address: 164 Ossington Avenue
Toronto, ON M6J 2Z7
Phone: (647) 343-4698

#104
Cherry Cola's Rock N' Rolla Cabaret Lounge
Category: Bar
Average price: Modest
Area: Alexandra Park, Trinity Bellwoods
Address: 200 Bathurst Street
Toronto, ON M5T 2R7
Phone: (416) 703-6969

#105
The Pilot Tavern
Category: Bar
Average price: Modest
Area: Yorkville
Address: 22 Cumberland St
Toronto, ON M4W 1J5
Phone: (416) 923-5716

#106
Lolabar
Category: Lounge, Pub
Average price: Inexpensive
Area: Leslieville
Address: 1173 Dundas Street E
Toronto, ON M4M 3P1
Phone: (416) 849-5331

#107
Duke of Kent
Category: Pub, British
Average price: Modest
Area: Mount Pleasant and Davisville, Yonge and Eglinton
Address: 2315 Yonge St
Toronto, ON M4P 2C6
Phone: (416) 485-9507

#108
Baby Huey
Category: Dance Club, Bar
Average price: Inexpensive
Area: Ossington Strip, Trinity Bellwoods, Beaconsfield Village
Address: 70 Ossington Avenue
Toronto, ON M6J 2Y7
Phone: (416) 419-3832

#109
Clinton's
Category: Pub, Music Venues
Average price: Modest
Area: Koreatown, Bickford Park
Address: 693 Bloor Street W
Toronto, ON M6G 1L5
Phone: (416) 535-9541

#110
Parts & Labour
Category: Bar, Canadian
Average price: Expensive
Area: Parkdale
Address: 1566 Queen St W
Toronto, ON M6R 1A3
Phone: (416) 588-7750

#111
Impatient Theatre Co.
Category: Comedy Club
Average price: Modest
Area: Parkdale, Roncesvalles
Address: 319 Spadina Avenue
Toronto, ON M5T 2E9
Phone: (416) 238-7337

#112
El Mocambo
Category: Music Venues
Average price: Inexpensive
Area: Chinatown, Kensington Market
Address: 464 Spadina Ave
Toronto, ON M5T 2G8
Phone: (647) 748-6969

#113
Squirly's
Category: American, Cocktail Bar
Average price: Modest
Area: Niagara, West Queen West, Trinity Bellwoods
Address: 807 Queen Street W
Toronto, ON M6J 1G1
Phone: (416) 703-0574

#114
The Monarch Tavern
Category: Pub, Gluten-Free, Sandwiches
Average price: Modest
Area: Little Italy
Address: 12 Clinton St
Toronto, ON M6J 2N8
Phone: (416) 531-5833

#115
Les 3 Brasseurs
Category: Pub, Burgers
Average price: Modest
Area: Downtown Core
Address: 275 Yonge St
Toronto, ON M5B 1N8
Phone: (647) 347-6286

#116
Wrongbar
Category: Dance Club, Music Venues
Average price: Modest
Area: Parkdale
Address: 1279 Queen Street W
Toronto, ON M6K 1L6
Phone: (416) 516-8677

#117
Kamasutra Indian Restaurant & Wine Bar
Category: Indian, Wine Bar
Average price: Modest
Area: Mount Pleasant and Davisville
Address: 1522 Bayview Ave
Toronto, ON M4G 3B4
Phone: (416) 489-4899

#118
Wallflower
Category: Canadian, Bar
Average price: Modest
Area: Brockton Village
Address: 1665 Dundas Street W
Toronto, ON M6K
Phone: (647) 352-5605

#119
Tequila Bookworm
Category: Bar, Sandwiches
Average price: Modest
Area: Alexandra Park, Queen Street West
Address: 512 Queen Street W
Toronto, ON M5V 2B3
Phone: (416) 504-2334

#120
East Thirty-Six
Category: Cocktail Bar
Average price: Modest
Area: St. Lawrence, Downtown Core
Address: 36 Wellington Street E
Toronto, ON M5E 1C7
Phone: (647) 350-3636

#121
Stratengers Bar & Restaurant
Category: Dive Bar, Canadian
Average price: Modest
Area: Leslieville
Address: 1130 Queen St E
Toronto, ON M4M 1L1
Phone: (416) 466-8934

#122
Czehoski
Category: Polish, Lounge
Average price: Modest
Area: Niagara, West Queen West, Trinity Bellwoods
Address: 678 Queen Street W
Toronto, ON M6J 1E5
Phone: (416) 366-6111

#123
Brazen Head Irish Pub
Category: Irish, Pub
Average price: Modest
Area: Liberty Village
Address: 165 E Liberty Street
Toronto, ON M6K 3P6
Phone: (416) 535-8787

#124
Thymeless Bar & Grill
Category: Bar, Caribbean
Average price: Inexpensive
Area: Kensington Market
Address: 355 College Street
Toronto, ON M5T 1S5
Phone: (416) 928-0556

#125
TALLBOYS - Craft Beer House
Category: Pub, Canadian
Average price: Modest
Area: Christie Pits, Bickford Park
Address: 838 Bloor Street W
Toronto, ON M6G 1M2
Phone: (416) 535-7486

#126
Woody's
Category: Gay Bar
Average price: Modest
Area: Church-Wellesley Village, Downtown Core
Address: 467 Church St
Toronto, ON M4Y 2C5
Phone: (416) 972-0887

#127
Wide Open
Category: Lounge, Dive Bar, Music Venues
Average price: Inexpensive
Area: Entertainment District, Downtown Core
Address: 139A Spadina Ave
Toronto, ON M5V
Phone: (416) 727-5411

#128
The Piston
Category: Music Venues, Lounge
Average price: Modest
Area: Dovercourt
Address: 937 Bloor St
Toronto, ON M6H 1L5
Phone: (416) 532-3989

#129
Nirvana
Category: Asian Fusion, Bar
Average price: Modest
Area: Kensington Market
Address: 434 College St
Toronto, ON M4W 1A7
Phone: (416) 927-8885

#130
Einstein Cafe & Pub
Category: Pub
Average price: Inexpensive
Area: Downtown Core
Address: 229 College Street
Toronto, ON M5T 1R4
Phone: (416) 597-8346

#131
Revival
Category: Dance Club, Venues
Average price: Modest
Area: Little Italy, Bickford Park
Address: 783 College Street
Toronto, ON M6G 1C5
Phone: (416) 535-7888

#132
The Hoxton
Category: Dance Club, Music Venues
Average price: Modest
Area: Niagara
Address: 69 Bathurst Street
Toronto, ON M5V 1M5
Phone: (416) 456-7321

#133
The Henhouse
Category: Bar
Average price: Inexpensive
Area: Brockton Village
Address: 1532 Dundas Street W
Toronto, ON M6K 1T5
Phone: (416) 534-5939

#134
Wish
Category: Breakfast & Brunch, Canadian
Average price: Modest
Area: Church-Wellesley Village, Downtown Core
Address: 3 Charles Street E
Toronto, ON M4Y 1R9
Phone: (416) 935-0240

#135
The Loose Moose
Category: Sports Bar, Gastropub
Average price: Modest
Area: Downtown Core
Address: 146 Front Street West
Toronto, ON M5J 1G2
Phone: (416) 977-8840

#136
The Wilson 96
Category: Pub, Karaoke
Average price: Inexpensive
Area: Little Italy, Bickford Park
Address: 615 College Street
Toronto, ON M6G 1B4
Phone: (416) 516-3237

#137
Fionn MacCool's
Category: Pub, Irish
Average price: Modest
Area: Church-Wellesley Village, Downtown Core
Address: 235 Bloor Street E
Toronto, ON M4W 3Y3
Phone: (416) 966-3006

#138
Archive
Category: Wine Bar
Average price: Modest
Area: Little Italy, Trinity Bellwoods
Address: 909 Dundas Street W
Toronto, ON M6J 1V9
Phone: (647) 748-0909

#139
Stock Restaurant Bar & Lounge
Category: Canadian, Bar, American
Average price: Exclusive
Area: Financial District, Downtown Core
Address: 325 Bay Street, Floor 31
Toronto, ON M5H 4G3
Phone: (416) 637-5550

#140
Roux
Category: Bar
Average price: Modest
Area: The Junction
Address: 2790 Dundas Street W
Toronto, ON M6P 2J3
Phone: (647) 343-3600

#141
Sneaky Dee's
Category: Tex-Mex, Dive Bar
Average price: Modest
Area: Kensington Market
Address: 431 College Street
Toronto, ON M5T 1T1
Phone: (416) 603-3090

#142
Boo Radley's Junction Bar and Grill
Category: Bar, Barbeque
Average price: Modest
Area: The Junction
Address: 1482 Dupont Street
Toronto, ON M6P
Phone: (416) 516-9992

#143
Dave's... On St Clair
Category: Breakfast & Brunch, Music Venues
Average price: Modest
Area: Wychwood
Address: 730 St Clair Ave W
Toronto, ON M6C 1B3
Phone: (416) 657-3283

#144
Artful Dodger Pub
Category: Pub
Average price: Modest
Area: Church-Wellesley Village, Downtown Core
Address: 10 Isabella Street
Toronto, ON M4Y 1N1
Phone: (416) 964-9511

#145
Hitch
Category: Bar
Average price: Modest
Area: Leslieville
Address: 1216 Queen Street E
Toronto, ON M4M
Phone: (647) 352-7781

#146
Duke of York
Category: Pub
Average price: Modest
Area: The Annex
Address: 39 Prince Arthur Ave
Toronto, ON M5R 1B2
Phone: (416) 964-2441

#147
Velvet Underground
Category: Music Venues, Dance Club
Average price: Inexpensive
Area: Alexandra Park,
Queen Street West
Address: 510 Queen St W
Toronto, ON M5V 2B3
Phone: (416) 504-6688

#148
Hemingway's Restaurant
Category: Bar, American
Average price: Modest
Area: Yorkville
Address: 142 Cumberland St
Toronto, ON M5R 1A8
Phone: (416) 968-2828

#149
Latinada Tapas Restaurant
Category: Latin American,
Music Venues
Average price: Modest
Area: High Park
Address: 1671 Bloor Street W
Toronto, ON M6P 1A6
Phone: (416) 913-9716

#150
The Garrison
Category: Music Venues
Average price: Modest
Area: Little Portugal,
Beaconsfield Village
Address: 1197 Dundas St W
Toronto, ON M6J
Phone: (416) 519-9439

#151
Remington's Men of Steel
Category: Adult Entertainment
Average price: Modest
Area: Ryerson, Downtown Core
Address: 379 Yonge Street
Toronto, ON M5B 1S1
Phone: (416) 977-2160

#152
El Caballito Tequila Bar
Category: Bar, Mexican
Average price: Modest
Area: Entertainment District,
Downtown Core
Address: 220 King St West
Toronto, ON M5H 1K4
Phone: (416) 628-9838

#153
The Ossington
Category: Dive Bar
Average price: Modest
Area: Ossington Strip, Trinity Bellwoods,
Beaconsfield Village
Address: 61 Ossington Avenue
Toronto, ON M6J 2Y9
Phone: (416) 850-0161

#154
Comfort Zone
Category: Dance Club, Music Venues
Average price: Modest
Area: University of Toronto,
Downtown Core
Address: 480 Spadina Avenue
Toronto, ON M5S 2H1
Phone: (416) 975-0909

#155
Spirits Bar & Grill
Category: Pub, American
Average price: Modest
Area: Church-Wellesley Village,
Downtown Core
Address: 642 Church Street
Toronto, ON M4Y 2G3
Phone: (416) 967-0001

#156
Snakes & Lattes
Category: Bar, Cafe
Average price: Inexpensive
Area: Koreatown, Palmerston,
Seaton Village
Address: 600 Bloor Street W
Toronto, ON M6G 1K4
Phone: (647) 342-9229

#157
McSorley's Wonderful Saloon & Grill
Category: American, Sports Bar
Average price: Modest
Area: Mount Pleasant and Davisville
Address: 1544 Bayview Avenue
Toronto, ON M4P 1Y5
Phone: (416) 932-0655

#158
Reds Wine Tavern
Category: Wine Bar, Beer, Wine & Spirits, Seafood
Average price: Expensive
Area: Financial District, Downtown Core
Address: 77 Adelaide St.W.
Toronto, ON M5X 1B1
Phone: (416) 862-7337

#159
Duke's Refresher + Bar
Category: Sports Bar, American
Average price: Modest
Area: Ryerson, Downtown Core
Address: 382 Yonge Street
Toronto, ON M5B 1S8
Phone: (416) 979-8529

#160
The Richmond Rogue
Category: Pub
Average price: Modest
Area: Corktown
Address: 284 Richmond Street E
Toronto, ON M5A 1P4
Phone: (416) 868-0506

#161
The Duke of Devon
Category: Pub
Average price: Modest
Area: Financial District, Downtown Core
Address: 66 Wellington St W
Toronto, ON M4W 1A7
Phone: (416) 642-3853

#162
Gate 403 Bar & Grill
Category: Jazz & Blues, American
Average price: Modest
Area: High Park, Roncesvalles
Address: 403 Roncesvalles Avenue
Toronto, ON M6R 2N1
Phone: (416) 588-2930

#163
Kilgour's Bar Meets Grill
Category: Pub
Average price: Modest
Area: The Annex
Address: 509 Bloor St W
Toronto, ON M5S 1Y2
Phone: (416) 923-7680

#164
The Rose & Crown
Category: Music Venues, Pub
Average price: Modest
Area: Mount Pleasant and Davisville, Yonge and Eglinton
Address: 2335 Yonge St
Toronto, ON M4P 2C8
Phone: (416) 487-7673

#165
Unlovable
Category: Bar
Average price: Inexpensive
Area: Little Portugal, Beaconsfield Village
Address: 1415B Dundas Street W
Toronto, ON M6J 1Y4
Phone: (416) 532-6669

#166
Suits
Category: Lounge
Average price: Expensive
Area: Downtown Core
Address: 325 Bay Street
Toronto, ON M5H 3C2
Phone: (416) 637-5555

#167
The Black Bull
Category: Bar
Average price: Modest
Area: Queen Street West, Downtown Core
Address: 298 Queen Street W
Toronto, ON M5V 2A1
Phone: (416) 593-2766

#168
Zanzibar
Category: Adult Entertainment, Dance Club
Average price: Modest
Area: Ryerson, Downtown Core
Address: 359 Yonge Street
Toronto, ON M5B 1S1
Phone: (416) 977-4642

#169
McGugan's
Category: Pub, Comfort Food, Breakfast & Brunch
Average price: Modest
Area: Leslieville
Address: 1058 Gerrard Street E
Toronto, ON M4M 3A3
Phone: (416) 901-9859

#170
The Ceili Cottage
Category: Irish, Pub
Average price: Modest
Area: Leslieville
Address: 1301 Queen Street East
Toronto, ON M4L 1C2
Phone: (416) 406-1301

#171
Crews And Tangos
Category: Gay Bar
Average price: Expensive
Area: Church-Wellesley Village, Downtown Core
Address: 508 Church Street
Toronto, ON M4Y 2C8
Phone: (647) 349-7469

#172
The Rhino
Category: Bar
Average price: Modest
Area: Parkdale
Address: 1249 Queen St W
Toronto, ON M6K 1L5
Phone: (416) 535-8089

#173
Duffy's Tavern
Category: Pub
Average price: Modest
Area: Brockton Village, Bloordale Village, Wallace Emerson
Address: 1238 Bloor Street W
Toronto, ON M6H 1N3
Phone: (416) 628-0330

#174
Jack Astor's Bar & Grill
Category: Canadian, Sports Bar
Average price: Modest
Area: Downtown Core
Address: 144 Front Street West
Toronto, ON M5J 2L7
Phone: (416) 585-2121

#175
The Irv Gastro Pub
Category: Pub, Burgers
Average price: Modest
Area: Cabbagetown
Address: 195 Carlton Street
Toronto, ON M5A
Phone: (647) 350-4787

#176
Hey Lucy
Category: Bar, Pizza, Italian
Average price: Modest
Area: The Annex
Address: 440 Bloor Street W
Toronto, ON M5R
Phone: (416) 967-9670

#177
Boutique Bar
Category: Bar
Average price: Modest
Area: Church-Wellesley Village, Downtown Core
Address: 506 Church Street
Toronto, ON M4Y 2C8
Phone: (647) 705-0006

#178
Pour Boy Pub
Category: Pub
Average price: Inexpensive
Area: Koreatown, Seaton Village
Address: 666 Manning Ave
Toronto, ON M6G 2W4
Phone: (647) 343-7969

#179
Mr. Pong's Bar
Category: Bar
Average price: Modest
Area: Brockton Village
Address: 1576 Dundas Street W
Toronto, ON M6K 1T5
Phone: (647) 748-6627

#180
Eat My Martini
Category: Lounge
Average price: Inexpensive
Area: Bickford Park
Address: 648 College St
Toronto, ON M6G 1B8
Phone: (416) 516-2549

#181
The Red Room
Category: Indian, Asian Fusion, Pub
Average price: Inexpensive
Area: Chinatown, Kensington Market
Address: 444 Spadina Ave
Toronto, ON M5T 2G8
Phone: (416) 929-9964

#182
PicNic Wine Bar
Category: Wine Bar, Canadian
Average price: Modest
Area: Riverdale
Address: 747 Queen Street E
Toronto, ON M4M 1H3
Phone: (647) 435-5298

#183
The Miller Tavern
Category: Bar
Average price: Expensive
Area: Harbourfront
Address: 31 Bay Street
Toronto, ON M5J 3B2
Phone: (416) 366-5544

#184
Lolita's Lust
Category: Lounge
Average price: Expensive
Area: Greektown, Riverdale
Address: 513 Danforth Avenue
Toronto, ON M4K 1P5
Phone: (416) 465-1751

#185
Poetry Jazz Cafe
Category: Music Venues
Average price: Modest
Area: Kensington Market
Address: 224 Augusta Avenue
Toronto, ON M5T 1M5
Phone: (416) 599-5299

#186
BassLine Music Bar
Category: Bar, Music Venues,
Comfort Food
Average price: Modest
Area: Bickford Park
Address: 865 Bloor Street W
Toronto, ON M6G 1M5
Phone: (416) 732-7513

#187
The Local
Category: Bar
Average price: Modest
Area: High Park, Roncesvalles
Address: 396 Roncesvalles Ave
Toronto, ON M6R 2M9
Phone: (416) 535-6225

#188
PACT
Category: Bar
Average price: Inexpensive
Area: Little Italy
Address: 768 Dundas W
Toronto, ON M6J 1T9
Phone: (647) 240-0738

#189
Crown & Dragon Pub
Category: Pub
Average price: Modest
Area: Yorkville
Address: 890 Yonge Street
Toronto, ON M4W 3P4
Phone: (416) 927-7976

#190
Japas
Category: Bar, Japanese
Average price: Modest
Area: Koreatown, Seaton Village
Address: 692 Bloor Street W
Toronto, ON M6G 1L2
Phone: (647) 748-8847

#191
Ferro Bar & Cafe
Category: Bar, Italian
Average price: Modest
Area: Wychwood
Address: 769 St Clair Avenue W
Toronto, ON M6C 1B4
Phone: (416) 654-9119

#192
The Steady Cafe & Bar
Category: Bar, Vegan,
Breakfast & Brunch
Average price: Modest
Area: Dovercourt, Dufferin Grove
Address: 1051 Bloor Street W
Toronto, ON M6H 1M4
Phone: (416) 536-4162

#193
Brass Taps Pizza Pub
Category: Bar, Pizza
Average price: Modest
Area: Greektown, Riverdale
Address: 493 Danforth Avenue
Toronto, ON M4K 1P5
Phone: (416) 466-3403

#194
Mezzrow's
Category: Pub
Average price: Inexpensive
Area: Parkdale
Address: 1546 Queen St W
Toronto, ON M6R 1A6
Phone: (416) 535-4906

#195
Salvador Darling
Category: Lounge
Average price: Modest
Area: Parkdale
Address: 1237 Queen Street W
Toronto, ON M6K 1L5
Phone: (416) 822-0891

#196
The Wine Bar
Category: Wine Bar, Tapas, Canadian
Average price: Expensive
Area: St. Lawrence
Address: 9 Church Street
Toronto, ON M5E 1M2
Phone: (416) 504-9463

#197
Granite Brewery & Restaurant
Category: Pub, Brewery, American
Average price: Modest
Area: Mount Pleasant and Davisville, Yonge and Eglinton
Address: 245 Eglinton Avenue E
Toronto, ON M4P 3B7
Phone: (416) 322-0723

#198
Bricco Wine Bar
Category: Wine Bar, Italian
Average price: Expensive
Area: The Junction
Address: 3047 Dundas Street W
Toronto, ON M6P
Phone: (416) 901-4536

#199
Duke of Somerset
Category: Pub, British
Average price: Modest
Area: Discovery District, Downtown Core
Address: 655 Bay St
Toronto, ON M5G 2K4
Phone: (416) 640-0921

#200
Spacco Restaurant and Bar
Category: Pool Hall, Italian, Mediterranean
Average price: Modest
Area: Mount Pleasant and Davisville, Yonge and Eglinton
Address: 2415 Yonge St
Toronto, ON M4P 2E7
Phone: (416) 489-4163

#201
Drake One Fifty
Category: Canadian, Brasserie, Cocktail Bar
Average price: Expensive
Area: Financial District, Downtown Core
Address: 150 York Street
Toronto, ON M5H 3S5
Phone: (416) 363-6150

#202
Scallywags
Category: Pub
Average price: Modest
Area: Yonge and St. Clair, Deer Park
Address: 11 St Clair Ave W
Toronto, ON M4V 1K6
Phone: (416) 922-3737

#203
Babaluu
Category: Spanish, Basque, Bar
Average price: Expensive
Area: Yorkville
Address: 136 Yorkville Ave
Toronto, ON M5R 1C2
Phone: (416) 515-0587

#204
Church Aperitivo Bar
Category: Bar, Italian, Music Venues
Average price: Expensive
Area: West Queen West, Beaconsfield Village
Address: 1090 Queen Street W
Toronto, ON M6J 1H7
Phone: (416) 537-1090

#205
The Beaver
Category: Bar, Cafe, Canadian
Average price: Modest
Area: West Queen West, Beaconsfield Village
Address: 1192 Queen St W
Toronto, ON M6J 1J6
Phone: (416) 537-2768

#206
Foggy Dew Irish Pub
Category: Irish, Pub
Average price: Modest
Area: Niagara
Address: 803 King St W
Toronto, ON M5V 1N4
Phone: (416) 703-4042

#207
The Flying Beaver Pubaret
Category: Music Venues, Pub
Average price: Modest
Area: Cabbagetown
Address: 488 Parliament St
Toronto, ON M4X 1P3
Phone: (647) 347-6567

#208
Red Sauce
Category: Cocktail Bar, Italian
Average price: Modest
Area: Palmerston, Bickford Park
Address: 50c Clinton Street
Toronto, ON M6G 2Y3
Phone: (416) 792-6002

#209
Hoops Sports Bar & Grill
Category: Sports Bar
Average price: Modest
Area: Downtown Core
Address: 458 Yonge St
Toronto, ON M4Y 1W9
Phone: (416) 929-3324

#210
Foxes Den Bar & Grill
Category: Pub
Average price: Modest
Area: Discovery District, Downtown Core
Address: 1075 Bay St
Toronto, ON M5S 2B1
Phone: (416) 961-1975

#211
Social Dance Spot
Category: Dance Club, Dance Studio
Average price: Inexpensive
Area: Corso Italia
Address: 1209 Saint Clair Avenue W
Toronto, ON M6E 1B5
Phone: (647) 718-0067

#212
Absolute Comedy
Category: Comedy Club
Average price: Modest
Area: Mount Pleasant and Davisville, Yonge and Eglinton
Address: 2335 Yonge Street
Toronto, ON M4P 2C8
Phone: (416) 486-7700

#213
Farmer's Daughter Eatery
Category: Cocktail Bar, Seafood, Breakfast & Brunch
Average price: Modest
Area: The Junction
Address: 1558 Dupont Street
Toronto, ON M6P 3S6
Phone: (416) 546-0626

#214
Murphy's Law Irish Pub
Category: Pub
Average price: Modest
Area: The Beach, Upper Beach
Address: 1702 Queen St E
Toronto, ON M4L 1G6
Phone: (416) 690-5516

#215
Firkin On Yonge
Category: Pub, Canadian
Average price: Modest
Area: Downtown Core
Address: 207 Yonge Street
Toronto, ON M5B 2H1
Phone: (647) 345-0455

#216
MacKenzies High Park
Category: Pub
Average price: Modest
Area: High Park
Address: 1982 Bloor St W
Toronto, ON M6P 3K9
Phone: (416) 767-7246

#217
Churchill
Category: Bar
Average price: Modest
Area: Dufferin Grove, Little Portugal, Beaconsfield Village
Address: 1212 Dundas St W
Toronto, ON M6J
Phone: (416) 588-4900

#218
The Yukon
Category: Bar
Average price: Modest
Area: Parkdale, Roncesvalles
Address: 1592 Queen Street W
Toronto, ON M6R
Phone: (647) 348-8400

#219
Turf Lounge
Category: Lounge, Canadian
Average price: Expensive
Area: Financial District, Downtown Core
Address: 330 Bay Street
Toronto, ON M5H 2S8
Phone: (416) 367-2111

#220
The Old Nick
Category: Pub, Breakfast & Brunch, Music Venues
Average price: Modest
Area: Riverdale
Address: 123 Danforth Ave
Toronto, ON M4K 1N2
Phone: (416) 461-5546

#221
Remy's Restaurant
Category: Bar, Canadian
Average price: Modest
Area: Yorkville
Address: 115 Yorkville Ave
Toronto, ON M5R 1C1
Phone: (416) 968-9429

#222
Mill Street Beer Hall
Category: Gastropub, Bar, Canadian
Average price: Modest
Area: Distillery District
Address: 21 Tank House Lane
Toronto, ON M5A 3C4
Phone: (416) 681-0338

#223
My Place in the Beach
Category: Pub
Average price: Modest
Area: The Beach
Address: 2066 Queen St E
Toronto, ON M4E 1E5
Phone: (416) 698-9885

#224
Alleycatz Restaurant Jazz Bar
Category: Greek, Canadian, Bar
Average price: Expensive
Area: Mount Pleasant and Davisville, Yonge and Eglinton
Address: 2409 Yonge Street
Toronto, ON M4P 2E7
Phone: (416) 481-6865

#225
Tryst Nightclub
Category: Lounge, Dance Club
Average price: Modest
Area: Entertainment District, Downtown Core
Address: 82 Peter Street
Toronto, ON M5V 2G5
Phone: (416) 588-7978

#226
Courthouse
Category: Bar, Canadian
Average price: Modest
Area: Downtown Core
Address: 57 Adelaide St E
Toronto, ON M5C 1K6
Phone: (416) 214-9379

#227
Amsterdam Bicycle Club
Category: Pub
Average price: Modest
Area: St. Lawrence
Address: 54 The Esplanade
Toronto, ON M5E 1A6
Phone: (416) 864-9996

#228
Bloke & 4th
Category: Dance Club, Canadian, Tapas Bar
Average price: Expensive
Area: Entertainment District, Downtown Core
Address: 401 King St W
Toronto, ON M5V 1K1
Phone: (416) 477-1490

#229
Mullins Irish Pub
Category: Pub
Average price: Modest
Area: Discovery District, Downtown Core
Address: 1033 Bay St
Toronto, ON M4W 1A7
Phone: (416) 963-3000

#230
Cake Night Club
Category: Dance Club, Bar
Average price: Modest
Area: Entertainment District, Downtown Core
Address: 214 Adelaide Street W
Toronto, ON M5H 1L3
Phone: (416) 599-2253

#231
Playa Cabana
Category: Mexican, Bar
Average price: Modest
Area: The Annex
Address: 111 Dupont St
Toronto, ON M5R 1V4
Phone: (416) 929-3911

#232
Oasis Aqualounge
Category: Adult Entertainment, Lounge
Average price: Modest
Area: Downtown Core
Address: 231 Mutual Street
Toronto, ON M5B 2B4
Phone: (416) 599-7665

#233
Scruffy Murphy's Irish Pub
Category: Pub
Average price: Modest
Area: Mount Pleasant and Davisville, Yonge and Eglinton
Address: 150 Eglinton Ave E
Toronto, ON M4P 1E8
Phone: (416) 484-6637

#234
Stones Place
Category: Bar
Average price: Modest
Area: Parkdale
Address: 1255 Queen Street W
Toronto, ON M6K 1L5
Phone: (416) 536-4242

#235
Three Speed
Category: Bar
Average price: Modest
Area: Brockton Village, Bloordale Village, Wallace Emerson
Address: 1163 Bloor St W
Toronto, ON M6H 1M9
Phone: (647) 430-3834

#236
Amsterdam BrewHouse
Category: Bar
Average price: Modest
Area: Harbourfront
Address: 245 Queens Quay W
Toronto, ON M5J 2K9
Phone: (416) 504-1020

#237
Phoenix Concert Theatre
Category: Music Venues
Average price: Modest
Area: Cabbagetown
Address: 410 Sherbourne St
Toronto, ON M4X 1K2
Phone: (416) 323-1251

#238
Two Bite Saloon
Category: Barbeque, Bar
Average price: Modest
Area: Christie Pits, Bickford Park
Address: 840 Bloor Street W
Toronto, ON M6G 1M3
Phone: (416) 536-8682

#239
Osteria Dei Ganzi
Category: Italian, Cocktail Bar, Pizza
Average price: Modest
Area: Church-Wellesley Village, Downtown Core
Address: 504 Jarvis Street
Toronto, ON M4Y 2H6
Phone: (647) 348-6520

#240
Motel
Category: Dive Bar
Average price: Inexpensive
Area: Parkdale
Address: 1235 Queen Street W
Toronto, ON M6K 1L5
Phone: (647) 381-6246

#241
Comedy Bar
Category: Comedy Club
Average price: Modest
Area: Dovercourt, Dufferin Grove
Address: 945 Bloor St W
Toronto, ON M6H 1L5
Phone: (416) 551-6540

#242
Philthy McNastys
Category: Bar
Average price: Modest
Area: Mount Pleasant and Davisville, Yonge and Eglinton
Address: 130 Eglinton Ave E
Toronto, ON M4P 2X9
Phone: (416) 482-2273

#243
The Fox and Firkin
Category: Pub
Average price: Modest
Area: Mount Pleasant and Davisville, Yonge and Eglinton
Address: 51 Eglinton Ave E
Toronto, ON M4P 1G7
Phone: (416) 480-0200

#244
Rakia Bar
Category: Modern European, Lounge
Average price: Expensive
Area: Leslieville
Address: 1402 Queen Street E
Toronto, ON M4L
Phone: (416) 778-8800

#245
Ted's Collision
Category: Dive Bar, Pub
Average price: Inexpensive
Area: Little Italy, Palmerston, Bickford Park
Address: 573 College St
Toronto, ON M6G 1B2
Phone: (416) 533-2430

#246
Not My Dog
Category: Bar, Music Venues
Average price: Inexpensive
Area: Parkdale
Address: 1510 Queen St W
Toronto, ON M6R 1A4
Phone: (416) 532-2397

#247
Fionn MacCool's
Category: Pub
Average price: Modest
Area: St. Lawrence
Address: 70 The Esplanade
Toronto, ON M5E 1R2
Phone: (416) 362-2495

#248
The County Cocktail and Snack Bar
Category: Bar, Cafe
Average price: Modest
Area: Riverdale
Address: 798 Queen Street E
Toronto, ON M4M 1H4
Phone: (416) 781-4743

#249
Gladstone Hotel
Category: Hotel, Lounge
Average price: Modest
Area: West Queen West, Beaconsfield Village
Address: 1214 Queen Street W
Toronto, ON M6J 1J6
Phone: (416) 531-4635

#250
Underground Garage
Category: Dive Bar, Music Venues
Average price: Modest
Area: Entertainment District, Downtown Core
Address: 365 King St W
Toronto, ON M5V 1K1
Phone: (416) 340-0365

#251
Mullins'
Category: Irish, Pub
Average price: Modest
Area: Little Italy, Palmerston
Address: 537 College St W
Toronto, ON M6J 2K2
Phone: (416) 972-6859

#252
Andy Poolhall
Category: Pool Hall, Dance Club
Average price: Modest
Area: Little Italy
Address: 489 College Street
Toronto, ON M6G 1A5
Phone: (416) 923-5300

#253
The Press Club
Category: Lounge
Average price: Modest
Area: Little Italy
Address: 850 Dundas Street W
Toronto, ON M6J 1V5
Phone: (416) 364-7183

#254
Sheesha Lounge and Cafe
Category: Lounge
Average price: Modest
Area: Dovercourt, Dufferin Grove
Address: 901 Bloor St W
Toronto, ON M6G 3T6
Phone: (647) 351-0251

#255
Hogtown Pub & Oysters
Category: Pub, Seafood
Average price: Expensive
Area: Little Italy, Bickford Park
Address: 633 College Street W
Toronto, ON M6G 3A7
Phone: (416) 645-0285

#256
Grossman's Tavern
Category: Dive Bar
Average price: Inexpensive
Area: Chinatown, Kensington Market, Downtown Core
Address: 379 Spadina Ave
Toronto, ON M5T 2G3
Phone: (416) 977-7000

#257
Fox and Fiddle
Category: Pub
Average price: Modest
Area: Yonge and St. Clair, Deer Park
Address: 1535 Yonge St
Toronto, ON M4T 1Z2
Phone: (416) 967-3400

#258
Form Lounge
Category: Bar
Average price: Modest
Area: Koreatown, Palmerston, Seaton Village
Address: 593 Bloor St W
Toronto, ON M6G 1K5
Phone: (416) 516-8998

#259
Eton Tavern
Category: Pub, Comedy Club
Average price: Inexpensive
Area: The Danforth, Greektown
Address: 710 Danforth Avenue
Toronto, ON M4J 1L1
Phone: (416) 466-6161

#260
Smiling Buddha
Category: Jazz & Blues, Comedy Club
Average price: Inexpensive
Area: Dufferin Grove
Address: 961 College Street
Toronto, ON M6H 1A6
Phone: (416) 519-3332

#261
Hard Rock Café
Category: Canadian, Music Venues
Average price: Modest
Area: Downtown Core
Address: 279 Yonge St
Toronto, ON M5B 1N8
Phone: (416) 362-3636

#262
Jack Astor's Bar & Grill
Category: Sports Bar, Canadian
Average price: Modest
Area: Downtown Core
Address: 2 Bloor Street East
Toronto, ON M4W 1A8
Phone: (416) 923-1555

#263
The Raq
Category: Pool Hall, Bar, Dance Club
Average price: Modest
Area: Niagara, West Queen West
Address: 739 Queen St W
Toronto, ON M6J 1G1
Phone: (416) 504-9120

#264
Lion On the Beach
Category: Pub
Average price: Modest
Area: The Beach
Address: 1958 Queen St E
Toronto, ON M4L 1H6
Phone: (416) 690-1984

#265
BerBer SOCIAL
Category: Lounge, Dance Club, Tapas
Average price: Modest
Area: St. Lawrence, Downtown Core
Address: 49 Front Street E
Toronto, ON M5E
Phone: (416) 860-9000

#266
Bull and Firkin
Category: Pub
Average price: Modest
Area: Mount Pleasant and Davisville
Address: 1835 Yonge Street
Toronto, ON M4S 1X8
Phone: (416) 485-2290

#267
Wicked Club
Category: Adult Entertainment
Average price: Expensive
Area: West Queen West, Beaconsfield Village
Address: 1032 Queen Street W
Toronto, ON M6J 1H7
Phone: (416) 669-5582

#268
BMB Karaoke and Music Studio
Category: Specialty School, Karaoke
Average price: Inexpensive
Area: Koreatown, Palmerston
Address: 593 Bloor St W
Toronto, ON M6G 1K5
Phone: (416) 533-8786

#269
Boxcar Social
Category: Wine Bar, Cafe, Coffee & Tea
Average price: Modest
Area: Summer Hill
Address: 1208 Yonge Street
Toronto, ON M4T 1W1
Phone: (416) 792-5873

#270
Fox and Fiddle
Category: Pub
Average price: Modest
Area: Church-Wellesley Village, Downtown Core
Address: 27 Wellesley Street East
Toronto, ON M4Y 1Z2
Phone: (416) 944-9369

#271
Shark Club Sports Bar & Grill
Category: Sports Bar, Lounge, Canadian
Average price: Modest
Area: Ryerson, Downtown Core
Address: 10 Dundas St East
Toronto, ON M5B
Phone: (416) 506-0753

#272
Dominion On Queen Restaurant Bar & Lounge
Category: Lounge
Average price: Modest
Area: Corktown
Address: 500 Queen Street E
Toronto, ON M5A 1T7
Phone: (416) 368-6893

#273
The Sister
Category: Pub, Breakfast & Brunch
Average price: Modest
Area: Parkdale
Address: 1554 Queen Street W
Toronto, ON M6R 1A6
Phone: (416) 532-2570

#274
The Bishop & the Belcher
Category: Pub, British
Average price: Modest
Area: Church-Wellesley Village, Downtown Core
Address: 175 Bloor Street E
Toronto, ON M4W 3R8
Phone: (416) 591-2352

#275
Black Moon Bar & Lounge
Category: Lounge, Beer, Wine & Spirits
Average price: Modest
Area: Financial District, Downtown Core
Address: 67 Richmond Street W
Toronto, ON M5H 2S9
Phone: (416) 603-3100

#276
The Fox
Category: Pub, Gastropub
Average price: Modest
Area: Harbourfront
Address: 35 Bay Street
Toronto, ON M5J 1J5
Phone: (416) 869-3535

#277
Auld Spot Pub
Category: Pub
Average price: Modest
Area: Riverdale
Address: 347 Danforth Ave
Toronto, ON M4K 1N7
Phone: (416) 406-4688

#278
Fionn MacCool's
Category: Pub
Average price: Modest
Area: Financial District, Downtown Core
Address: 181 University Ave
Toronto, ON M5H 3M7
Phone: (416) 363-1944

#279
The Paddock Tavern
Category: Lounge, Canadian, Gastropub
Average price: Inexpensive
Area: Niagara, Queen Street West
Address: 178 Bathurst Street
Toronto, ON M5V 2R4
Phone: (416) 504-9997

#280
Screen Lounge
Category: Lounge, Dance Club
Average price: Expensive
Area: Downtown Core
Address: 20 College St
Toronto, ON M5G 2B3
Phone: (647) 351-2040

#281
College Street Bar
Category: Bar, Italian
Average price: Modest
Area: Little Italy, Palmerston, Bickford Park
Address: 574 College Street
Toronto, ON M6G 1B3
Phone: (416) 521-7200

#282
Firkin on Harbour
Category: Pub
Average price: Modest
Area: Harbourfront
Address: 10 Yonge Street
Toronto, ON M5E 1R4
Phone: (416) 519-9949

#283
The Longest Yard Restaurant
Category: Gastropub, Pub
Average price: Modest
Area: Mount Pleasant and Davisville
Address: 535 Mt Pleasant Road
Toronto, ON M4S 2M5
Phone: (416) 487-6468

#284
Gull & Firkin
Category: Pub
Average price: Modest
Area: The Beach
Address: 1943 Queen Street E
Toronto, ON M4L 1H7
Phone: (416) 693-9337

#285
Fat Cat Wine Bar
Category: Wine Bar
Average price: Expensive
Area: High Park, Roncesvalles
Address: 331 Roncesvalles Ave
Toronto, ON M6R 2M8
Phone: (416) 535-4064

#286
Troika Vodka Boutique
Category: Lounge
Average price: Expensive
Area: St. Lawrence, Downtown Core
Address: 95 King Street E
Toronto, ON M5C 1G3
Phone: (416) 361-0404

#287
Downtown Echo Karaoke Box
Category: Karaoke
Average price: Expensive
Area: Alexandra Park, Chinatown, Downtown Core
Address: 280 Spadina Ave
Toronto, ON M5T 3A5
Phone: (416) 596-6800

#288
Tortilla Flats
Category: Tex-Mex, Mexican, Bar
Average price: Modest
Area: Alexandra Park
Address: 458 Queen St W
Toronto, ON M5V 2A8
Phone: (416) 203-0088

#289
Shakey's Original Bar & Grill
Category: Sports Bar, Canadian
Average price: Modest
Area: Swansea
Address: 2255 Bloor Street W
Toronto, ON M6S 1N8
Phone: (416) 767-0608

#290
Captain Jack
Category: Pub
Average price: Inexpensive
Area: The Beach
Address: 2 Wheeler Avenue
Toronto, ON M4L 3V2
Phone: (416) 691-5433

#291
The Groove Bar & Grill
Category: Pub, Sports Bar, American
Average price: Inexpensive
Area: The Danforth
Address: 1952 Danforth Avenue
Toronto, ON M4C 1J4
Phone: (647) 350-1917

#292
The Keg Steakhouse + Bar
Category: Steakhouse, Bar, Seafood
Average price: Expensive
Area: Mount Pleasant and Davisville, Yonge and Eglinton
Address: 2201 Yonge St
Toronto, ON M4S 2B2
Phone: (416) 484-4646

#293
Old York Bar & Grill
Category: Pub, Breakfast & Brunch
Average price: Modest
Area: Niagara
Address: 167 Niagara St
Toronto, ON M5V 1C9
Phone: (416) 703-9675

#294
Momofuku Nikai
Category: Lounge, Beer, Wine & Spirits
Average price: Expensive
Area: Financial District, Downtown Core
Address: 190 University Avenue
Toronto, ON M5H 0A3
Phone: (647) 253-8000

#295
Overdraught Irish Pub
Category: Irish, Pub
Average price: Modest
Area: Downtown Core
Address: 156 Front St W
Toronto, ON M5J 2L6
Phone: (416) 408-3925

#296
Ascari Enoteca
Category: Italian, Bar
Average price: Expensive
Area: Leslieville
Address: 1111 Queen Street E
Toronto, ON M4M
Phone: (416) 792-4157

#297
The Roncy Public
Category: Lounge, Canadian
Average price: Modest
Area: High Park, Roncesvalles
Address: 390 Roncesvalles Avenue
Toronto, ON M6R 2N1
Phone: (416) 516-8112

#298
The Marquis of Granby
Category: Pub
Average price: Modest
Area: Downtown Core
Address: 418 Church Street
Toronto, ON M5B 2A3
Phone: (416) 599-0418

#299
Domani Restaurant & Wine Bar
Category: Wine Bar, Italian
Average price: Modest
Area: High Park, Roncesvalles
Address: 335 Roncesvalles Ave
Toronto, ON M6R 2M8
Phone: (416) 516-2147

#300
Annex Billiards Club
Category: Pool Hall
Average price: Inexpensive
Area: The Annex
Address: 507 Bloor St W
Toronto, ON M5S 1Y2
Phone: (416) 972-6588

#301
The Dizzy
Category: Pub, Chicken Wings
Average price: Modest
Area: High Park, Roncesvalles
Address: 305 Roncesvalles Ave
Toronto, ON M6R 2M6
Phone: (416) 538-8484

#302
Rhum Corner
Category: Caribbean, Cocktail Bar
Average price: Modest
Area: Little Italy, Trinity Bellwoods
Address: 926 Dundas Street W
Toronto, ON M6J 1W3
Phone: (647) 346-9356

#303
Byzantium
Category: Gay Bar, Canadian
Average price: Expensive
Area: Church-Wellesley Village, Downtown Core
Address: 499 Church St
Toronto, ON M4Y 2C6
Phone: (416) 922-3859

#304
King Rustic
Category: Comfort Food, Seafood, Lounge
Average price: Modest
Area: Niagara
Address: 926 King Street W
Toronto, ON M5V 1P5
Phone: (416) 792-5910

#305
Bite Bar
Category: Bakeries, Cocktail Bar
Average price: Modest
Area: Discovery District, Downtown Core
Address: 57 Elm Street
Toronto, ON M5G 1H3
Phone: (647) 907-4465

#306
The Roosevelt Room Supper Club
Category: French, Bar
Average price: Expensive
Area: Entertainment District, Downtown Core
Address: 328 Adelaide Street West
Toronto, ON M5V 0A5
Phone: (416) 599-9000

#307
Black Swan Tavern
Category: Pub, Music Venues
Average price: Inexpensive
Area: The Danforth
Address: 154 Danforth Avenue
Toronto, ON M4K 1N1
Phone: (416) 469-0537

#308
Freezone Karaoke
Category: Karaoke
Average price: Modest
Area: Koreatown, Bickford Park
Address: 721 Bloor Street W
Toronto, ON M6G 1L5
Phone: (416) 530-2781

#309
Shoeless Joe's
Category: Sports Bar, Canadian
Average price: Modest
Area: Harbourfront
Address: 249 Queens Quay W
Toronto, ON M5J
Phone: (416) 915-7478

#310
The Banknote Bar & Supergrill
Category: Pizza, Pub
Average price: Modest
Area: Niagara
Address: 663 King St W
Toronto, ON M5V 1M5
Phone: (416) 947-0404

#311
The Pour House Irish Pub
Category: Pub, Irish
Average price: Modest
Area: The Annex
Address: 182 Dupont St
Toronto, ON M5R 2E6
Phone: (416) 967-7687

#312
Dark Horse
Category: Pub
Average price: Modest
Area: Swansea
Address: 2401 Bloor St W
Toronto, ON M6S 1P7
Phone: (416) 769-4696

#313
Weldon Park
Category: Bar
Average price: Expensive
Area: Little Italy, Palmerston, Bickford Park
Address: 569 College Street
Toronto, ON M6G 1B1
Phone: (416) 551-7055

#314
Jazz Bistro
Category: Jazz & Blues
Average price: Expensive
Area: Downtown Core
Address: 251 Victoria Street
Toronto, ON M5B 1T8
Phone: (416) 363-5299

#315
Jingles II
Category: Lounge
Average price: Modest
Area: Yonge and St. Clair, Deer Park
Address: 1378 Yonge St
Toronto, ON M4T 1Y5
Phone: (416) 960-1500

#316
The Silver Dollar Room
Category: Music Venues
Average price: Inexpensive
Area: University of Toronto, Downtown Core
Address: 486 Spadina Avenue
Toronto, ON M5S 2H1
Phone: (416) 975-0909

#317
The Roxton
Category: Pub, Canadian
Average price: Modest
Area: Bickford Park
Address: 379 Harbord Street
Toronto, ON M6G 1H8
Phone: (416) 535-8181

#318
Club Paradise
Category: Bar
Average price: Modest
Area: Brockton Village, Wallace Emerson
Address: 1313 Bloor Street W
Toronto, ON M6H 1P1
Phone: (416) 535-0723

#319
751 Lounge
Category: Pub
Average price: Modest
Area: Niagara, West Queen West, Trinity Bellwoods
Address: 751 Queen Street W
Toronto, ON M6J 1G1
Phone: (647) 436-6681

#320
The Danforth Music Hall
Category: Music Venues
Average price: Modest
Area: Riverdale
Address: 147 Danforth Avenue
Toronto, ON M4K 1N2
Phone: (416) 778-8163

#321
Parlour
Category: Venues, Event Space, Lounge, Dance Club
Average price: Expensive
Area: Entertainment District, Downtown Core
Address: 270 Adelaide Street West
Toronto, ON M5H 1Y2
Phone: (416) 408-3666

#322
The Midtown
Category: Dance Club, Canadian
Average price: Inexpensive
Area: Palmerston
Address: 552 College St
Toronto, ON M6G 1B1
Phone: (416) 920-4533

#323
Sangria Lounge
Category: Lounge
Average price: Inexpensive
Area: High Park, Roncesvalles
Address: 145 Roncesvalles Avenue
Toronto, ON M6R 2K9
Phone: (416) 533-9939

#324
The Central
Category: Bar, Music Venues, Canadian
Average price: Modest
Area: Palmerston
Address: 603 Markham St
Toronto, ON M6G 2L7
Phone: (416) 913-4586

#325
Fabulous Bar & Cafe
Category: Dive Bar
Average price: Expensive
Area: Discovery District, Downtown Core
Address: 635 Bay St
Toronto, ON M5G 1M7
Phone: (416) 593-1423

#326
Shangri-La Toronto
Category: Canadian, Lounge
Average price: Exclusive
Area: Downtown Core
Address: 200 Avenue University
Toronto, ON M5H 3C6
Phone: (416) 599-0333

#327
Zipperz
Category: Nightlife
Average price: Modest
Area: Church-Wellesley Village, Downtown Core
Address: 72 Carlton Street
Toronto, ON M5B 1L6
Phone: (416) 921-0066

#328
Lula Lounge
Category: Latin American, Music Venues
Average price: Modest
Area: Brockton Village
Address: 1585 Dundas Street W
Toronto, ON M6K 1T9
Phone: (416) 588-0307

#329
The Jason George
Category: Pub
Average price: Modest
Area: Corktown, St. Lawrence
Address: 100 Front St E
Toronto, ON M5A 1E1
Phone: (416) 363-7100

#330
The Devil's Advocate
Category: Pub
Average price: Modest
Area: Discovery District, Downtown Core
Address: 655 Bay St
Toronto, ON M5G
Phone: (416) 595-1105

#331
Il Gatto Nero
Category: Italian, Nightlife
Average price: Modest
Area: Bickford Park
Address: 720 College Street
Toronto, ON M6G 1C4
Phone: (416) 536-3132

#332
O'Grady's Tap & Grill
Category: Pub, Irish
Average price: Modest
Area: University of Toronto, Downtown Core
Address: 171 College Street
Toronto, ON M5T 1P7
Phone: (416) 596-0327

#333
Ice Lounge
Category: Lounge
Average price: Modest
Area: The Danforth, Greektown
Address: 785 Carlaw Avenue
Toronto, ON M4K 3L1
Phone: (416) 469-6749

#334
Sopra Upper Lounge
Category: Lounge
Average price: Expensive
Area: The Annex
Address: 265 Davenport Road
Toronto, ON M5R 1J9
Phone: (416) 929-9006

#335
Shibui Robata Bar
Category: Japanese, Bar
Average price: Expensive
Area: Entertainment District, Downtown Core
Address: 230 Adelaide Street W
Toronto, ON M5H
Phone: (647) 748-3211

#336
N'awlins Jazz Bar & Dining
Category: American, Jazz & Blues
Average price: Expensive
Area: Entertainment District, Downtown Core
Address: 299 King St W
Toronto, ON M5V 1J5
Phone: (416) 595-1958

#337
Camp 4
Category: Bar
Average price: Modest
Area: Little Portugal, Beaconsfield Village
Address: 1173 Dundas Street W Toronto, ON M6J 1X4
Phone: (416) 546-6780

#338
Coda
Category: Dance Club
Average price: Modest
Area: Seaton Village
Address: 794 Bathurst Street Toronto, ON M5R 3G1
Phone: (416) 536-0346

#339
Adelaide Hall
Category: Music Venues, Performing Arts
Average price: Expensive
Area: Entertainment District, Downtown Core
Address: 250 Adelaide Street W Toronto, ON M5H 1X6
Phone: (416) 205-1234

#340
Remarks Bar & Grill
Category: Pub
Average price: Modest
Area: East York
Address: 1026 Coxwell Avenue Toronto, ON M4J 2W9
Phone: (416) 429-9889

#341
Lot 16
Category: Lounge
Average price: Modest
Area: West Queen West, Beaconsfield Village
Address: 1136 Queen W Toronto, ON M6J 1J3
Phone: (416) 531-6556

#342
Amnesia Bar & Grill
Category: Dive Bar
Average price: Modest
Area: The Annex
Address: 526 Bloor Street W Toronto, ON M5S 1Y3
Phone: (416) 538-3335

#343
Moskito Bite
Category: Dance Club
Average price: Modest
Area: Kensington Market
Address: 423 College Street Toronto, ON M5T 1S9
Phone: (416) 862-2323

#344
Wildfire Steakhouse & Wine Bar
Category: Wine Bar, Steakhouse
Average price: Expensive
Area: St. Lawrence, Downtown Core
Address: 8 Colborne St Toronto, ON M5E 1E1
Phone: (416) 350-8188

#345
Johnny Jackson
Category: Pub, American, Music Venues
Average price: Inexpensive
Area: Little Italy, Palmerston, Bickford Park
Address: 587 College Street Toronto, ON M6G 1A9
Phone: (416) 546-0330

#346
Gorhegorhe
Category: Karaoke
Average price: Expensive
Area: Koreatown, Bickford Park, Seaton Village
Address: 708 Bloor Street W Toronto, ON M6G 1L4
Phone: (416) 916-2720

#347
Duke of Westminster
Category: Pub
Average price: Modest
Area: Financial District, Downtown Core
Address: 77 Adelaide Street W Toronto, ON M5X 1A6
Phone: (416) 368-2761

#348
Tilted Kilt Pub & Eatery
Category: Sports Bar, American, Pub
Average price: Modest
Area: St. Lawrence
Address: 38 The Esplanade Toronto, ON M5E 1A1
Phone: (416) 364-3764

#349
The Duke Live
Category: Sports Bar, Karaoke, Music Venues
Average price: Modest
Area: Leslieville
Address: 1225 Queen Street E
Toronto, ON M4M 1L6
Phone: (416) 463-5302

#350
The Charlotte Room
Category: Pool Hall, Lounge, Venues
Average price: Modest
Area: Entertainment District, Downtown Core
Address: 19 Charlotte Street
Toronto, ON M5V 2H5
Phone: (416) 591-1738

#351
Cabin Five
Category: Dance Club
Average price: Modest
Area: Entertainment District, Downtown Core
Address: 225 Richmond Street W
Toronto, ON M5V 1W2
Phone: (416) 979-3000

#352
Hugh's Room
Category: Music Venues
Average price: Expensive
Area: High Park, Roncesvalles
Address: 2261 Dundas St W
Toronto, ON M6R 1X6
Phone: (416) 531-6604

#353
St. Louis Bar and Grill
Category: Chicken Wings, Pub
Average price: Modest
Area: The Annex
Address: 376 Bloor Street W
Toronto, ON M5R
Phone: (416) 925-6689

#354
Duke of Gloucester
Category: Pub
Average price: Modest
Area: Downtown Core
Address: 649 Yonge St
Toronto, ON M4Y 1Z9
Phone: (416) 961-9704

#355
The Strathcona Hotel
Category: Pub, Hotel
Average price: Modest
Area: Financial District, Downtown Core
Address: 60 York St
Toronto, ON M5J 1S8
Phone: (416) 363-3321

#356
Duke of Richmond Pub
Category: Pub
Average price: Modest
Area: Downtown Core
Address: 20 Queen St W
Toronto, ON M5H 3R3
Phone: (416) 340-7887

#357
Tota Lounge
Category: Lounge
Average price: Inexpensive
Area: Niagara, West Queen West, Trinity Bellwoods
Address: 592 Queen Street W
Toronto, ON M6J 1E6
Phone: (416) 580-9983

#358
Darwin Bistro & Bar
Category: Bar, Canadian
Average price: Expensive
Area: Little Italy, Bickford Park
Address: 651 College Street
Toronto, ON M6G 3A7
Phone: (647) 348-9347

#359
The Office Pub
Category: Pub, Sports Bar, American
Average price: Modest
Area: Entertainment District, Downtown Core
Address: 117 John Street
Toronto, ON M5V 2E2
Phone: (416) 977-1900

#360
Bar Milano
Category: Italian, Pizza, Bar
Average price: Modest
Area: Harbourfront
Address: 207 Queens Quay W
Toronto, ON M5J 1A7
Phone: (416) 306-0424

#361
Hoops
Category: Sports Bar
Average price: Modest
Area: Niagara, West Queen West, Trinity Bellwoods
Address: 735 Queen Street W
Toronto, ON M6J 1E5
Phone: (416) 800-8864

#362
StrangeLove
Category: Dance Club
Average price: Modest
Area: Little Italy, Palmerston, Bickford Park
Address: 587 College Street
Toronto, ON M6G 1B2
Phone: (416) 588-7625

#363
Rockwood Nightclub
Category: Lounge, Dance Club
Average price: Modest
Area: Entertainment District, Downtown Core
Address: 31 Mercer Street
Toronto, ON M5V 1H2
Phone: (416) 979-7373

#364
The Social Bar & Nightclub
Category: Dance Club
Average price: Modest
Area: West Queen West, Beaconsfield Village
Address: 1100 Queen Street W
Toronto, ON M6J 1A9
Phone: (416) 532-4474

#365
Paully's Pub
Category: Bar
Average price: Inexpensive
Area: Summer Hill
Address: 1240 Yonge Street
Toronto, ON M4T 1W5
Phone: (416) 921-7782

#366
Media Bar
Category: Dance Club
Average price: Modest
Area: Entertainment District, Downtown Core
Address: 77 Peter Street
Toronto, ON M5V 2G4
Phone: (416) 260-6111

#367
Gabby's
Category: Pub
Average price: Modest
Area: The Beach
Address: 2076 Queen St E
Toronto, ON M4E 1E1
Phone: (416) 699-5699

#368
Saviari Tea & Cocktail Lounge
Category: Lounge
Average price: Expensive
Area: Niagara
Address: 926 King Street W
Toronto, ON M7A 2A9
Phone: (647) 349-8077

#369
Grace O'Malley's
Category: Pub, American
Average price: Modest
Area: Entertainment District, Downtown Core
Address: 14 Duncan Street
Toronto, ON M5H 3G8
Phone: (416) 596-1444

#370
Jekyl and Hyde Pub
Category: Pub, Pool Hall, Karaoke
Average price: Modest
Area: High Park
Address: 2340 Dundas St W
Toronto, ON M6P 4A9
Phone: (416) 535-0547

#371
D.W. Alexander
Category: Cocktail Bar
Average price: Modest
Area: St. Lawrence, Downtown Core
Address: 19 Church Street
Toronto, ON M5E 1M2
Phone: (416) 364-8368

#372
CAMERA
Category: Cinema, Art Galleries, Bar
Average price: Modest
Area: West Queen West, Beaconsfield Village
Address: 1026 Queen Street W
Toronto, ON M6J 1H6
Phone: (416) 530-0011

#373
Urban House Cafe
Category: Pub, Canadian, Sandwiches
Average price: Modest
Area: Church-Wellesley Village, Downtown Core
Address: 4 Dundonald Street
Toronto, ON M4Y 1K2
Phone: (416) 915-0113

#374
The Keg Steakhouse + Bar
Category: Steakhouse, Bar, Seafood
Average price: Expensive
Area: St. Lawrence
Address: 26 The Esplanade
Toronto, ON M5E 1A7
Phone: (416) 367-0685

#375
Randolph Theatre
Category: Music Venues
Average price: Modest
Area: Palmerston
Address: 736 Bathurst St.
Toronto, ON M5S 2R4
Phone: (855) 985-5000

#376
Mayday Malone's Pub & Ristorante
Category: Italian, Pub
Average price: Modest
Area: Seaton Village
Address: 1078 Bathurst Street
Toronto, ON M5R 3G9
Phone: (416) 531-8064

#377
McQueen's
Category: Pub
Average price: Modest
Area: Leslieville
Address: 993 Queen Street E
Toronto, ON M5V
Phone: (647) 748-7740

#378
McVeigh's New Windsor Tavern
Category: Pub
Average price: Modest
Area: Corktown, Downtown Core
Address: 124 Church St
Toronto, ON M5C 2G8
Phone: (416) 364-9698

#379
Hey Lucy
Category: Bar, Italian, Pizza
Average price: Modest
Area: Entertainment District, Downtown Core
Address: 295 King Street W
Toronto, ON M5V 1J5
Phone: (416) 979-1010

#380
Mike's Place
Category: American, Wine Bar
Average price: Exclusive
Area: Downtown Core
Address: 1408-15 Richmond Street East
Toronto, ON M5C 1N2
Phone: (416) 382-5968

#381
Teranga African Bar & Restaurant
Category: African, Bar
Average price: Modest
Area: Kensington Market
Address: 159 Augusta Avenue
Toronto, ON M5T 2L4
Phone: (416) 849-9777

#382
Bambi's
Category: Dive Bar, Karaoke
Average price: Modest
Area: Little Portugal
Address: 1265 Dundas Street W
Toronto, ON M6J
Phone: (647) 351-1100

#383
Rush Lane & Co
Category: Cocktail Bar, Gastropub
Average price: Modest
Area: Alexandra Park
Address: 563 Queen Street W
Toronto, ON M5V 2B3
Phone: (416) 551-7540

#384
Baltic Avenue
Category: Lounge, Dance Club
Average price: Modest
Area: Bickford Park
Address: 875 Bloor Street W
Toronto, ON M6H 1M4
Phone: (647) 898-5324

#385
Paaeez
Category: Hookah Bar
Average price: Expensive
Area: Little Italy, Palmerston, Bickford Park
Address: 569 College St
Toronto, ON M6G 1B2
Phone: (416) 537-0767

#386
On Cue Bar & Billiards
Category: Pool Hall, Bar
Average price: Modest
Area: Bloor-West Village
Address: 349 Jane St
Toronto, ON M6S 3Z3
Phone: (416) 761-9245

#387
The Tap House
Category: Gastropub, Music Venues
Average price: Modest
Area: Entertainment District, Downtown Core
Address: 250 Adelaide Street W
Toronto, ON M5H
Phone: (416) 205-1234

#388
This End Up
Category: Sandwiches, Bar
Average price: Modest
Area: Dufferin Grove, Little Portugal, Beaconsfield Village
Address: 1454 Dundas Street W
Toronto, ON M6J 1Y6
Phone: (647) 347-8700

#389
The Parkdale Drink
Category: Lounge, Sushi Bar
Average price: Modest
Area: Parkdale
Address: 1292 Queen Street W
Toronto, ON M6K 1L4
Phone: (416) 778-8822

#390
Gabby's
Category: Bar
Average price: Modest
Area: Roncesvalles
Address: 157 Roncesvalles Ave
Toronto, ON M6R 2L3
Phone: (416) 533-9000

#391
On The Rocks
Category: Chinese, Dive Bar
Average price: Modest
Area: Corktown, St. Lawrence
Address: 169 Front St E
Toronto, ON M5A 3Z4
Phone: (416) 862-2901

#392
Legends Bar & Eatery
Category: Sports Bar, Dive Bar
Average price: Modest
Area: Wychwood
Address: 517 St Clair Ave W
Toronto, ON M6C 1A1
Phone: (416) 535-2715

#393
Empire Restaurant and Lounge
Category: Lounge, Canadian
Average price: Expensive
Area: Yorkville
Address: 50 Cumberland Street
Toronto, ON M4W 1J5
Phone: (416) 840-8440

#394
The Spotted Dick
Category: Pub
Average price: Modest
Area: Church-Wellesley Village, Downtown Core
Address: 81 Bloor Street East
Toronto, ON M4W 1A9
Phone: (416) 929-3425

#395
Shoeless Joe's
Category: Sports Bar
Average price: Modest
Area: Entertainment District, Downtown Core
Address: 276 King St W
Toronto, ON M5V 3C6
Phone: (416) 596-4203

#396
Suite 106 and Wet Bar
Category: Lounge
Average price: Exclusive
Area: Entertainment District, Downtown Core
Address: 106 Peter Street
Toronto, ON M5V 2G7
Phone: (416) 599-2224

#397
The Foundation Room
Category: Lounge, Dance Club
Average price: Modest
Area: St. Lawrence, Downtown Core
Address: 19 Church Street
Toronto, ON M5E 1M2
Phone: (416) 364-8368

#398
The Antler Room
Category: Music Venues, Sports Bar
Average price: Modest
Area: Downtown Core
Address: 146 Front Street West
Toronto, ON M5J 1G2
Phone: (416) 977-8840

#399
The Grover Pub & Grub
Category: Pub
Average price: Modest
Area: Upper Beach
Address: 676 Kingston Rd
Toronto, ON M4E 1R4
Phone: (416) 691-9200

#400
Plaza Flamingo Banquet & Catering
Category: Caterer, Dance Club, Breakfast & Brunch
Average price: Modest
Area: Kensington Market
Address: 423 College Street
Toronto, ON M5T 1T1
Phone: (416) 603-8884

#401
Le Petit Castor
Category: Lounge
Average price: Expensive
Area: Summer Hill
Address: 1118 Yonge St
Toronto, ON M4W 2L6
Phone: (416) 968-7366

#402
Cinema Nightclub
Category: Dance Club
Average price: Exclusive
Area: Liberty Village
Address: 135 Liberty Street
Toronto, ON M6K 3H5
Phone: (416) 588-2888

#403
Loons Restaurant & Pub
Category: Pub, American
Average price: Modest
Area: High Park, Roncesvalles
Address: 416 Roncesvalles Avenue
Toronto, ON M6R 2N2
Phone: (416) 535-2196

#404
The Wallace Gastropub
Category: Pub
Average price: Modest
Area: Mount Pleasant and Davisville
Address: 1954 Yonge St
Toronto, ON M4S 1Z4
Phone: (416) 489-3500

#405
Mata Petisco Bar
Category: Brazilian, Bar, Latin American
Average price: Modest
Area: Parkdale, Roncesvalles
Address: 1690 Queen Street W
Toronto, ON M6R 1B3
Phone: (647) 691-0234

#406
Black Knight Restaurant & Tavern
Category: Breakfast & Brunch, Dive Bar
Average price: Inexpensive
Area: Dufferin Grove
Address: 858 College St
Toronto, ON M6H 1A2
Phone: (416) 536-1877

#407
Gabby's Bistro
Category: Pub
Average price: Modest
Area: Mount Pleasant and Davisville
Address: 383 Eglinton Ave E
Toronto, ON M4P 1M5
Phone: (416) 484-4101

#408
May
Category: Music Venues, Lounge
Average price: Modest
Area: Little Italy, Trinity Bellwoods
Address: 876 Dundas Street W
Toronto, ON M6J 1V7
Phone: (416) 568-5510

#409
House of Lancaster II
Category: Adult Entertainment
Average price: Modest
Area: Brockton Village, Bloordale Village, Wallace Emerson
Address: 1215 Bloor St W
Toronto, ON M6H
Phone: (416) 534-2385

#410
Blue Moon Pub
Category: Pub
Average price: Inexpensive
Area: Riverdale
Address: 725 Queen Street E
Toronto, ON M4M 1H1
Phone: (416) 463-8868

#411
Food & Liquor
Category: Bar, Asian Fusion
Average price: Modest
Area: Parkdale, Roncesvalles
Address: 1610 Queen St W
Toronto, ON M6R 1A8
Phone: (647) 748-7113

#412
Linsmore Hotel
Category: Hotel, Bar
Average price: Inexpensive
Area: The Danforth
Address: 1298 Av Danforth
Toronto, ON M4J 1M6
Phone: (416) 466-5130

#413
Wild Indigo
Category: Bar
Average price: Modest
Area: Little Italy, Bickford Park
Address: 607 College Street
Toronto, ON M6G 1B5
Phone: (416) 536-8797

#414
Owls Club
Category: Bar
Average price: Inexpensive
Area: Dovercourt
Address: 847 Dovercourt Rd
Toronto, ON M6H 2X4
Phone: (416) 532-6920

#415
Fox and Fiddle
Category: Pub
Average price: Modest
Area: City Place
Address: 17 Fort York Boulevard
Toronto, ON M5V 3Y2
Phone: (416) 623-0390

#416
Black Eagle
Category: Gay Bar
Average price: Modest
Area: Church-Wellesley Village, Downtown Core
Address: 457 Church St
Toronto, ON M4Y 2C5
Phone: (416) 413-1219

#417
Monica's Bar and Grill
Category: Dive Bar, Karaoke
Average price: Inexpensive
Area: Christie Pits, Bickford Park
Address: 881 Bloor Street W
Toronto, ON M6G 1M2
Phone: (647) 341-8885

#418
Lola
Category: Bar
Average price: Inexpensive
Area: Kensington Market
Address: 40 Kensington Avenue
Toronto, ON M5T 2J9
Phone: (416) 348-8645

#419
Metropolitan Resto Bar
Category: Italian, Brasserie, Cocktail Bar
Average price: Modest
Area: Downtown Core
Address: 20 Victoria St
Toronto, ON M5C
Phone: (416) 868-6748

#420
The Abbey Pub & Steak House
Category: Pub, Steakhouse
Average price: Modest
Area: Dufferin Grove
Address: 989 College St
Toronto, ON M6H 1A6
Phone: (416) 530-5954

#421
Gravity SoundBar
Category: Dance Club
Average price: Modest
Area: Entertainment District, Downtown Core
Address: 296 Richmond Street W
Toronto, ON M5V 1X2
Phone: (416) 977-8900

#422
Local Kitchen & Winebar
Category: Wine Bar, Canadian, Italian
Average price: Expensive
Area: Parkdale, Roncesvalles
Address: 1710 Queen Street W
Toronto, ON M6N
Phone: (416) 534-6700

#423
Carens Wine and Cheese Bar
Category: Wine Bar, French
Average price: Expensive
Area: Yorkville
Address: 158 Cumberland St
Toronto, ON M5R 1A8
Phone: (416) 962-5158

#424
Rails & Ales Billards Lounge
Category: Pool Hall
Average price: Inexpensive
Area: The Danforth
Address: 1106 Danforth Avenue
Toronto, ON M4J 1L5
Phone: (416) 462-9555

#425
SpeakEasy 21
Category: Bar
Average price: Expensive
Area: Downtown Core
Address: 21 Adelaide St W
Toronto, ON M5H
Phone: (416) 601-0210

#426
1st Thursdays at the AGO
Category: Bar
Average price: Modest
Area: Downtown Core
Address: 317 Dundas Street W
Toronto, ON M5T 1G4
Phone: (416) 977-0414

#427
Red Cranberries Restaurant
Category: Bar
Average price: Modest
Area: Cabbagetown
Address: 601 Parliament St
Toronto, ON M4X 1P9
Phone: (416) 925-6330

#428
Cornerstone Pub
Category: Pub
Average price: Modest
Area: Little Italy
Address: 537 College St W
Toronto, ON M6G 1A9
Phone: (647) 430-7111

#429
Li'ly Resto Lounge
Category: Italian, Dance Club, Lounge
Average price: Modest
Area: Little Italy, Bickford Park
Address: 656 College St
Toronto, ON M6G 1B8
Phone: (416) 532-0419

#430
Statler's Lounge
Category: Lounge
Average price: Modest
Area: Church-Wellesley Village, Downtown Core
Address: 471 Church Street
Toronto, ON M4Y 2C5
Phone: (416) 925-0341

#431
The Annex Wreckroom
Category: Bar
Average price: Inexpensive
Area: Seaton Village
Address: 794 Bathurst St
Toronto, ON M5R 3G1
Phone: (416) 536-0346

#432
The Pint House
Category: Sports Bar, Diner, Breakfast & Brunch
Average price: Modest
Area: Downtown Core
Address: 678 Yonge Street
Toronto, ON M4Y 2A6
Phone: (416) 962-6092

#433
The Dog's Bollocks
Category: Pub, Canadian, Karaoke
Average price: Inexpensive
Area: Niagara, West Queen West
Address: 817 Queen Street W
Toronto, ON M6J 1G1
Phone: (647) 350-6496

#434
Maison Mercer
Category: Dance Club, Music Venues
Average price: Expensive
Area: Entertainment District, Downtown Core
Address: 15 Mercer Street
Toronto, ON M5V 3C6
Phone: (416) 341-8777

#435
Porteree
Category: Pub, Italian, Indian
Average price: Modest
Area: Little Italy, Palmerston, Bickford Park
Address: 583 College Street
Toronto, ON M6G 1B2
Phone: (416) 532-1250

#436
Planet of Sound
Category: Electronics, Jazz & Blues
Average price: Exclusive
Area: Corktown
Address: 263 Queen St E
Toronto, ON M5A 1S6
Phone: (416) 601-1313

#437
The Kathedral
Category: Music Venues
Average price: Modest
Area: Alexandra Park, Niagara, Queen Street West, West Queen West, Trinity Bellwoods
Address: 651 Queen Street W
Toronto, ON M5V 2B7
Phone: (416) 504-6699

#438
Nocturne
Category: Bar, Music Venues
Average price: Expensive
Area: Alexandra Park
Address: 550 Queen Street W
Toronto, ON M5V 2B5
Phone: (416) 504-2178

#439
Wild Wing on King
Category: Chicken Wings, Karaoke
Average price: Modest
Area: Niagara
Address: 675 King Street W
Toronto, ON M5V 1M9
Phone: (416) 777-9464

#440
Dora Keogh Irish Pub
Category: Pub, Irish
Average price: Modest
Area: Riverdale
Address: 141 Danforth Ave
Toronto, ON M4K 1N2
Phone: (416) 778-1804

#441
Church St. Garage
Category: Bar, Canadian
Average price: Modest
Area: Church-Wellesley Village, Downtown Core
Address: 477 Church Street
Toronto, ON M4Y 2C6
Phone: (647) 352-5508

#442
Elephant & Castle
Category: British, Pub
Average price: Modest
Area: Entertainment District, Downtown Core
Address: 212 King Street West
Toronto, ON M5H 1K5
Phone: (416) 598-4455

#443
Mana Bar & Lounge
Category: Lounge, Dance Club
Average price: Modest
Area: Bickford Park
Address: 722 College Street
Toronto, ON M6G 1C4
Phone: (416) 537-9292

#444
Cube
Category: Dance Club
Average price: Modest
Area: Entertainment District, Queen Street West, Downtown Core
Address: 314 Queen Street West
Toronto, ON M5V 2A4
Phone: (416) 263-0330

#445
The City
Category: Dance Club
Average price: Modest
Area: Entertainment District, Downtown Core
Address: 296 Richmond St W
Toronto, ON M5V 1X2
Phone: (416) 977-8900

#446
Gabby's
Category: Fish & Chips, Pub, Canadian
Average price: Modest
Area: The Junction
Address: 3026 Dundas Street W
Toronto, ON M6P 1Z2
Phone: (416) 766-3026

#447
Grasslands
Category: Vegan, Lounge, European
Average price: Modest
Area: Alexandra Park
Address: 478 Queen Street W
Toronto, ON M5V 2B4
Phone: (416) 504-5127

#448
Teatro Restaurant
Category: Italian, Lounge
Average price: Modest
Area: Little Italy, Palmerston
Address: 505 College Street
Toronto, ON M6G 1A5
Phone: (416) 972-1475

#449
Churrasqueira Do Sardinha
Category: Portuguese, French, Wine Bar
Average price: Inexpensive
Area: Little Italy, Bickford Park
Address: 707 College Street W
Toronto, ON M6G 1C2
Phone: (416) 531-1120

#450
XS Nightclub
Category: Dance Club
Average price: Modest
Area: Entertainment District, Downtown Core
Address: 261 Richmond Street West
Toronto, ON M5V
Phone: (416) 598-1632

#451
Christie Pits Pub
Category: Pub
Average price: Modest
Area: Christie Pits, Bickford Park
Address: 814 Bloor Street W
Toronto, ON M6G 1M1
Phone: (416) 535-8287

#452
Epique Lounge
Category: Nightlife
Average price: Modest
Area: Yorkville
Address: 120 Cumberland Street
Toronto, ON M5R 1A6
Phone: (416) 880-8940

#453
The Last Temptation
Category: Bar
Average price: Inexpensive
Area: Kensington Market
Address: 12 Kensington Avenue
Toronto, ON M5T 2J7
Phone: (416) 599-2551

#454
Ole Ole
Category: Mexican, Wine Bar
Average price: Modest
Area: Corktown, Downtown Core
Address: 169 King St E
Toronto, ON M5A 1J4
Phone: (416) 363-9000

#455
Cafe Restaurant Peppers
Category: Bar, American
Average price: Inexpensive
Area: Wallace Emerson
Address: 189 Wallace Ave
Toronto, ON M6H 1V5
Phone: (416) 531-3146

#456
OurHouse
Category: Bar
Average price: Modest
Area: Little Portugal, Ossington Strip, Trinity Bellwoods, Beaconsfield Village
Address: 214 Ossington Ave
Toronto, ON M6J 2Z7
Phone: (647) 341-4477

#457
8090 KTV
Category: Pub, Karaoke
Average price: Expensive
Area: Kensington Market
Address: 530 Dundas Street W
Toronto, ON M5T 1H3
Phone: (647) 973-8090

#458
Little Anthony's
Category: Bar, Italian
Average price: Modest
Area: Financial District, Downtown Core
Address: 121 Richmond Street W
Toronto, ON M5H 3K6
Phone: (416) 368-2223

#459
Monarchs Pub
Category: Pub
Average price: Modest
Area: Downtown Core
Address: 33 Gerrard Street W
Toronto, ON M5G 1Z4
Phone: (416) 585-4352

#460
Salute Piano Bar
Category: Piano Bar
Average price: Modest
Area: Yorkville
Address: 29 Bellair Street
Toronto, ON M5R 3N7
Phone: (647) 748-1770

#461
St. Louis Bar and Grill
Category: Pub, Canadian
Average price: Modest
Area: The Beach
Address: 1963 Queen Street E
Toronto, ON M4L 1H9
Phone: (416) 637-7427

#462
Churchmouse & Firkin
Category: Pub, British
Average price: Modest
Area: Church-Wellesley Village, Downtown Core
Address: 475 Church Street
Toronto, ON M4Y 2C5
Phone: (416) 927-1735

#463
Rivoli Cafe & Club
Category: Pool Hall, Music Venues
Average price: Modest
Area: Entertainment District, Queen Street West, Downtown Core
Address: 334 Queen St W
Toronto, ON M5V 2A2
Phone: (416) 596-1908

#464
Vip Billiard Club
Category: Pool Hall
Average price: Modest
Area: Ryerson, Downtown Core
Address: 385 Yonge St
Toronto, ON M5B 1S1
Phone: (416) 977-1011

#465
Annie's Bar & Grill
Category: Bar
Average price: Modest
Area: Corktown
Address: 372 Queen Street E
Toronto, ON M5A 1T1
Phone: (416) 366-3366

#466
Copacabana Brazilian Steak House
Category: Brazilian, Bar, Barbeque
Average price: Expensive
Area: Entertainment District, Downtown Core
Address: 230 Adelaide Street W
Toronto, ON M5H
Phone: (647) 748-3211

#467
Riva
Category: Italian, Lounge
Average price: Modest
Area: Little Italy, Palmerston
Address: 584 College St
Toronto, ON M6G
Phone: (416) 588-7377

#468
The Whippoorwill Restaurant & Tavern
Category: Canadian, Cocktail Bar
Average price: Modest
Area: Brockton Village, Bloordale Village
Address: 1285 Bloor St W
Toronto, ON M6H 1N7
Phone: (416) 530-2999

#469
The Court Jester Pub
Category: Pub
Average price: Modest
Area: Greektown, Riverdale
Address: 609 Danforth Ave
Toronto, ON M4K 1R2
Phone: (416) 465-6247

#470
Burgundy's Bar & Eatery 780
Category: Pub, Mediterranean
Average price: Modest
Area: Yorkville, Downtown Core
Address: 780 Yonge Street
Toronto, ON M4Y 2B6
Phone: (416) 924-1186

#471
ZippersZ
Category: Gay Bar
Average price: Modest
Area: Church-Wellesley Village, Downtown Core
Address: 72 Carlton Street
Toronto, ON M5B
Phone: (416) 921-0066

#472
The Fox & Fiddle
Category: Pub
Average price: Modest
Area: Greektown, Riverdale
Address: 535 Danforth Ave
Toronto, ON M4K 1P7
Phone: (416) 462-9830

#473
Imperial Pub
Category: Pub
Average price: Modest
Area: Ryerson, Downtown Core
Address: 58 Dundas Street E
Toronto, ON M5B 1C7
Phone: (416) 977-4667

#474
Lot 332
Category: Dance Club
Average price: Modest
Area: Entertainment District, Downtown Core
Address: 332 Richmond Street W
Toronto, ON M5V 1X2
Phone: (416) 850-6821

#475
The Tap
Category: Nightlife
Average price: Inexpensive
Area: The Annex
Address: 517 Bloor Street W
Toronto, ON M5S 1Y4
Phone: (416) 533-5321

#476
Pogue Mahone Irish Pub
Category: Pub
Average price: Modest
Area: Downtown Core
Address: 777 Bay St
Toronto, ON M5G 2C8
Phone: (416) 598-3339

#477
Terri O's Sports Bar & Grill
Category: Sports Bar
Average price: Inexpensive
Area: Riverdale
Address: 185 Danforth Ave
Toronto, ON M4K 1N2
Phone: (416) 462-0038

#478
Ciao Wine Bar
Category: Italian, Wine Bar
Average price: Expensive
Area: Yorkville
Address: 133 Yorkville Avenue
Toronto, ON M5R 1C4
Phone: (416) 925-2143

#479
Fionn MacCools
Category: Irish, Bar
Average price: Modest
Area: Entertainment District, Downtown Core
Address: 310 Front Street W
Toronto, ON M5V 3B5
Phone: (416) 340-1917

#480
Aria Entertainment Complex
Category: Dance Club
Average price: Modest
Area: Entertainment District, Downtown Core
Address: 108 Peter Street
Toronto, ON M5V 1R4
Phone: (647) 228-2434

#481
Aristotle & McGregor's
Category: Pub
Average price: Modest
Area: Mount Pleasant and Davisville
Address: 525 Mount Pleasant Road
Toronto, ON M4S 2M4
Phone: (416) 480-2252

#482
Dufferin Gate Tavern
Category: Bar
Average price: Inexpensive
Area: Parkdale
Address: 1204 King St W
Toronto, ON M6K 1G4
Phone: (416) 534-2238

#483
New Times Square Billiards
Category: Pool Hall
Average price: Inexpensive
Area: Ryerson, Downtown Core
Address: 356 Yonge Street
Toronto, ON M5B 1S5
Phone: (416) 979-7537

#484
Honora Wise Guys Bar & Grill
Category: Bar
Average price: Inexpensive
Area: Wychwood
Address: 682 Street Clair Avenue W
Toronto, ON M6C 1B1
Phone: (416) 651-3881

#485
Chelsea Room
Category: Bar
Average price: Modest
Area: Little Italy, Trinity Bellwoods
Address: 923 Dundas Street W
Toronto, ON M6J 1W2
Phone: (416) 364-0553

#486
Brass Taps Pizza Pub
Category: Pizza, Pub
Average price: Modest
Area: Dufferin Grove
Address: 934 College St
Toronto, ON M6H 1A4
Phone: (416) 533-4333

#487
73 Stirs
Category: Bar
Average price: Modest
Area: St. Lawrence, Downtown Core
Address: 73 King Street E
Toronto, ON M5C 1G3
Phone: (416) 362-4342

#488
If Lounge
Category: Lounge
Average price: Modest
Area: Dufferin Grove, Little Portugal, Beaconsfield Village
Address: 1212 Dundas St W
Toronto, ON M6J 1X5
Phone: (416) 588-4900

#489
Novo Horizonte Sports Bar
Category: Sports Bar
Average price: Inexpensive
Area: Dufferin Grove, Little Portugal, Beaconsfield Village
Address: 1430 Dundas St W
Toronto, ON M6J 1Y5
Phone: (416) 534-5355

#490
Tommy's Bar and Grill
Category: Pub
Average price: Inexpensive
Area: The Danforth
Address: 1206 Danforth Ave
Toronto, ON M4J 1M6
Phone: (416) 462-9537

#491
Skål Rock Bar
Category: Bar, Music Venues
Average price: Modest
Area: Corktown
Address: 474 Adelaide Street E
Toronto, ON M5A 1N6
Phone: (416) 603-7525

#492
Regal Beagle Pub
Category: Pub
Average price: Modest
Area: University of Toronto, Downtown Core
Address: 335 Bloor St W
Toronto, ON M5S 1W7
Phone: (416) 591-6859

#493
Neutral
Category: Dance Club, Karaoke
Average price: Inexpensive
Area: Kensington Market
Address: A-349 College Street
Toronto, ON M5T 1S5
Phone: (416) 926-1212

#494
Aji Sai Plus Resto Lounge
Category: Japanese, Lounge, Sushi Bar
Average price: Modest
Area: Downtown Core
Address: 637 Yonge Street
Toronto, ON M4Y 1Z5
Phone: (647) 748-3866

#495
XO Karaoke
Category: Karaoke
Average price: Modest
Area: Koreatown, Bickford Park, Seaton Village
Address: 693 Bloor St W
Toronto, ON M6G 1L5
Phone: (416) 535-3734

#496
Crown Bar & Lounge
Category: Bar, Dance Club
Average price: Expensive
Area: Entertainment District, Downtown Core
Address: 393 King Street W
Toronto, ON M5V 3G8
Phone: (416) 341-2345

#497
Mapleleaf Sports Bar & Grill
Category: Sports Bar
Average price: Inexpensive
Area: Greektown, Riverdale
Address: 828 Danforth Ave
Toronto, ON M4J 1L6
Phone: (416) 466-0521

#498
Wise Guys Deluxe Grill & Bar
Category: Dive Bar
Average price: Inexpensive
Area: The Danforth
Address: 2301 Avenue Danforth
Toronto, ON M4C 1K5
Phone: (416) 690-8343

#499
Geraldine
Category: Cocktail Bar, Seafood
Average price: Expensive
Area: Parkdale
Address: 1564 Queen Street W
Toronto, ON M6R 1A6
Phone: (647) 352-8827

#500
Studio Restaurant Tavern
Category: Bar, Canadian
Average price: Inexpensive
Area: Downtown Core
Address: 389 Church Street
Toronto, ON M5B 2E5
Phone: (416) 977-4777

Made in the USA
Columbia, SC
03 April 2019